Entrepreneurship in the Catholic Tradition

STUDIES IN ETHICS AND ECONOMICS

Series Editor
Samuel Gregg, Acton Institute

Economics as a discipline cannot be detached from a historical background that was, it is increasingly recognized, religious in nature. Adam Ferguson and Adam Smith drew on the work of sixteenth- and seventeenth-century Spanish theologians, who strove to understand the process of exchange and trade in order to better address the moral dilemmas they saw arising from the spread of commerce in the New World. After a long period in which economics became detached from theology and ethics, many economists and theologians now see the benefit of studying economic realities in their full cultural, often religious, context. This new series, Studies in Ethics and Economics, provides an international forum for exploring the difficult theological and economic questions that arise in the pursuit of this objective.

Titles in the Series

Entrepreneurship in the Catholic Tradition

Anthony G. Percy

LEXINGTON BOOKS
A division of
ROWMAN & LITTLEFIELD PUBLISHERS, INC.
Lanham • Boulder • New York • Toronto • Plymouth, UK

Published by Lexington Books
A division of Rowman & Littlefield Publishers, Inc.
A wholly owned subsidiary of The Rowman & Littlefield Publishing Group, Inc.
4501 Forbes Boulevard, Suite 200, Lanham, Maryland 20706
http://www.lexingtonbooks.com

Estover Road, Plymouth PL6 7PY, United Kingdom

British Library Cataloguing in Publication Information Available

Library of Congress Cataloging-in-Publication Data
Percy, Anthony.
  Entrepreneurship in the Catholic tradition / Anthony G. Percy.
      p. cm. — (Studies in ethics and economics)
  Includes bibliographical references (p.   ) and index.
  ISBN: 978-0-7391-2514-4
  1. Entrepreneurship. 2. Business—Religious aspects—Catholic Church. I. Title.
  HF5388.P47 2010
  261.8'5—dc22   2010015815

♾™ The paper used in this publication meets the minimum requirements of American
National Standard for Information Sciences—Permanence of Paper for Printed Library
Materials, ANSI/NISO Z39.48-1992.

Printed in the United States of America

CONTENTS

ACKNOWLEDGMENTS

I would principally like to thank Samuel Gregg of the Acton Institute for his editorial work and for helping to bring this text to publication. It would not have occurred without him. I also wish to thank the scholars, especially Professor William E. May, at the John Paul II Institute for Studies on Marriage and the Family, Washington, D.C., who supervised this work when it was a doctoral thesis. Thanks are also owed to my ecclesiastical authorities in Australia for permission to undertake the doctorate. Finally, I want to thank my parents and family who have done so much to form my mind and heart as a man, priest, and seeker of the truth.

Permission to cite from the following documents has been granted by Libreria Editrice Vaticana, which retains full copyright ©. Leo XIII, *Rerum Novarum* (1891); Pius XI, *Quadragesimo Anno* (1931); Pius XII, "Function of Bankers" (1951); Pius XII, "Christmas Address" (1952); Pius XII, "Christmas Address" (1955); Pius XII, "Business and the Common Good" (1956); Pius XII, "The Small Business Manger" (1956); Pius XII, "Small Business in Today's Economy" (1957); John XXIII, *Mater et Magistra* (1961); Second Vatican Council, *Lumen Gentium* (1964); Second Vatican Council, *Dei Verbum* (1965); Second Vatican Council, *Gaudium et Spes* (1965); Paul VI, *Populorum Progressio* (1967); John Paul II, *Redemptor Hominis* (1979); John Paul II, *Laborem Exercens* (1981); John Paul II, *Sollicitudo Rei Socialis* (1987); John Paul II, *Centesimus Annus* (1991).

FOREWORD

At the beginning of the twenty-first century, the figure of the entrepreneur looms perhaps larger than in the nineteenth century and even larger than the period when capitalism first emerged: the Middle Ages. Few would claim, however, that there is enhanced understanding of entrepreneurship's significance in the modern economy. The word "entrepreneur" is often used, for instance, interchangeably with that of "business executive" or "manager." As economic thinkers such as Israel Kirzner to Ludwig von Mises have illustrated, entrepreneurship is something quite distinct, with specific characteristics. It plays a crucial economic role very different from that of a manager or executive—even those with immense responsibilities.

But reflection on the nature and purpose of entrepreneurship is most decidedly not new. Though the word is of relatively modern lineage, humans have been—by necessity and by nature—entrepreneurial from the very beginning. Unlike all other creatures, humans have shaped the world around them in new and innovative ways. Man, it seems, cannot help but change the material context in which he finds himself—for better or worse. At the source of the ability of humans to do so is the human reason and free will with which all have been endowed.

Consideration of the role of human reason inevitably and eventually raises theological questions, and it is little wonder that some of the first and most profound reflections upon entrepreneurship have come from within Roman Catholicism. Yet relatively few scholars have looked carefully at the history of Catholic analysis of entrepreneurship. Since the time of Joseph Schumpeter's magisterial *History of Economic Analysis*, there has been wider acknowledgment—grudgingly, one may say—of the crucial, indeed indispensible role played by Catholic theologians in intellectually facilitating the rise of capitalism. Careful attention, however, to this research indicates that Catholic thinking about entrepreneurship *per se* has been neglected.

This book by Anthony Percy does a great deal to diminish this gap in contemporary knowledge. Percy draws upon his own deep theological and economic knowledge to demonstrate that there *is* a strong tradition of Catholic reflection upon entrepreneurship. Apart from drawing upon Scripture, Percy illustrates that the Church Fathers did not neglect the subject of human economic creativity. Indeed, he demonstrates that, while deeply censorious of materialism and greed, the Church Fathers held economic entrepreneurship in high esteem, seeing in it reflections of the divine. Percy then proceeds to trace the history of Catholic interest in entrepreneurship through the Middle Ages, all the way through to the modern period, ending with John Paul II's 1991 social encyclical *Centesimus Annus*.

Several key points emerge from Percy's analysis. The first is the Catholic integration of entrepreneurship into a concrete theology of work which is as much directed to humanity's moral flourishing as its material well-being. The second is that, from a Catholic standpoint, entrepreneurship is about meeting human needs. "It is from this foundation—the primordial foundation of love—that," Percy writes, "the dignity of the entrepreneur and his work arises." This association with love is not at all a common way of reflecting upon the ultimate origins and direction of entrepreneurship, even though the attention to need finds echoes in the writings of economists such as von Mises and business figures such as François Michelin.

Finally, Percy's analysis provides an excellent insight into how Catholic teaching on something as pivotal to humanity's continued existence as entrepreneurship has undergone development over the centuries. Certainly this has occurred within the larger context of Catholic thinking about economic activity in general. But there are distinct continuities across the centuries, some of which feature more prominently at different times, often depending on the circumstances.

Entrepreneurship in the Catholic Tradition is a distinctly original contribution to Catholic social thought about the economy. Herein is to be found its achievement. By focusing on entrepreneurship, Percy allows new insights into the history and nature of Catholic social teaching. He also lays the ground for more innovative thinking within the Catholic tradition about free enterprise, business, and market economies in our globalized world. For a truly global church that has always by definition had global aspirations, this cannot be an optional extra. It is a necessity.

—Samuel Gregg
Director of Research
Acton Institute

1

Introduction

The Church's social teaching proposes principles for reflection; it provides criteria for judgment; it gives guidelines for action.

—Catechism of the Catholic Church[1]

The story is told of an Irish priest who took his regular afternoon walk around his small country parish. Each afternoon the priest would survey the beautiful countryside, breathe in the fresh air and converse occasionally with a member of his flock. One day he stopped to talk to an elderly man. He was a wise and gentle Irishman. The priest said to him, "Paddy, what a wonderful garden you have." To which his loyal son replied, "O Father, it was much better when God had it on his own!"

God and His Creation

In the opening chapters of the Book of Genesis, Adam finds himself in the Garden of Eden. It is there that God and he first converse. That garden—a symbol of innocence, peace, beauty, joy, and order—had been given to man, who was placed there "to till it and keep it."[2] The garden, like man, was created out of nothing. The world, and everything in it, is the result of an infinite act of love. It is a gift to man.[3] Originally, God intended man to experience this kind of life on earth as well

1

as in heaven. In their encounter with the serpent, however, Adam and Eve betrayed their call to be loyal stewards of creation.

That wise and gentle Irishman, apparently, was incorrect: the garden would not have been best left to God, for despite man's mistrust, suspicion, and disobedience, God did not abandon man. On the contrary, in the Old and New Testaments God continually searches for man and in the process reveals himself more fully to him.[4] In the garden, God spoke briefly, but in his Son, Jesus Christ, God speaks with complete clarity and plenitude. As *Dei Verbum* teaches: "In His goodness and wisdom God chose to reveal Himself and to make known to us the hidden purpose of His will by which through Christ, the Word made flesh, man might in the Holy Spirit have access to the Father and come to share in the divine nature."[5]

Christ was conceived in a little village called Nazareth, a town unknown to the world at large and not even mentioned in the Old Testament. He was born in Bethlehem, popularly interpreted as the *House of Bread*, but spent the majority of his life in Nazareth with the Blessed Virgin and her husband, St. Joseph. There he learned how to talk, to read, to live, to work, to pray, and to love through his human parents, Mary Most Holy and Joseph, whom scripture calls "a just man." At the same time, and without any diminution, Jesus is the Only-Begotten Son of the Father—a Divine Person.

Christ Jesus is, as John Paul II reminds us, "a man of work" and he therefore proclaims "the gospel of work."[6] That Jesus is a man of work can hardly be denied. His life and the lives of Mary and Joseph—full of the mundanity of work—is a source of scandal for his contemporaries (and perhaps for moderns, as well). In *Jesus Christ: The Holy One of God*, Raniero Cantalamessa writes of the act of faith in Christ's divinity and notes the "scandal" of Christ's ordinary life. "The divinity of Christ is the highest peak, the Everest, of faith. Much more difficult than just believing in God."[7]

> The difficulty is linked to the possibility of and so to the inevitability of 'scandal': 'Blessed is he,' says Jesus, 'who takes no offence at me' (Mt. 11:6). The scandal arises from the fact that the man proclaiming himself to be 'God' is someone about whom everything is known: 'We know where this man comes from,' say the Pharisees (Jn. 7:27). 'Son of God!' sneered Celsus. 'A man living only a few years ago?' Someone 'of yesterday or the day before?' A man 'who came from a village in Judaea and whose mother was a poor country woman who earned a living by spinning?'[8]

Jesus is indeed a "man of work." His followers, recreated anew in baptism, are called to follow him in "tilling" and "keeping" the garden. They, too, are called to "fill the earth and subdue it" and to "have dominion over the fish of the sea and over the birds of the air and over every living thing that moves upon the earth."[9] Scripture makes it evident that God has a plan. His garden, given to man, is to be cultivated and man is to be the instrument of this loving plan. So much so, that the Word of God, through the Book of Revelation, seems intent on moving from the garden to the city. Indeed, there are no less than twenty-nine references to the city in this book attributed to the apostle John.

But Revelation 21 reveals that the city does not belong to man and is not of his making. It belongs to the Father, who builds it with the help of man: "And I saw the holy city, new Jerusalem, coming down out of heaven from God, prepared as a bride adorned for her husband; and I heard a loud voice from the throne saying, "Behold, the dwelling of God is with men. He will dwell with them, and they shall be his people, and God himself will be with them."[10] Man must know and recognize his place in this loving and providential plan. When he fails to do so, confusion and fragmentation ensues. The Tower of Babel in the Old Testament illustrates that cities built to "make a name" for man—cities that are expressions of vainglory—are headed for ruin:

> Then they said, "Come, let us build ourselves a city, and a tower with its top in the heavens, and let us make a name for ourselves, lest we be scattered abroad upon the face of the whole earth." And the Lord came down to see the city and the tower, which the sons of men had built. And the Lord said, "Behold, they are one people, and they have all one language; and this is only the beginning of what they will do; and nothing that they propose to do will now be impossible for them. Come, let us go down, and there confuse their language, that they may not understand one another's speech." So the Lord scattered them abroad from there over the face of all the earth, and they left off building the city.[11]

James Schall, in his recent work *On the Unseriousness of Human Affairs*, cites the Angelic Doctor, St. Thomas Aquinas, to highlight the preeminence of God and his grace in man's life.

> In his question of the "Governance of Things," Saint Thomas observed: "For as 'it belongs to the best to produce the best,' it is not fitting that the supreme goodness of God should produce things without giving them their perfection. Now a thing's ultimate perfection consists in the attainment of its end. Therefore, it belongs to the Divine goodness, as it brought things into existence, so to lead them to their end... " (*ST*, I, 103, I). If this passage means anything, it means that no external condition can ultimately interfere with our freely reaching our end. We are the only thing that can prevent it. The governance of God over his creation, His ability to bring it to its end, does not depend on the affairs of men, though it does include them. He is present in our tragedies as in our elations. The Cross is, as à Kempis said, a way, a "royal road."[12]

Thus, in free cooperation with God's providential plan, man and his works will be brought to a fruitful conclusion. The governance of the world does not depend on man, but on God and his grace, granted in Jesus Christ. But it certainly does not exclude man. Man is a partner in this most magnificent, beautiful, and wondrous work. The Church teaches what Saint Thomas taught so eloquently:

Nothing is impossible with God, who disposes his works according to his will. He is the Lord of the universe, *whose order he established and which remains wholly subject to him and at his disposal.* He is the master of history, governing hearts and events in keeping with his will: 'It is always in your power to show great strength, and who can withstand the strength of your arm.'[13]

However, this trust in divine providence does not permit any presumption on man's part. Neither does it mean abrogation of responsibility. God's almighty power does not allow man to live in a state of inertia. Man is called to a task that is both human and divine. God has entrusted the world to him, and together, God and man must cultivate the earth and perfect the creation. Trust in divine providence instead assures that man fulfills his vocation to subdue the earth without needless anxiety. God is a provident Father, and man is a son of God. With a spirit of faith and trust in God's mercy, the earth will be perfected. There is no need for agitation and anxiety, as Christ taught in the Sermon on the Mount:

> And why are you anxious about clothing? Consider the lilies of the field, how they grow; they neither toil nor spin; yet I tell you, even Solomon in all his glory was not arrayed like one of these. But if God so clothes the grass of the field, which today is alive and tomorrow is thrown into the oven, will he not much more clothe you, O men of little faith? Therefore do not be anxious, saying, 'What shall we eat?' or 'What shall we drink?' or 'What shall we wear?' For the Gentiles seek all these things; and your heavenly Father knows that you need them all. But seek first his kingdom and his righteousness, and all these things shall be yours as well.[14]

Ultimately, therefore, progress is a question of faith in both God and man. Man is called to work, conscious of the task entrusted to him and conscious of the One who gave him this gracious task. God is generous with his governance of the world and in the gifts He grants freely to man. This is clear from the words of the Psalmist, who writes,

> *In vain you get up earlier,*
> *And put off going to bed,*
> *Sweating to make a living,*
> *Since he provides for his beloved*
> *as they sleep.*[15]

But man must also be conscious of himself, for he rises above the material creation with his transcendental dignity and singular place in the eternal plan of God:

> *When I look at thy heavens,*
> *the work of thy fingers,*
> *the moon and the stars which thou hast established;*
> *what is man that thou art mindful of him,*
> *and the son of man that thou dost care for him?*
> *Yet thou hast made him little less than God*
> *and dost crown him with glory and honor.*[16]

Man is the pinnacle of creation. He shares and possesses a human nature which far exceeds the material creation. God so clothes the birds of the air and cares even more deliberately for His chosen ones. Such is this paternal care and love of God, as the Psalmist says, that he pours gifts on his chosen ones even while they slumber.

The Social Doctrine of the Church

God is, therefore, the starting point for theological reflection as well as for the Church's social teaching. It is commonly recognized that the "social doctrine of the Church developed in the nineteenth century when the Gospel encountered modern industrial society with its new structures for the production of consumer goods, its new concepts of society, the state and authority, and its new forms of labor and ownership."[17] Clearly this does not mean that there never existed a body of social teaching in the Church prior to the middle and late nineteenth century. The Old Testament is particularly sensitive to social matters, as is the New Testament. The new law of love, first lived and then taught by Jesus Christ, has many applications (and implications) for society. For instance, in Matthew 25:31–46 Jesus identifies himself with the hungry and thirsty, the stranger, the naked, the sick, and the imprisoned. The Church Fathers also make it clear that they were deeply concerned with the alleviation of injustice and poverty. Clearly, Catholic social teaching underwent major development before the nineteenth century. Rodger Charles' work *Christian Social Witness and Teaching* is perhaps the best evidence of this truth.[18]

Instead, the changes in the middle to late nineteenth century were the occasion for, not the catalyst of, significant development in the social teaching in the Catholic Church. The development began with Leo XIII's now-famous encyclical *Rerum Novarum* in 1891. It was followed by *Quadragesimo Anno* (Pius XI) in 1931, *Mater et Magistra* (John XXIII) in 1961, *Pacem in Terris* (John XXIII) in 1963, *Populorum Progressio* (Paul VI) in 1967, *Laborem Exercens* (John Paul II) in 1981, *Sollicitudo Rei Socialis* (John Paul II) in 1987, and finally *Centesimus Annus* (John Paul II) in 1991. All in all, eight social encyclicals have been written, three of them by Pope John Paul II.

In these eight social encyclicals, the Church has compiled a significant body of social thought in the modern age. Strategically and providentially placed in the middle of this developing thought and teaching is the Second Vatican Council's Pastoral Constitution on the Church in the Modern World, *Gaudium et Spes*. One of the most important documents of the Catholic Church's social teaching, it was promulgated on December 7, 1965. Thus, twenty-first-century Catholics are the inheritors and custodians of a truly significant advancement of social teaching in the Catholic Church. This great burst of understanding carries with it responsibility: John Paul II writes in *Centesimus Annus*, "As far as the Church is concerned, the social message of the Gospel must not be considered a theory, but above all else a basis and a motivation for *action*."[19]

The social teaching, therefore, needs to be believed and given the full assent that all the truths of the Catholic faith require. As *Lumen Gentium* teaches, the faithful are required to give a "loyal submission of the will and intellect" "to the authentic teaching authority of the Roman Pontiff, even when he does not speak *ex cathedra*."[20] And according to *Dei Verbum*, believing entails more than giving mere intellectual assent. It is the surrender of the entire human person to God as he reveals himself. "By faith man freely commits his *entire self to God,* making 'the full submission of his intellect and will to God who reveals,' and willingly assenting to the Revelation given by him."[21]

The Entrepreneur in the Social Doctrine of the Church

Notwithstanding the preeminence of assimilation and action, study is required. This book embarks on such a project. It focuses on the figure of the entrepreneur and his work as it has appeared in the social teaching of the Church, not only from the time of Leo XIII, but since the inception of the Church herself. Such a task is important, particularly given the events of the latter part of the twentieth century. In 1989, one of the chief symbols of communism, the Berlin Wall, crumbled under the weight of its own oppression. The desire of the human spirit for freedom could not be extinguished. On the western side of the wall stood capitalism, free markets, and free institutions, while little remained on the eastern side. Here was a people, not unlike the Jews centuries before them, who had been held in captivity for seventy years. The effect on the human spirit would be deep. The task of rebuilding those eastern bloc countries would be no small feat. Pope John Paul II addressed these important issues in *Centesimus Annus*. He expressed the desire that the social teaching of the Church be applied not only in formerly communist countries, but also in Western countries that, while enjoying free markets and institutions, have many serious problems to address.[22] This book confines itself to one important teaching that has emerged in the social teaching of the Church, particularly since *Rerum Novarum*: the importance of private initiative and, in particular, the theological significance of the entrepreneur in the life of society.

This study will hopefully contribute to a deeper understanding of the entrepreneur, what he does and why his activities are important. Significantly, this work also will attempt to understand the entrepreneur through the eyes of faith, explicating the theological meaning of the entrepreneur and the principles that might guide an entrepreneurial corporation.

The Fruits of This Study

By the end of Chapter 6 of *Centesimus Annus*, it becomes clear that the Church has long held a deep appreciation for the work of the entrepreneur. This may be surprising for some, whose concerns about avarice have colored people's view of the entrepreneur (and businesspersons). But it is the love of money that is condemned in scripture, not money itself: "For the love of money is the root of all evils; it is through this craving that some have wandered away from the faith and pierced their hearts with many pangs."[23] As we shall see, the entrepreneur is present both in the Old and New Testaments and he appears occasionally in the writings of the Fathers. True, the Word of God is not concerned primarily with the entrepreneur, or with any particular profession. The New Testament principally is concerned with revealing the person of Christ to those who hear the Word of God. But the entrepreneur makes intermittent appearances, and he and his behavior are met with approval.

The Church Fathers highlight this in their writings, as well. It is particularly interesting to note that a number of Fathers use the merchant and his work of exchange as a metaphor for Christ's redemptive activity. This hardly would be appropriate unless the merchant and his work were held in high esteem. St. Jerome goes so far as to say that capital is a metaphor for grace. Then there is the Angelic Doctor, whose work on the virtue of magnificence is often neglected. Pius XI in *Quadragesimo Anno* alerted me to this reference,[24] in which St. Thomas appears to foresee one of the principles of modern finance theory: the relationship between risk and return. Thomas tends to focus on the risks the entrepreneur takes rather than the return he expects. Through moderating the love of money, Thomas teaches, the entrepreneur embarks on risky and magnificent projects.

One important finding of this thesis is the extraordinary contribution of Pius XII. His contribution comes to us in the form of papal addresses to various gatherings of entrepreneurs, businessmen, and bankers. So while his teachings do not come to us with the gravity of a papal encyclical, his teachings are nevertheless a very significant contribution to the development of Catholic social thought in the area of entrepreneurial activity. In particular, Pius focuses on the transcendental source of entrepreneurial activity—the human person. The human person is free and transcendent and this forms the basis for entrepreneurial action. In this he prefigures Pope John Paul II in both *Laborem Exercens* and *Centesimus Annus*.

Laborem Exercens is also the first social encyclical devoted exclusively to work. It is arguably the most original and important contribution John Paul II has made to the development of social thought in the life of the Church. John Paul II delivers three theological meanings of work: it has an objective meaning, a subjective meaning, and a spiritual meaning. Every person who works, whether he receives payment or not, stands to gain by reading this encyclical.

Laborem Exercens and *Centesimus Annus* were written ten years apart to commemorate *Rerum Novarum*. It becomes clear that John Paul II is indebted to Leo's famous encyclical. But he is not content to simply repeat the doctrine contained therein. Rather, he uses the changes in work (*Laborem Exercens*) and the collapse of communism (*Centesimus Annus*) as catalysts for developing his own thought. Some have even claimed that *Centesimus Annus* represents a fundamental shift in Catholic social thought away from a suspicion—perhaps even a rejection—of capitalism to an acceptance of it. These two encyclicals together, particularly in the light of *Rerum Novarum*, prove this analysis false. It is true that the Church has always been somewhat reserved in her assessment of capitalist thought and activity. If one lived from the middle of the nineteenth century to the first half of the twentieth, the reasons for this would become abundantly clear. The divisions created by the industrial revolution and the early forms of capitalism were abysmal, and the Church could not fail to be on the side of the less fortunate.

For John Paul II, it is less a question of systems and more a question of freedom; or, more precisely, of the relationship between freedom and truth as it manifests itself in the human person. Karol Wojtyla has always had a fascination with man. He makes this clear in his first encyclical, *Redemptor Hominis*, when he writes, "Man is the primary route that the Church must travel in fulfilling her mission."[25] And so, understanding man in light of the true man, Jesus Christ, John Paul II is able to distinguish the nuances of capitalism per se and economies that might be termed business, free, or market economies. It is the full truth of man, disclosed through Jesus Christ, that enables him (in *Centesimus Annus*) to call for a society of free work, enterprise, and participation.

Besides discovering the contribution of Pius XII in his papal addresses, two matters from the writings of John Paul II were especially evocative in the process of researching for this book. Relevant sections of *Laborem Exercens* and *Centesimus Annus* in the official Latin text also proved useful. As a consequence of this, it became clear that in his activity of working, man is given the task of participating in the *opus* of God himself. Work can be toilsome, exhausting, monotonous, and tedious. John Paul II does not deny this evident truth. For many people, no doubt, work has no meaning. Even worse, it has become a disease, a form of slavery, due to the long and hideous hours that many people seem to spend at work. John Paul II speaks directly to this destructive culture. He suggests that man, in working and resting, is actually participating in and perfecting God's *opus*. This is a marvelous discovery—one that speaks eloquently to every man and woman.

In addition, John Paul II sees something very important in entrepreneurial work. For him, entrepreneurial work is marvelous because it foresees and satisfies the needs of others. It is the *other*—other human persons who are deeply relational in their existence—that grants entrepreneurial work much of its dignity. Philosophical and theological concepts are clearly in play. But for Karol Wojtyla, the needs of others cannot be reduced to theory. Recognizing the needs of others is the beginning of love.

In his definitive biography of Pope John Paul II, George Weigel has bequeathed to us some correspondence between the young Father Wojtyla and a woman named Teresa Heydel. It took place between December 1956 (Wojtyla was then thirty-six years old and ten years a priest) and January 1957. In this first letter to Teresa, Father Wojtyla writes:

Dear Teresa,

> ... Everyone ... lives, above all, for love. The ability to love authentically, not great intellectual capacity, constitutes the deepest part of a personality. It is no accident that the greatest commandment is to love. Authentic love leads us outside ourselves to affirming others: devoting oneself to the cause of man, to people, and, above all, to God.[26]

Obviously wishing to clarify his thoughts and above all to help Teresa, he takes up his pen again a month later and writes:

Dear Teresa,

> Before I leave for Warsaw I have to tell you a few things (think together with you): 1) I don't want you ever to think this way: that life forces me to move away from the perspective of something that is better, riper, fuller, to something that is less good, less mature, less attractive. I am convinced that life is a constant development toward that which is better, more perfect—if there is no stagnation *within* us. 2) After many experiences and a lot of thinking, I am convinced that the (objective) starting point of love is the realization that I am needed by another. The person who *objectively* needs me most is also, for me, *objectively*, the person I most need. This is a fragment of life's deep logic, and also a fragment of trusting in the Creator and in Providence. 3) People's values are different and they come in different configurations. The great achievement is always to *see* values that others don't see and to *affirm* them. The even greater achievement is to *bring out* of people the values that would perish without us. In the same way, we bring our values out in ourselves. 4) This is what I wanted to write you. Don't ever think that I want to cut short your way. I want your way. Wujek[27]

In *Centesimus Annus* John Paul II affirms the entrepreneur and his work. In a sense, why would he not? On the one hand, man is called to see value where others don't. On the other hand, John Paul II is convinced on the intellectual level that man is free and responsible. How can anyone deny the entrepreneur freedom of action in the economic sphere without thereby wresting his dignity from him? But John Paul II's affirmation of the entrepreneur arises, too, from a deep personal conviction. It is a conviction that is the fruit not only of thought, but also of personal experience. The entrepreneur is *needed* by others. It is from this foundation—the primordial foundation of love—that the dignity of the entrepreneur and his work arises. There is little doubt, therefore, that entrepreneurs are both affirmed and challenged by this pope who, as Andre Frossard has insightfully noted, is not so much a pope from Poland, as one from Galilee.[28]

The Development of Doctrine

Finally, a word on the development of doctrine as it applies to this book. St. Vincent of Lerins has provided a simple framework for this topic.[29] His goal is to protect the deposit of faith, while admitting growth in the understanding of the content of faith in both the soul of the individual and of the Church.[30] He uses the analogy of the human body, writing,

> The growth of religion in the soul must be analogous to the growth of the body, which, though in process of years it is developed and attains its full size, yet remains still the same. There is a wide difference between the flower of youth and the maturity of age; yet they who were once young are still the same now that they have become old, insomuch that though the stature and outward form of the individual are changed, yet his nature is one and the same, his person is one and the same.[31]

So the Church, while never changing anything of the deposit of faith—neither subtracting from it nor adding to it—"keeps this one object carefully in view."

> [If] there is anything which antiquity has left shapeless and rudimentary, to fashion and polish it, if anything already reduced to shape and developed, to consolidate and strengthen it, if any already ratified and defined to keep and guard it. Finally, what other object have Councils ever aimed at in their decrees, than to provide that what was before believed in simplicity should in future be believed intelligently, that what was before preached coldly should in future be preached earnestly, that what was before practised negligently should henceforward be practised with double solicitude.[32]

It would seem that in regard to the entrepreneur, the Church has focused magnificently on this "object." Beginning with *Rerum Novarum*, the eight social encyclicals of the Catholic Church have certainly fashioned and polished, consolidated and strengthened, kept and guarded the deposit of faith in its social dimension. *Rerum Novarum* scrupulously defended the right to private property. *Quadragesimo Anno* then developed and transformed this right into action. Pius XII and John Paul II would then focus attention specifically on the entrepreneur and his virtues. And while these developments took place, there was another underlying development. Where *Rerum Novarum* emphasized and almost exclusively based its arguments on human nature, the Second Vatican Council and Pope John Paul II would present and develop the social doctrine based on the human person. This truth was established via reference to the true and definitive man Jesus Christ: "the same yesterday and today and for ever."[33]

In short, this work sets out to define the entrepreneur and then hold this definition up to the light of faith in subsequent chapters. In doing so, it becomes clear that the Church is indeed "like a householder who brings out of his treasure what is new and what is old."[34] By the end of Chapter 6 it is evident that the Church has developed and deepened her understanding of the entrepreneur with the passage of time. The entrepreneur is (or can be) a Christian who stands beside other Christians in his intimate participation in the mystery of Jesus Christ.

Notes

1. *Catechism of the Catholic Church*, 2d ed. (Citta del Vaticano: Libreria Editrice Vaticana, 1997), paragraph 2423. When referring to the *Catechism* I will use the abbreviation CCC, followed by the paragraph number. (Hence this first reference is CCC 2423.) The Latin text is from: *Catechismus Catholicae Ecclesiae* (Citta del Vaticano: Libreria Editrice Vaticana, 1997).

2. Gen. 2:15. All biblical references are taken from the Revised Standard Version of the Bible. I use the *Jerusalem Bible* on occasion and indicate when this is so.

3. CCC 1.

4. See CCC 50–65. "Through an utterly free decision, God has revealed himself and given himself to man. This he does by revealing the mystery, his plan of loving goodness, formed from all eternity in Christ, for the benefit of all men. God fully revealed this plan by sending us his beloved Son, our Lord Jesus Christ, and the Holy Spirit" (CCC 50).

5. Second Vatican Ecumenical Council, Dogmatic Constitution on Divine Revelation, *Dei Verbum*, 2, in: *Vatican Council II: The Conciliar and Post Conciliar Documents*, New Revised Study Edition, ed. Austin Flannery, O.P. (New York: Costello Publishing Company, 1992), 750–65. All references to the documents of the Second Vatican Council will be taken from this edition of Flannery.

6. John Paul II, Encyclical Letter *Laborem Exercens*, 26, in *The Encyclicals of John Paul II*, ed. J. Michael Miller (Huntington, IN: Our Sunday Visitor Publishing Division, 2001), 153–93. The Latin text from *Acta Apostolicae Sedis* 73 (1981) 577–647. All references to the encyclicals of Pope John Paul II are taken from Miller's book. I will first give the full title of the encyclical and then in subsequent references use the commonly acknowledged Latin title with the relevant paragraph number. In addition, I will use AAS in referring to the Official Commentary from the Holy See (*Acta Apostolicae Sedis*).

7. Raniero Cantalamessa, *Jesus Christ: The Holy One of God*, trans. Alan Neame (Collegeville, MN: The Liturgical Press, 1991), 56.

8. Ibid. The reference given is to Origen. See Origen, *Contra Celsum*, I, 26, 28; VI, 10 (SCh 132, 146f; SCh 147: 202f).

9. Gen. 1:28–29.

10. Rev. 21:2–3.

11. Gen. 11:4–8.

12. James V. Schall S.J., *On the Unseriousness of Human Affairs: Teaching, Writing, Playing, Believing, Lecturing, Philosophizing, Singing, Dancing* (Wilmington, DE: ISI Books, 2001), 6–7.

13. CCC 269. Emphasis added.

14. Matt. 6:28–33.

15. Ps. 127:2. *The Jerusalem Bible*, ed. Alexander Jones (Garden City, NY: Doubleday & Company, Inc, 1966).

16. Ps. 8:3–5.

17. CCC 2421. While most scholars would not take issue with this claim, it is true that there is a significant body of social thought that developed in the pre-Leonine period: 1740–1877. Michael Schuck, in *That They Be One: The Social Teaching of the Papal Encyclicals 1740-1989*, highlights this point. He writes: "Following Benedict XIV's inception of modern encyclical writing, nine popes produce seventy-seven letters antedating Leo XIII. Most addressees are bishops. There are thirty-four *litterae encyclicae* (letters to all bishops) and thirty-six *epistolae encyclicae* (letters to bishops of specific countries)...

The pope's major interests are morality and worship." See *That They Be One: The Social Teaching of the Papal Encyclicals 1740-1989*, ed. Michael J. Schuck (Washington, D.C.: Georgetown University Press, 1991), 1.

18. See Rodger Charles S.J., *Christian Social Witness and Teaching: The Catholic Tradition from Genesis to Centesimus Annus*, 2 vols., vol. 1: From Biblical Times to the Late Nineteenth Century; vol. 2: The Modern Social Teaching Contexts: Summaries: Analysis (Trowbridge: Cromwell Press, 1998).

19. *Centesimus Annus*, 57. Emphasis added.

20. Second Vatican Ecumenical Council, Dogmatic Constitution on the Church, *Lumen Gentium*, 25, in *Vatican Council II: The Conciliar and Post Conciliar Documents*, ed. Austin Flannery, OP (New York: Costello Publishing Compnay, 1992), 350–426.

21. *Dei Verbum*, 5. Emphasis added.

22. See *Centesimus Annus*, 56.

23. 1 Tim. 6:10.

24. See Pius XI. Encyclical Letter *Quadragesimo Anno*, 51 in *Catholic Social Thought: The Documentary Heritage*, ed. David J. O'Brien and Thomas A. Shannon (Maryknoll, NY: Orbis Books, 2000), 42–79.

25. John Paul II. Encyclical Letter *Redemptor Hominis*, 14, in *The Encyclicals*, ed. J. Michael Miller (Huntington, IN: Our Sunday Visitor Publishing Division, 2001), 47–89.

26. Quoted in: George Weigel, *Witness To Hope: The Biography of Pope John Paul II* (New York: Cliff Street Books, 2001), 101.

27. Ibid., 101–2.

28. "Now, on seeing the new Pope and sensing in him the power of a witness, Andre Frossard wired back to his Parisian newspaper: 'This is not a Pope from Poland; this is a Pope from Galilee.'" (Ibid., 258).

29. St. Vincent of Lerins, *A Commonitory: For the Antiquity and Universality of the Catholic Faith against the Profane Novelties of all Heresies*, Chapter XXIII, "On Development in Religious Knowledge" in *Sulpitius Severus, Vincent of Lerins, John Cassian*, 14 vols., vol. 11, *Nicene and Post-Nicene Fathers: Second Series*, ed. Philip Schaff and Henry Wace (Peabody: Hendrickson Publishers, 1999), 147–49.

30. Ibid., 148. He writes: "The intelligence, then, the knowledge, the wisdom, as well of individuals as of all, as well of one man as of the whole Church, ought, in the course of ages and centuries, to increase and make much and vigorous progress; but yet only in its own kind; that is to say, in the same doctrine, in the same sense, and in the same meaning."

31. Ibid.

32. Ibid., 149.

33. Heb. 13:8.

34. Matt. 13:52.

2

Entrepreneurial Work: Toward a Definition

*Of the following things do not be ashamed,… of profit from
dealing with merchants.*

—Sirach[1]

This chapter seeks to develop a definition of entrepreneurial work. After giving
a basic definition of work, the remainder of the chapter will be concerned with
developing the elements of entrepreneurial work, providing a definition that will
help to focus the study. Various secular definitions of the entrepreneur will be examined. To this end, it is helpful to examine not only the work of the entrepreneur
but also the type of person who is likely to be an entrepreneur. Proceeding in this
manner allows the work itself and the person himself to manifest and contribute
to an understanding of entrepreneurial activity.

The Human Dimension of Work

Since an entrepreneur is involved in an activity that we appropriately call *work*, it
is necessary to define what we mean and understand by the word *work*. According
to *The Concise Oxford Dictionary*, work is defined as an "activity involving mental
or physical effort done in order to achieve a result… Such activity [is] a means of
earning income."[2] This latter observation—the earning of income—while critical for

13

man's human existence, does not form part of the essence of the definition. Many people work, such as stay-at-home mothers (and fathers), volunteers, and many others, without earning money. Therefore, in one sense work is a human activity that is directed to some end, the achievement of some predetermined purpose. Work, in this first sense, is understood as *action*.

But work also refers to an *object* that is produced by this action. "Thus the craftsman, writer, artist, or industrial worker may produce an object which is termed his *work*."[3] In *The Theology of Work*, Gideon Goosen brings these two elements of work together—action and object. In doing so, he helps provide a more succinct definition of work.

> We do not only look at the final object, but together with it, at the way in which it was produced. When one praises another with the expression, 'what a lovely piece of work,' or 'what a fine job,' the meaning of this definition becomes clear. This is a good definition, because it considers both the *perfectio operis* and the *perfectio operantis* (the perfection of the thing and the doer). One can regard the end of work as firstly, exterior to the subject (i.e., the *perfectio operis*), and the effect it has on the worker (the *perfectio operantis*) as secondary, but necessary. (Hegel said that it was the opposite—that it was more the man than the matter that took shape in work.) Christianity, too, has traditionally tended to stress this aspect, namely that work can be made to promote man's spiritual perfection.[4]

Thus, work refers not only to what is produced (the object); it also refers to action (what we commonly refer to as working). In addition, it refers to the person who is doing the action. Work not only produces an object, it has a personal value. In and through the action of working, man himself is perfected. In addition, work has a moral value, which is intimately related to this personal value. This is encapsulated by Goosen's reference to the various expressions that may be used to describe a person's work. When a person says, "what a lovely piece of work," or "what a fine job," the comment brings together the object, action, and subject of work. It is also a comment on the goodness and therefore the moral dimension of work. It is also a commentary on the way in which a person works. Work, then, has undeniable moral overtones. Man can work well or badly, and this affects not only the object he produces—it affects man himself.

Work is necessary for man's existence on earth. Without work, man could not provide for his needs or the needs of his family. Work is necessary in this sense, but also in the sense that man is confronted by a world that requires work. Man needs to develop and transform the earth to satisfy these needs. In this, it can be distinguished from play. Work involves toil, hardship and strain, things which further distinguish it from play. But as Kaiser writes: "It is equally apparent that some activities may be classed as work under some aspects or conditions and as sport or play or recreation under others. This is particularly true of the activity of the professional athlete, the professional actor or entertainer. Often the distinction between work and play *is the motive or purpose* for the activity."[5]

The Divine Dimension of Work

Work also has a theological dimension. It can be viewed as a task that the creature is given by the Creator. With the light of faith, work is understood as part of the original vocation of every man and woman—a vocation attested to by the early texts of Genesis and confirmed by Jesus Christ in his years of hidden work in Nazareth. The *Catechism of the Catholic Church* teaches the following about human work: "The sign of man's familiarity with God is that God places him in the garden. There he lives 'to till it and keep it.' Work is not yet a burden, but rather the collaboration of man and woman with God in perfecting the visible creation."[6]

In working, then, man not only attempts to satisfy his own needs and desires, but is also attempting to fulfill a command of God himself. Genesis 1:28 depicts the vocation man has received from God to till, keep, and subdue the earth. John Paul II comments directly on the last point, which is crucial to understanding man's interaction with creation:

When man, who had been created "in the image of God ... male and female," hears the words: "Be fruitful and *multiply, and fill the earth and subdue it,*" even though these words do not refer directly and explicitly to work, beyond any doubt they indirectly indicate it as an activity for man to carry out in the world. Man is the image of God partly through the mandate received from his Creator to subdue, to dominate, the earth. In carrying out this mandate, man, every human being, reflects the very action of the Creator of the universe.[7]

Thus, man is given the original vocation by God to be fruitful and multiply, and to fill the earth and subdue it. When man cultivates and transforms the products of the earth, adapting them to his own use, he is fulfilling this God-given call. Man's activity is directed toward himself and the community in which he lives, and this activity is part of a divine vocation.

Work, then, has both an immediate and obvious human meaning. In addition, it has a profound theological meaning when understood in the context of the category of creation. John Paul II teaches in *Laborem Exercens* that man, by working, reflects the very action of God himself. This latter point will be dealt with more comprehensively in Chapter 5. It is sufficient to note in passing that it gives rise to the crucial distinction between work as *labor* and work as *opus*. God's work of creating the world is an *opus* and man is called to participate in God's marvelous works. God's *opus* is entirely free, without necessity. It is a gift of love. Man, called to participate in God's *opus*, is also called to work with a spirit of freedom and love. But, as a consequence of original sin, man now finds that his work is also *labor*, which involves fatigue and toil: "In the sweat of your face you shall eat bread till you return to the ground, for out of it you were taken; you are dust, and to dust you shall return."[8]

In addition, the Church teaches that work takes on a redemptive meaning because of the life and work of Jesus Christ.

By enduring the hardship of work in union with Jesus, the carpenter of Nazareth and the one crucified on Calvary, man collaborates in a certain fashion with the Son of God in his redemptive work. He shows himself to be a disciple of Christ by carrying the cross, daily, in the work he is called to accomplish. Work can be a means of sanctification and a way of animating earthly realities with the Spirit of Christ.[9]

By his hidden life and work in Nazareth, Christ gives man an example. Man is called to work, oftentimes far from the gaze of the world, but never from the sight of God. God's call to Adam in the Book of Genesis, "Where are you?" echoes throughout each generation. *The Catechism of the Catholic Church* teaches: "[A]t every time and in everyplace, God draws close to man. [God] calls man [and helps him] to seek him, to know him, to love him with all his strength."[10]

God calls Adam and he does not cease to call the men and women of every generation and of every time. God calls them to himself not only in every epoch, but in every place and situation. God is interested in all of man's activities. Jesus Christ, through his hidden life in Nazareth, confirms man's vocation to work. He confirms God's interest in the ordinary and thereby confirms man in his work. Man discovers and fulfills the will of God in and through his daily work. Then by his work of salvation in his death and resurrection, Jesus Christ *elevates* man's work. Now man works not only to perfect and prolong the visible creation, but he works in union with Jesus Christ in redeeming the world. And not only does work have a *creative* and *redemptive* meaning, it also *sanctifies* man. It has the potential, in union with Christ, to make man holy.

Work as an Expression of Love

From its human and divine perspectives, work can be viewed as an expression of love. John Paul II underscores this in his letter *Redemptoris Custos*—man's work has human significance. Man works with the intention of carrying out specific tasks that enable him to live his daily life. In addition, he carries out certain tasks in order to be of service to others. He works to support his family, friends, and society. Work is thus not only a personal reality, but also has an important social dimension which can and should be understood as an expression of love for oneself and one's neighbor.

Man can also discover, with the light of faith, that his work shares in God's creative and redemptive act and that his work becomes a means to personal growth and holiness. God's creative and redemptive acts are works of love. They are works of freedom. Man, created in the image and likeness of God, is called to participate, perpetuate and perfect God's work. Such is the lot of all men and women, whether they receive remuneration for their work or not. This is true of work that may be witnessed by thousands, perhaps millions of people. It is true of work that may be seen by only a few persons or perhaps just one, the subject who is doing the work himself. Clearly, it is true of the work of the entrepreneur, as it is of a doctor, an engineer, a mother, a father, a nurse, etc. All work, in the eyes of God—and subsequently in the eyes of the Christian—is an expression of love. The prototype of the daily life and work of man is the life and work of the Holy Family of Nazareth. It is precisely here, in Nazareth, that work is clearly seen and understood to be an expression of love.

Entrepreneurial Theory and Activity:
Some General Observations

In their work, entrepreneurs carry out specific activities aimed at achieving certain goals. Like other men and women, especially Christians, they are called to see, in the light of faith, that their work is a share in the creative and redemptive work of God. Thus their work is also an expression of love.

Before attempting to define entrepreneurial work more precisely, it seems useful to make some brief observations about economics, business, and finance. To which theoretical field does the work of the entrepreneur belong? Does entrepreneurial work form part of the theory of economics, or does it fit better with the theory of finance, or the theory of business? Some beginning definitions will help to clarify discussion of this question. First, economics can be defined as: "[T]he branch of knowledge concerned with the production, consumption, and transfer of wealth."[11] Paul Samuelson's classic definition expounds this basic idea.

> Economics is the study of how men *choose* to use scarce or limited productive resources (land, labor, capital goods such as machinery, technical knowledge) to *produce* various commodities (such as wheat, beef, overcoats, yachts; concerts, roads, bombers) and *distribute* them to various members of society for their consumption.[12]

Finance may be defined as: "[T]he management of large amounts of money, especially by governments or large companies."[13] In fact, however, financial theory takes up two interrelated questions: the investment decision and the financing decision.[14] Alexander Robichek and Stewart Myers, in *Optimal Financing Decisions*, outline the function of finance, utilizing the thoughts of Solomon. They argue that the modern approach to financial management as the attempt to provide answers to these questions. What specific assets should an enterprise acquire? What volume of funds should an enterprise commit? How should the funds required be financed?[15] The objective of finance, they conclude, "is to *maximize the value of the firm to its shareholders.*"[16]

Business is perhaps a little harder to define. The word itself would seem to have its origin from Old English *bisignis* and thus refers to "anxiety."[17] But clearly a businessman refers to "a *person who works in commerce*, especially at executive level."[18] It is here, in the world of business and in the world of investment and finance, that the entrepreneur seems to fit. Economics covers the vast field of choice with respect to the use of resources and their subsequent transformation and distribution. It is concerned with human activity given certain assumptions about resources and human behavior. It assumes that there are limited resources[19] and that man will make decisions that will maximize or optimize his returns. For instance, microeconomic theory holds that the producer will attempt to sell his product at the highest possible price, while the consumer will attempt to buy a product at the lowest possible price. The intersection of supply and demand will be the equilibrium price for a given product. Economic theory postulates that increases or decreases in either supply or demand (due to changes in the conditions behind supply and demand) will have an effect on the price of products. But the price of the goods will always tend toward equilibrium. Dealing with these and related issues, economics studies the vast field of human action in the economic sphere and therefore tends to have a universal character that finance and business theory do not. In addition, when dealing with possible solutions to difficult economic issues, it tends to place greater trust in the adjustment of certain economic variables.

Economic theory clearly is important, but because of its universal character and reliance on economic variables as well as its assumptions concerning human behavior, it tends to miss the importance of individual initiative in building and sustaining the economy. While economics studies what we call "the economy," finance and business theory and practice is involved in the study and practice of the actual creation and sustaining of the economy. Economics studies the economy as it exists, so to speak, while finance and business appears as one of the most important protagonists in creating the economy.

Thus, the entrepreneur, while fully part of the economy, is in some sense *prior* to it. He would appear to belong more to the world of finance and business than economics. Having made this observation, it becomes clear that the entrepreneur is himself not primarily concerned with the investment and finance decision. To be sure, he will be interested in what assets should be acquired by his company and how the company will finance the decision. But he and his entrepreneurial activity exist prior to these decisions. This becomes clear when we examine an accurate definition of the entrepreneur. Two words are crucial here: *entrepreneur* and *enterprise*.

The term *entrepreneur* has its origin in the nineteenth-century word "denoting the director of a musical institution" and comes from the French *entreprendre*,[20] which is based on the Latin word *prendere* ("to take"[21] or to "seize, catch, lay hold of"[22]). The word itself would seem to imply a taking up of things with or between other people, or perhaps an entering into and taking up of a task among other possible tasks. In the *Concise Oxford Dictionary*, the entrepreneur is defined as: "[A] person who *sets up a business* or businesses, taking on *greater than normal financial risks* in order to do so."[23] Enterprise is defined as: "[A] project or undertaking, especially a bold one."[24] Hence, the term *entrepreneur* is of recent origin, but the activity that it describes is not. In pre-industrial societies, the term *merchant* or *trader* was used to cover a large range of business activities, but also behavior that particularly can be called entrepreneurial, which is developed below.

The preliminary definition that is provided above highlights two of the essential elements of entrepreneurial work: (1) *undertaking* a business project and (2) the *risk* involved in such a decision. While economic theory and practice concern the interplay of economic variables within the economy as such, the theory and practice of entrepreneurial activity concerns the decision which creates a business or project that will enable the creation, functioning, and sustaining of the economy.

In *Entrepreneurship: A Comparitive and Historical Study*, Paul Wilken illuminates this important distinction. First, he takes note of the view that regards the entrepreneur as a critical figure in the development of economic growth. Second, he takes note of the view that simply regards the entrepreneur as a conductor or transmitter of more fundamental causes of economic growth. This latter view belongs to the sphere of economic theory, while the former relates clearly to entrepreneurial and business theory.

> Entrepreneurship has been regarded by many as one, perhaps the most, *significant causal factor in the process of economic growth* and development. Hence differences in entrepreneurship among societies are believed to account for their differential rates of growth and development.... advocates of this point of view are most likely to *attribute the amount of entrepreneurship within society to a constellation of factors that are generally non-economic in nature.* According to them, entrepreneurship is most likely to emerge either under a specific set of social conditions or when a society has a sufficient supply of individuals possessing particular psychological characteristics.
>
> But some students of the problem offer an opposite argument regarding the significance of entrepreneurship and its causes. *From this point of view entrepreneurship is neither a significant causal factor in economic growth* and development, nor are social and psychological factors crucial facilitating factors. Rather, entrepreneurship is regarded as fulfilling the function of a conductor or transmitter of more fundamental causes. And these causes are economic in nature. Thus the argument can be simply summarized as follows: *Economic growth and development, and entrepreneurship are most likely to occur in situations where particular economic conditions are most favorable.*[25]

The first categorization might be termed the "business-finance" view of the entrepreneur, while the second might be termed the "economic" view of the entrepreneur. I am inclined to side with the business view of the entrepreneur. Surely the economic view is correct in pointing out that economic conditions are important in either fostering or hampering the entrepreneur. But the business view of the entrepreneur places greater emphasis on and respect for human freedom. The economic and financial system is crucial, as are proper legislative and judiciary processes that protect and promote private property. But it is human persons who make decisions and take risks. Without this basic freedom of the human person, expressed by specific choices, there would be no economic development, let alone economic and financial system.

Australian entrepreneur Christopher Golis takes a balanced approach, noting the importance of entrepreneurs and describing how governments can thwart their crucial role in economic development. Making his comments in the midst of a debate on possible solutions to the problem of unemployment in Australia, Golis writes, "Employment growth does not come from achieving certain levels of economic growth and productivity gains (as most economists suggest), but rather from entrepreneurs launching new companies based on new ideas and technologies."[26] He continues:

> Crushing enterprise out of a nation is easy. Governments need only lower the tax and interest cost for large corporations and shift the burden increasingly onto individuals and families and lift the rate of Capital Gains Tax. By putting in programs that favor established companies, institutionalize savings and wealth, and *move against mobile capital*, personal savings and disposable savings, governments thwart the creative and unpredictable processes of growth and innovation.[27]

Golis captures well the distinction between the approach of economists and business theorists. As he notes concerning the issue of employment growth, economists typically place great trust in achieving certain levels of economic growth through various changes in fiscal and monetary policy. Undoubtedly, reductions in interest rates and alterations in government spending will aid employment growth. But Golis' point is most accurate: wealth needs to be spent, rather than hoarded by individuals and corporations. And when governments allow capital to be transferred and used productively, entrepreneurs are given breathing space—they are allowed to retain the capital made on previous investments. Consequently, they have at their disposal a significant source of capital that permits them to undertake new projects. Thus, unemployment rates decline. It is for these reasons that the business-finance view of the entrepreneur is to be preferred.

Finally, an underlying assumption of economic theory is that each individual has access to certain and predictable information that allows the maximization of his needs and wants. This knowledge allows the price to tend toward equilibrium. The difficulty here is not so much with the concept of the equilibrium price, but rather with the assumption that everyone has access to adequate information. As Israel Kirzner notes in *Competition and Entrepreneurship*, this assumption of perfect knowledge that characterizes economic theory needs to be qualified, and when it is, one begins to notice the crucial role of the entrepreneur.

> In other words, where the circumstances of a decision are believed to be certainly known to the decision-maker, we can "predict" what form that decision will take merely by identifying the optimum course of action relevant to the known circumstance. Now this "mechanical" interpretation of decision-making would be entirely acceptable for a world of perfect knowledge and prediction. In such

a world there would be no scope for the entrepreneurial element... But of course we know that human beings do not operate in a world of perfect knowledge, and it was this that led us to emphasize the importance of the *alertness* individuals display toward new information.[28]

Kirzner's points are crucial: we do not live in a world of perfect knowledge, nor does every person share an identical interest in or desire for the same types of information.

The Entrepreneur and Alertness: *Creative Knowledge*

Kirzner's introduction of the alertness concept brings us to the heart of the difference between the economic and business view of the entrepreneur. Economists are interested in the likely effects of changes in certain variables in the economy—such as interest rates, taxation, money supply—while entrepreneurs are interested in innovation and new projects and enterprises. The interests of economists and financiers are different but are not necessarily opposed. The entrepreneur should stay attuned to critical economic information that will allow him to seize the opportunity for new possibilities. His interest is in new movements of thought, of developments in technology and business practice. Through alertness, the entrepreneur desires and obtains access to information that others do not have.

In *The Spirit of Enterprise*, George Gilder offers insights that pertain to alertness. The prologue of his book critiques Adam Smith's "concept of the economy as a great invisibly guided 'machine' in which capitalists are tools of the 'market.'"[29] In other words, the capitalist is not a "tool" or "instrument" placed in the grasp of the "invisible hand." He quotes what he deems to be Smith's most famous lines in *The Wealth of Nations.*

> In perhaps Smith's most famous lines he wrote of capitalists: "In spite of their *natural selfishness and rapacity*, though they *mean only their own conveniency*, though the sole end which they proposed from the labours of all the thousands they employ, be *gratification of their own vain and insatiable desires ... they are led by an invisible hand* ... and *without intending it, without knowing it*, advance the interest of society.[30]

In rejecting the notion that the entrepreneur is simply an instrument of the market, Gilder expounds for us the meaning of what Kirzner means by alertness. The entrepreneur is a *protagonist*, a man who creates and sustains markets by developing business opportunities. All of this is far removed from the "unintentional" and "unknowing" entrepreneur Smith portrays. Rather, the entrepreneur's activity is intelligent and focused:

> The capitalist is not merely a dependent of capital, labor, and land; *he defines and creates capital, lends value to land*, and offers his own labor while *giving effect* to

the otherwise amorphous labor of others. He is not chiefly a tool of markets but the *maker of markets*; not a scout of opportunities but a *developer of opportunity*; not an optimizer of resources but an *inventor* of them; not a respondent to existing demands but an *innovator* who evokes demand; not chiefly a user of technology but a *producer* of it. He does not operate within a limited sphere of market disequilibria, marginal options and incremental advances. For small changes, entrepreneurs are unnecessary; even a lawyer or bureaucrat would do.[31]

Gilder paints a picture of the entrepreneur that is fundamentally different from Smith's. Besides being intelligent and diligent, Gilder claims that the entrepreneur demonstrates freedom and shows selfless behavior.

In their most inventive and beneficial role, capitalists seek monopoly: the unique product, the startling new fashion, the marketing breakthrough, the novel design. These ventures *disrupt existing equilibria* rather than restore a natural balance that outside forces have thrown awry. Because they can change the technical frontiers and reshape public desires, entrepreneurs may be even less limited by tastes and technologies than artists and writers, who are widely seen as supremely free. And because entrepreneurs *must necessarily work and share credit with others and produce for them, they tend to be less selfish than other creative people*, who often exalt happiness and self-expression as their highest goals.[32]

The concept of alertness seems crucial to entrepreneurial activity and it is intimately related to creativity in the marketplace, as will be seen in the definition of entrepreneurial work developed below. By alertness, the entrepreneur is able to *transcend* the existing order of the market. While working within the financial and economic system he is able to play the role of the "outsider," so to speak. He transcends it, crossing the boundaries where others have stopped. By being alert, he takes notice of changed conditions in the marketplace or he is attentive to possibilities that exist, either in the present or future. This alertness then leads to discoveries, to possibilities, of opportunities unforeseen by others.

Alertness forms the basis of creative knowledge. The entrepreneur, through his will and intelligence, reaches beyond the existing order, and with new information in hand, begins to think of new possibilities—of new creations. Can his work be compared to that of an artist? What the artist and entrepreneur create is of course quite dissimilar, but the process is not. Both appear to demonstrate what Joseph Pieper describes in *Living the Truth* as "creative knowing." Pieper speaks of the artist's mind:

The essential form of a statue, for example, lives most vividly and lucidly in the artist's mind (again, *inasmuch* as the sculpture is the creation of the artist; the marble is someone else's work). And in the conception of an inventor and builder—*as far as* being an original idea—a machine exists as much as in the eye of its operator, even more so. The creatively knowing mind of the artist (or technician) is present in the objective, material work as intimately as conversely the work is present in the mind of its creator.[33]

Both artists and entrepreneurs require great willpower and energy, but their intellectual capacities should be highlighted and appreciated, as well. In *Art and Scholasticism*, Jacques Maritain writes:

> The work of art has been pondered before being made, has been kneaded and prepared, formed, brooded over, and matured in a mind before emerging into matter. And there it will always retain the colour and the savour of the spirit. Its *formal* element, what constitutes it of its kind and makes it what it is, is its being controlled and directed by the mind.[34]

So while the work of the entrepreneur is undoubtedly that of the practical intellect,[35] it is first the fruit of creative knowledge. Like the artist, the projects of the entrepreneur have been *pondered*, kneaded, and prepared. Beginning with alertness to outside information, these projects have been brooded over and have matured in the mind even before they are carried out in the practical order.

The Entrepreneur: *Risk* and *Return*

Entrepreneurial work is first a work of the mind, and not in a merely reactive or responsive way. Rather, it is the fruit of freedom and intellect working in unison. It is man seeking, inventing, and desiring new works and possibilities in the marketplace and then bringing them to fruition. In this sense it can be compared to an *opus*, after the work of God himself.

Alertness and creative knowledge lead to action, and because the entrepreneur is dealing with matters that are new in the marketplace, he is involved in risk-taking enterprises. He is not afraid of startling new fashion, of marketing breakthrough and the novel design. In light of his notion of human action, Ludwig von Mises considers that everyone, because of the unevenness of data, can be considered, in some sense, an entrepreneur—a risk taker:

> As soon as one abandons this assumption of rigidity of data, one finds that action must needs be affected by every change in the data. As action necessarily is directed toward influencing a future state of affairs, even if sometimes only the immediate future of the next instant, it is affected by every incorrectly anticipated change in the data occurring in the period of time between its beginning and the end of the period for which it aimed to provide (period of provision). Thus the outcome of action is always uncertain. *Action is always speculation...* In the imaginary construction of an evenly rotating system nobody is an entrepreneur and speculator. *In any real and living economy every actor is always an entrepreneur and speculator* ...[36]

Three important elements here arise from von Mises' thought: uncertainty, some certainty, and purposeful action. Almost every decision that is made contains some element of uncertainty because of the variables that constitute the scenario.

If one of those variables is the human freedom of other individuals, then the outcome is perhaps less certain due to the nature of human persons. Thus, in some sense, everyone can be considered an entrepreneur. But the decisions an entrepreneur makes are characterized by more acute and deliberate risk. After all, it is an entrepreneur's business to effect change, to disrupt normal patterns of choice by introducing some new technology, product, or service into the market. His decisions are uniquely risky, since they are attempting something entirely new. In this sense, then, the behavior of the entrepreneur differs not only in degree, but in kind, from other professions.

The hope of changing the current state of affairs motivates and urges the individual to carry out those human tasks that will actually effect change. An entrepreneur would not act at all without the conviction that change was possible. Amidst whatever uncertainty an entrepreneur faces, there must be underlying data that gives rise to an element of certainty that makes his action seem feasible; otherwise, his action would be irrational, for acting without knowledge contradicts reason.

It is the entrepreneur, precisely with his alertness to information and his creative knowledge, who is able to discern new possibilities. Thus while he, like other human beings, is subject to uncertainty, his interest, alertness, intelligence and motivation enable the entrepreneur to sense and uncover some underlying certainties. It seems to me that this is the particular gift of the entrepreneur, best described as alertness and creative knowledge.[37] Living in and subject to the same world as other human beings are, the entrepreneur is able to see and understand in a different way. He sees new possibilities. He discovers information and realities that others overlook. In a sense, he creates them. He sees them precisely because he desires to see them. This sets him apart from others.

It is this paradox—uncertainty mingled with certainty—that gives rise to the notions of risk and return. These two realities form a key part of Modern Corporate Finance Theory. The relationship between the two is straightforward: "Investors demand and receive a risk premium for holding risky assets."[38] An investment with higher risks promises higher returns, while an investment with lower risks promises lower returns. The relationship between the two is clear and investors will attempt to reduce the amount of risk for a given rate of return, or increase the rate of return for a given level of risk. They will try to arbitrage away the risk.

This principle, the relationship between risk and return, is crucial for the entrepreneur. Clearly, an entrepreneur would not be interested in making a risky decision if the decision did not suggest significant returns. Like an investor who buys stocks or bonds or invests in some other financial instrument, the entrepreneur will make his decision after serious reflection on both the risk and return of a proposed project. Like investors, he will do his best to minimize risk and maximize return. But because of his disposition, the entrepreneur is more willing to take on projects where risk and return are higher. He will be less likely to settle for projects or investments that are safe or risk-free.

Von Mises writes that the true entrepreneur will demonstrate in his activity this fundamental disposition. He will be alert to changes and new possibilities—better prepared than others to assume the risk of a project in the expectation of future returns.[39] While von Mises focuses more on profit as the reward for that quickness of eye, others prefer to focus on risk. Other writers have emphasized the importance of appreciating the risks that entrepreneurs take in preference to being preoccupied with the profits entrepreneurs might make. Robert Sirico's comments in *The Entrepreneurial Vocation* are written within a framework that is more normative than descriptive, but they are very helpful in highlighting the risks entrepreneurs take in their activity. The entrepreneur often assumes great risks, which not only have the potential to bring large profits, but large losses as well. Risk, then, is a key component of entrepreneurial activity along with reward. [40]

Von Mises' observations are also useful for articulating a more exact definition of entrepreneurial work precisely because he makes a distinction between the particular character of entrepreneurial work and the type of person who is likely to be involved in this work. Entrepreneurial work is characterized by initiative in the production process and the promoting of economic and business development. And the person who involves himself in this process can be described as one who is a pacesetter, is agile, possesses a quick eye, is venturesome, is a promoter who is characterized by restlessness, and possesses an eagerness for profits. In the following sections I will provide a systematic definition of entrepreneurial work based on this distinction between the work itself and the type of person likely to be involved in the activity of work. Forming the cornerstone of this definition are the concepts of alertness, creative knowledge, and risk and return.

Entrepreneurial Work

For Kirzner, alertness is the key to entrepreneurial work, and has shown that alertness is intimately related to creative knowledge. In his earlier writings, Kirzner also defines entrepreneurial work:

> That is why, in this book, I speak of the essentially entrepreneurial element in human action in terms of *alertness to information*, rather than of its possession. The entrepreneur is the person who hires the services of factors of production. Among these factors may be persons with superior knowledge of market information, but the very fact that these hired possessors of information have not themselves exploited it shows that, in perhaps the truest sense, their knowledge is possessed not by them but by the one who is hiring them. It is the latter who "knows" whom to hire, who "knows" where to find those with the market information needed to locate profit opportunities. Without himself possessing the facts known to those he hires, the hiring entrepreneur does nonetheless "know" these facts, in the sense that his alertness—*his propensity to know where to look for information*—dominates the course of events.

Ultimately, then, the kind of "knowledge" required for entrepreneurship is *"knowing where to look for knowledge"* rather than knowledge of substantive market information. The word which captures most closely this kind of "knowledge" seems to be *alertness.*[41]

This alertness then leads to new opportunities—what Kirzner describes as *discovery*—and it manifests itself in what can appropriately be called *works of opportunity.* Thus Kirzner documents the various human activities that spring from alertness:

> The kinds of activities we associate with entrepreneurial vision and energy are varied and numerous. They include, certainly, forming new business ventures; introducing new products; initiating new techniques of production; altering prices (offers or bids) to meet or to forestall competitors; striking out in new territory to identify new markets for one's product; identifying new sources of finance; and streamlining internal patterns of organization.[42]

The four key elements in entrepreneurial work are, first, *alertness* to information. It leads to creative knowledge. *Discovery* is the second key element. With alertness, the entrepreneur either discovers changed conditions or overlooked possibilities, both of which have gone unnoticed by others in the marketplace. Such overlooked possibilities include both existing conditions and future conditions. In either scenario the entrepreneur is said to *transcend* the existing framework. Third, having discovered the changed conditions or overlooked possibilities, the entrepreneur acts by *engaging the factors of production* (land, labor, capital, and enterprise). Fourth, *profit* and *reward* enter into the very definition of entrepreneurial work. There must be sufficient compensation—return—for the risk undertaken in step three.

These four elements comprise a descriptive, rather than normative, definition of entrepreneurial work. The question of the common good—and whether this forms part of the essence of what entrepreneurial work can and should be—will be developed when we examine the sacred sources in Chapter 2.

The Entrepreneurial Personality

With the aid of Kirzner, it has been possible to further refine von Mises' general definition of entrepreneurial work, with its specific character of initiative in the production process and the promoting of economic and business development. Specifically, by enlisting Kirzner's notion of alertness, four key elements of entrepreneurial work have arisen. Alertness and creative knowledge are crucial to the entrepreneurial process of work, for it leads first to discovery, then to the engaging of the factors of production, and finally to profit—a necessary ingredient in the definition. Profit provides a crucial motivation for the risk of the decision to be undertaken and it also provides a financial base with which future decisions can be made.

In relation to identifying the entrepreneurial personality with precision, Kirzner notes a difficulty:

> It would certainly be desirable to be able to identify with precision those human qualities, personal and psychological, which are to be credited with successful entrepreneurial alertness, drive and initiative...
> *Research on Psychological Aspects Is Desirable.* Up to the present, little systematic work appears to have been done on these questions.... Indeed, an important frontier of knowledge, largely unexplored, appears to consist of those aspects of psychology, such as temperament, thirst for adventure, ambition, and imagination, that are likely to throw light on the development of the qualities of entrepreneurship and on the ways alternative institutional arrangements may affect such development. It is to be expected and very much to be desired that research should proceed on this frontier during the years ahead.[43]

Since the publication of Kirzner's work in 1985, there have been attempts to study this exact question. In 1999, Stewart, Watson, Carland and Carland published the results of a survey of 767 small business owner-managers and corporate managers from a twenty-state region, primarily from the southeastern part of the United States. Their article, *A Proclivity for Entrepreneurship: A Comparison of Entrepreneurs, Small Business Owners, and Corporate Managers*,[44] notes the purpose of the study: "to investigate the potential of psychological constructs to predict a proclivity for entrepreneurship." The methodology used by Stewart et al. consisted of a questionnaire "composed of the Achievement Scale of the Personality Research Form, the Risk-Taking and Innovation Scales of the Jackson Personality Inventory and questions pertaining to numerous individual and organizational variables."[45]
The results of the study confirmed their hypotheses:

> In terms of entrepreneurs, the findings were consistent with the majority of our rationale. Our portrait of an entrepreneur is an individual who is *highly driven to succeed*, a motivation that is also connected with a higher propensity for *risk-taking*. Concomitantly, the entrepreneur *sparks innovation* by altering the economic characteristics of products, markets or industries. Decades of research and theorizing about the entrepreneur indicate the confluence of these factors in distinguishing entrepreneurs from their corporate counterparts. The results of this study reinforce this conceptualization of the entrepreneur as an *achieving, creative risk-taker.*[46]

Three characteristics thus emerge about the personality of the entrepreneur. They confirm earlier theoretical literature on the subject. The entrepreneur is one who has a high need for achievement and "this predisposes a young person to seek out an entrepreneurial position to attain more achievement satisfaction than could be derived from other types of positions."[47] Second, the entrepreneur possesses a risk-taking propensity—grounded by a "focus on profits and growth."[48] Finally, the entrepreneur has a preference for innovation. Here the authors' research confirmed what Schumpeter and others had noted.

For instance, Schumpeter (1934) described entrepreneurial innovation in terms of introducing new products or methods of production, opening new markets or new sources of supply, or reorganizing industries. These behaviors are indicative of a level of creative ability possessed by entrepreneurs, as manifested by their strategic behavior."[49]

Innovation in the marketplace, therefore, is the result of creative ability. But the question arises: does the entrepreneur possess a temperament and personality that is unique? Or does he possess a personality type that is shared by others who express themselves, not in entrepreneurial activities, but in other creative activities? Would the founder of a religious order, for instance, possess the same personality type as that of an entrepreneur? It seems the entrepreneur shares a personality type which can find outlet in a variety of activities, but which he expresses in business and commerce.

Entrepreneurial Personality:
The Experience of Entrepreneurs

These qualities are confirmed by entrepreneurial self-reflection. Chris Golis is an Australian entrepreneur who has written on the topic in his book *Enterprise and Venture Capital*.[50] Also noteworthy is McGrath's and MacMillan's recently published, *The Entrepreneurial Mindset*.[51] Both speak from their experience of entrepreneurial work. Golis has been involved in this field of work for many years and McGrath and MacMillan speak from their experience of entrepreneurial work, research studies, and active teaching and working with business organizations.

The first chapter of Golis's work is entitled: *The Entrepreneur: Have You Got What It Takes?* In it Golis details the characteristics of entrepreneurs. They are persons who love to work outside defined parameters and categories. They are not pre-programmed.

Let us begin by considering some of the characteristics of entrepreneurs. One feature is *high energy level*. Entrepreneurs as a whole get up early in the morning. Entrepreneurs hate to stay in bed. They tend to be enthusiastic people who realise the only thing more contagious than enthusiasm is the lack of it.

The next quality is an *interest in money*. Typically a natural entrepreneur will have had jobs in childhood and understand naturally the value of money and how to use it as a resource. Bill Gates, for example, started his first business at the age of sixteen and was filling in company tax forms by the age of eighteen.

The third characteristic is a *creative attitude towards obstacles*. When faced with obstacles typical entrepreneurs find a new way of overcoming them. Most people are conservative. They do not like changes to occur and prefer life to become a habit. Consequently, most people respond to proposals for change with resistance and doubt. The role of the entrepreneur is to create new businesses. They conflict with this widespread conservatism. Most people are constantly putting obstacles in the paths of entrepreneurs trying to achieve their goals. The ability to overcome these obstacles with creative solutions and do it again and again and still maintain enthusiasm is a sign of an entrepreneur...

Entrepreneurs are famous for their *risk-taking ability*. However, it is my experience that successful entrepreneurs are not risk-takers when compared with gamblers or speculators. Entrepreneurs usually operate on stretched resources, yet carry out a realistic evaluation of the risks. They try to establish a position where risk is limited and the reward is substantial. In other words, they tend to look at risk-reward ratios while gamblers think only of the rewards.

The four qualities of *commercial focus, creativity, calculated risk-taking and energy* are necessary ingredients in the personality of an entrepreneur.[52]

Golis then lists a variety of skills the entrepreneur requires in order to function properly in his profession. There is a movement in his writings from temperament to character:

Running a business requires the same *communication skills* [he refers here to earlier comments related to the ability to sell] plus *the ability to negotiate with and analyze people*. Not only are these skills necessary when dealing with customers, but similar skills are necessary when recruiting and motivating employees. Finally, the entrepreneur must be able to convince financiers, be they the banks, finance companies or venture capitalists, that they are as important as the customers and employees. Many of the biographies of successful entrepreneurs demonstrate either a natural selling ability or several years learning the skills of selling.

A good entrepreneur is typically a *good communicator* and is interested in the English language. Most are excellent communicators in the written form and write business letters in strong, simple English...

The next skill one likes to see in the entrepreneur is an *understanding of numbers*. A businessperson needs to understand the principles of accounting...

Another skill the entrepreneur needs is an *understanding of financial and company structuring*;... Entrepreneurs should be familiar with the difference between equity and debt, the roles and responsibilities of directors and the law governing companies and shareholders. The other part of the legal process the entrepreneur must understand is the law of contract.[53]

The thoughts of McGrath and MacMillan are remarkably similar. They note that "habitual entrepreneurs have five characteristics in common."

1. They passionately *seek new opportunities*. Habitual entrepreneurs *stay alert*, always looking for the chance to profit from change and disruption in the way business is done. Their greatest impact occurs when they *create entirely new business models*. New business models revolutionize how revenues are made, costs are incurred, or operations are conducted, sometimes throughout an entire industry. One reason that the emergence of the Internet as

a new medium of business has been accompanied by dizzyingly high company valuations is that investors perceive its potential to profitably transform virtually every aspect of economic life.

2. They pursue opportunities with *enormous discipline.* Habitual entrepreneurs not only are alert enough to spot opportunities, but make sure they act on them. Most maintain some form of inventory, or register, of unexploited opportunities. They make sure that they revisit their inventory of ideas often but they take action only if the competitive arena is attractive and the opportunity is ripe.

3. They pursue only the very best opportunities and avoid exhausting themselves and their organizations by chasing after every option. Even though many habitual entrepreneurs are wealthy, the most successful *remain ruthlessly disciplined about limiting the number of projects they pursue.* They go after a tightly controlled portfolio of opportunities in different stages of development. They tightly link their strategy with their choice of projects, rather than diluting their efforts too broadly.

4. They focus on execution—specifically, *adaptive execution.* Both words are important. People with an entrepreneurial mindset execute, that is, they get on with it instead of analyzing new ideas to death. Yet they are also adaptive, able to change directions as the real opportunity, and the best way to exploit it, evolves.

5. They *engage the energies of everyone* in their domain. Habitual entrepreneurs involve many people—both inside and outside the organization—in their pursuit of an opportunity. *They create and sustain networks of relationships rather than going it alone, making the most of the intellectual and other resources people have to offer and helping those people to achieve their goals as well.*[54]

McGrath and MacMillan list five characteristics. Golis lists four characteristics, then adds another in his discussion of the skills that an entrepreneur requires. In fact, his fifth characteristic equates with that of McGrath and MacMillan. For Golis, an entrepreneur requires communication skills and the ability to negotiate with and analyze people. McGrath and MacMillan are perhaps a little more succinct when they note that the entrepreneur mobilizes everyone's energy. Specifically, the entrepreneur creates and sustains networks of relationships rather than going it alone, and in doing so make the most of the intellectual and human resources others have to offer.[55] Both of these writers highlight the relational aspect of entrepreneurial work.

Of the following five characteristics that serve as a definition of the entrepreneurial personality, in constructing the first four characteristics, I have compressed the thoughts of Golis, McGrath, and MacMillan together. There are slight differences between the two, but essentially they form a coherent definition. An entrepreneur is *commercially focused* (has an interest in money). He is *creative*, seeks out new opportunities and acts on them. He enjoys involvement in *calculated risk-taking* (decisions). He possesses *high energy levels* and is disciplined in the pursuit of commercial goals. Lastly, an entrepreneur enjoys working with others. He enlists the intellectual and human resources of others and in doing so *creates and sustains relationships* in his work. It is of the nature of entrepreneurial work to appreciate and utilize the intellectual and human resources of other human beings.

Entrepreneur, Businessman, Merchant, Manager: A Clarification of Terms

Having developed a definition of entrepreneurial work and personality, it becomes necessary to make some qualifying remarks about this definition. Stewart observes that a distinction is made between three types of persons involved in the world of business. They distinguish clearly between corporate managers and entrepreneurs and then make the further distinction within this latter term between entrepreneurs and small business owners.[56]

> The central problem addressed in this study is to investigate selected psychologi-
> cal predispositions of small business owner-managers and corporate managers to
> determine if there are significant differences... Carland et al (1984) elucidated two
> distinct types of small business owner-managers: entrepreneurs and small busi-
> ness owners. According to the authors, an entrepreneur capitalizes on innovative
> combinations of resources for the principal purposes of profit and growth, and uses
> strategic management practices. Alternatively, the small business owner operates
> a business as an extension of the individual's personality to further personal goals
> and to produce family income.[57]

While the wide ambit of human occupation is not the domain of scripture and tradition, the Word of God is concerned with mediating those events that display the free activity of God and man. The Word of God mediates the dialogue between Himself and mankind, making these events present to those who hear and receive them. In doing so, Scripture refers quite often to the different professions and activities man undertakes, but it will not be concerned to define those activities with great precision. The writings of theologians and the encyclicals and addresses of popes perhaps show more sensitivity to more exact definitions, although precise definitions will not be their main concern. Rather, the concern will be that of faith seeking understanding, beginning with the deposit of faith and proceeding with the light of faith and the gift of human reason. These observations will be important for identifying the entrepreneur in subsequent chapters. He is present in the sacred sources and in papal thought, but perhaps not with the same precision that defines him in this book.

It has been noted above that the term "entrepreneur" is of recent origin, nowhere to be found until roughly the nineteenth century. In the ancient world the terms "merchant," "trade," or "exchange" most likely denoted what is now understood as entrepreneurial activity. So in examining the sacred sources the goal is not to look for specific terms, but rather for activities that seem to mediate actual entrepreneurial work.

In addition, since there has been no real consensus about what constitutes entrepreneurial work itself, it will not be possible to apply the definition developed here rigorously. For instance, how is it possible to say what constitutes a project or enterprise? Is there some quantitative measure—a monetary value that operates as a benchmark? What constitutes alertness, creative knowledge, and new possibilities in the marketplace? Does the enterprise have to be something entirely new, or can a task be considered entrepreneurial if it builds upon previous insights but nevertheless significantly advances thought or production techniques or some other crucial aspect of the market? Again, while risk and return can be measured with accuracy, who is to determine the level of risk and return that constitutes entrepreneurial activity? These are difficult questions, perhaps are best left to those who work in the field. These questions do not disregard the precise definition developed here, but merely highlight some difficulties in application.

Furthermore, when examining the social teachings of the popes, there are some important observations that relate to the precise definition expounded here in Chapter 1. Chapter 3 examines the topic of private initiative in the social encyclicals since Leo XIII up until Pope John Paul II. The popes judge that business and enterprising activities are important for the common good, but they rarely, with the exception of Pius XII, use the word entrepreneur. Pius XII himself uses this word, and as we shall see, he of all the popes, including Pope John Paul II with his positive affirmations of the entrepreneur in *Centesimus Annus*, is the most affirming of the entrepreneur.[58] While Pius XII is the first pontiff to use the word entrepreneur, his preferred approach is to use words like businessman. Clearly, the activity that is envisaged by Pius XII (and other popes) is wider than the specialized activity of the entrepreneur. They seem to refer to the wider activity of businessmen, who may or may not be entrepreneurs according to the definition developed here.

Nevertheless, it becomes clear from the public addresses of Pius XII and the writings of the other popes that the entrepreneur, as has been defined above, cannot be excluded from their writings, even though the term is rarely used. It seems clear that the phrase "private initiative" and others terms such as business actually mediate entrepreneurial activity as well as business activities in a more general sense.

Therefore, while this thesis explores the theological meaning of entrepreneurial work, it also extends to the wider ambit of business or commercial activities that are not, strictly speaking, entrepreneurial. All entrepreneurs are businessmen, but not all businessmen are entrepreneurs. The focus of this thesis is the entrepreneur; but it will be of interest to those involved in business, even if their work is not exactly that of an entrepreneur. In *Centesimus Annus*, John Paul II directly deals with entrepreneurial activities and then moves into the wider arena of business when he calls for a society of free work, enterprise, and participation. He also calls for a business to be a communion of persons. He is clearly addressing all business people and not just entrepreneurs. So, the man at the corner store who has inherited his father's business, the woman who starts and works a fashion business from home, the CEO of a major company, partners who buy a landscaping business together, and even the small vendors at a baseball game, are all within John Paul's field of vision. Their work may not fit exactly the definition developed in Chapter 1, but much of their activity will include some elements of the definition. They cannot be excluded. The emphasis and focus is the entrepreneur—but this is not meant to exclude the wide variety of businessmen and businesswomen who live and breathe the air of the commercial and business world every day of their lives.

Conclusion

This chapter has developed a precise definition of the entrepreneur, first by identifying the key characteristics of the work itself, then by highlighting the personality characteristics of the entrepreneur. Entrepreneurial work is distinguished by alertness to information and creative knowledge. It discovers new possibilities in the marketplace, engages the factors of production, looks toward profit (return) as a compensation for the risks undertaken in engaging the factors of production. Finally, it is a work characterized by creating and sustaining relationships between human persons. The entrepreneur is a person who is commercially focused, creative, takes calculated risks, possesses high energy levels, and enjoys working with others. Chapter 3 examines the sacred sources to discover evidence of a positive appreciation of entrepreneurial work to see whether sacred scripture and tradition can further improve the definition developed in this chapter.

Notes

1. Sir. 42:1, 5.
2. *The Concise Oxford Dictionary*, 10th ed., s.v. "Work."
3. Edwin G. Kaiser, *Theology of Work* (Westminster: The Newman Press, 1966), 5.
4. Gideon Goosen, *The Theology of Work* in vol. 22 of *Theology Today*, ed. Edward Yarnold (Hales Corners, WI: Clergy, Book Service, 1974), 43.
5. Kaiser, *Theology of Work*, 6. Emphasis added.
6. CCC 378.
7. *Laborem Exercens*, 4.
8. Gen. 3:19.
9. CCC 2427.
10. CCC 1.
11. *The Concise Oxford Dictionary*, 10th ed., s.v. "Economics."
12. Paul A. Samuelson, *Economics*, 9th ed. (New York: McGraw-Hill Books, 1973), 3. Emphasis added.
13. *The Concise Oxford Dictionary*, 10th ed., s.v. "Finance."

14. See Alexander A. Robichek and Stewart C. Myers, *Optimal Financing Decisions*, ed. Ezra Solomon, *Prentice-Hall Foundations of Finance Series* (Englewood Cliffs: Prentice-Hall, Inc., 1965), 2.

15. Ibid.

16. Ibid.

17. *The Concise Oxford Dictionary*, 10th ed., s.v. "Business."

18. Ibid. Emphasis added.

19. If the crucial resource is man, and not land or capital, then to a certain extent resources can be viewed as infinite or at least indefinite and open.

20. *The Concise Oxford Dictionary*, 10th ed., s.v. "Entrepreneur."

21. Ibid.

22. Leo F. Stelten, *Dictionary of Ecclesiastical Latin* (Peabody: Hendrickson, 1997), 207.

23. *The Concise Oxford Dictionary*, 10th ed., s.v. "Entrepreneur." Emphasis added.

24. Ibid., s.v. "Enterprise."

25. Paul H. Wilken, *Entrepreneurship: A Comparitive and Historical Study* (Norwood, NJ: Ablex Publishing Corporation, 1979), 2–3. Emphasis added.

26. Quoted in: Anthony Percy, "Taxes and the Future of our Youth," *Catholic Voice*, December 1998, 1–8, 8.

27. Ibid. Emphasis added.

28. Israel M. Kirzner, *Competition and Entrepreneurship* (Chicago: The University of Chicago Press, 1973), 37–38.

29. George Gilder, *The Spirit of Enterprise* (New York: Simon and Schuster, 1984), 16.

30. Ibid., 16. Emphasis added.

31. Ibid., 16–17. Emphasis added.

32. Ibid., 17. Emphasis added.

33. Josef Pieper, *Living the Truth: The Truth of All Things and Reality and the Good*, trans. Lothar Krauth (San Francisco: Ignatius Press, 1989), 41.

34. Jacques Maritain, *Art and Scholasticism: With Other Essays*, trans. J. F. Scanlan, Reprint ed. (North Stratford: Ayer Company Publishers, 2002), 7.

35. Ibid., 3.

36. Ludwig von Mises, *Human Action: A Treatise on Economics* (New Haven: Yale University Press, 1949), 253–54. Emphasis added. For an excellent summary of the insights of the Austrian School of thought regarding the entrepreneur see: Samuel Gregg, "The Rediscovery of Entrepreneurship: Developments in the Catholic Tradition," in Samuel Gregg and Gordon Preece, "Christianity and Entrepreneurship: Protestant and Catholic Thoughts," CIS Policy Monograph 44 (Sydney: The Centre for Independent Studies, 1999). Gregg's article is particularly good at bringing out the importance of freedom and human action in entrepreneurial work. He follows von Mises' view of action presented in the citation above, but then notes that action also has a redounding effect.

37. Alertness and creative knowledge could be referred to as the "artistic" dimension of entrepreneurial work.

38. Richard A. Brealey, Stewart C. Myers, and Alan J. Marcus, *Fundamentals of Corporate Finance*, 2d ed. (Boston: Irwin/McGraw-Hill, 1999), 242.

39. Von Mises, *Human Action*, 255–56.

40. Robert A. Sirico, "The Entrepreneurial Vocation," *Markets & Morality* 3, no. 1 (2000): 1–22, 6. Emphasis added.

41. Israel M. Kirzner, *Competition and Entrepreneurship* (Chicago: The University of Chicago Press, 1973), 68. Emphasis added.

42. Israel M. Kirzner, *Discovery and the Capitalist Process* (Chicago: The University of Chicago Press, 1985), 6.

43. Ibid., 25–26.

44. Wayne H. Stewart et al., "A Proclivity for Entrepreneurship: A Comparison of Entrepreneurs, Small Business Owners, and Corporate Managers," *Journal of Business Venturing* 14, no. 20 (1999): 189–214.

45. Ibid., 189.

46. Ibid., 204. Emphasis added.

47. Ibid., 192.

48. Ibid., 195.

49. Ibid.

50. Christopher C. Golis, *Enterprise and Venture Capital: A Business Builders' an Investors' Handbook*, 3d ed. (Sydney: Allen & Unwin, 1998).

51. Rita G. McGrath and Ian MacMillian, *The Entrepreneurial Mindset* (Boston: Harvard Business School Press, 2000).

52. Christopher C. Golis, *Enterprise and Venture Capital: A Business Builders' and Investors' Handbook*, 3d ed. (Sydney: Allen & Unwin, 1998), 3–4. Emphasis added.

53. Ibid., 5–6. Emphasis added.

54. Rita G. McGrath and Ian MacMillan, *Entrepreneurial Mindset* (Boston: Harvard Business School Press, 2000), 2–3. Emphasis added.

55. In the chapter entitled "The Most Important Job: Entrepreneurial Leadership," McGrath and MacMillan expound on this fifth characteristic. "Your most important job as an entrepreneurial leader is not to find new opportunities or to identify the critical competitive insights. Your task is to create an organization that does these things for you as a matter of course. You will have succeeded when everyone in the organization takes it for granted that business success is about a continual search for new opportunities and a continual letting go of less productive activities" (Ibid., 301).

56. Stewart et al., "Proclivity for Entrepreneurship," 191.

57. Ibid.

58. As we shall see in Chapter 6, John Paul II does not use the word entrepreneur in *Centesimus Annus*. He does use it, however, in other less solemn addresses. Nevertheless, that he is referring to entrepreneurial activity in *Centesimus Annus* is made clear by the context of his discussion.

3

Entrepreneurial Work: Scripture and Tradition

*O Good Merchant, buy us. Why should I say buy us, when we
ought to give Thee thanks that Thou hast bought us? Thou dost
deal out our Price to us, we drink Thy Blood; so dost thou deal
out to us our Price.*

—St. Augustine[1]

Having developed a definition of entrepreneurial work, we will now examine
several questions. First, is it possible to identify the entrepreneur, his work, and
his personality in the sacred sources—that is, scripture and tradition as well as
the works of theologians who write within the tradition of the Catholic Church?
Second, do sacred scripture and tradition have anything to say about the meaning
of entrepreneurial work? Chapter 1 examined entrepreneurial work largely from a
secular standpoint. With the introduction of scripture and tradition, the normative
element of human behavior comes into play. Do the sacred sources contribute to a
deepening of the definition developed in Chapter 1 by introducing the normative
and moral dimensions of entrepreneurial activity, transforming it in light of faith?
Do the sacred sources speak directly to the entrepreneur and his work, encourag-
ing him to see dimensions in it that he would not have seen otherwise? It has been
noted already that entrepreneurial work creates and sustains human relationships.
This relational dimension forms, for John Paul II, the essential character of human

work. Does the light of faith suggest other dimensions that can and should form part of entrepreneurial work?

This question is critical. How is the meaning of entrepreneurial work deepened by contact with the Word of God? One great theme is introduced in this chapter that is repeated in subsequent chapters: entrepreneurial work should be oriented toward the common good.

Entrepreneurial Work in the Old Testament

All of the elements of entrepreneurial work found in Chapter 1 are discernible in the Old Testament. Likewise, the entrepreneurial personality emerges in several persons of the Old Testament and they are praised. And many instances of the broader definition of business provided in the previous chapter are disclosed by the reading of the sacred text. In *Christian Social Witness and Teaching*, Charles writes that:

> The basis of the economy of the people of God was land, and so it is the ethics of land distribution and use which is at the heart of their economic ethic. From the first chapter of Genesis, it is stressed that the land is God's gift, providing from its agricultural and other riches the means needed for man's support. It was a gift to all mankind. God planted a garden and settled man to cultivate it (Gen. 2:8, 15). He was to fill the earth and conquer it (Gen. 1:28), being given all the plants (Gen. 1:29) and animals for his use (Gen1:30), a gift which implied that that use must be such as would please the giver.[2]

Old Testament texts on the subject of work in general and of business in particular have this flavor: they all speak with an agrarian tone. And as Charles notes, the Chosen People—perhaps more so than their modern counterparts—see in the land a gift of God. As a consequence, they were to work with a sense of gratitude—or as Charles puts it, the gift of land implies "that that use must be such as would please the giver"—and the people were to work with a sense that the land was meant for all. "There were to be no poor among them (Deut. 15:4)."[3]

The nature of the gift of land, combined with the nature of man (free, intelligent, and creative), meant that business and commerce and trade would abound. "The particular land the Israelites were to have for themselves was a rich land of streams and springs, of wheat and barley, of vines and fig trees, of olives, oil, and honey, and in it they would want for nothing—a generous gift indeed (Deut. 8:7–10)."[4]

As Charles notes insightfully, the organization of property furthered this personal and economic initiative:

> The organization of the bounty given to them was through *individual property right*. Unlike the Canaanite kingdoms around them, where the king owned all the land and the people held it as his tenants, the Israelites had their own holdings

which they knew were Yahweh's gift to them. Hence Naboth's indignant protest when King Ahab sought to take his plot from him (1 Kings 21:1–3).[5]

Thus, all the ingredients for trade, exchange, commerce and initiative were present. This is what we find when we examine the sacred text. We find laborers, craftsmen, some large-scale commerce and foreign trade. But as Charles notes, there was no merchant class.[6]

Charles notices two predominant patterns in Old Testament thought which are also found in the New Testament: while all forms of work are praised, there is always a caveat. The worker, owner, or trader (merchant) must always be alert to the dangers of wealth, the possibility of avarice and, thus, the destruction of the soul. It is the recognition that work must be viewed from the perspective of the original and bountiful gift from God. Especially since the Fall (and man's tendency toward evil), the perception and recognition of the gift becomes that much more difficult. Thus, while man will out of necessity always work, since he is a social being and will always need to provide for his welfare, man will not always work within the category of the gift. As we will see in the section devoted to the Fathers of the Church, this too informs their reflections on the meaning of work. Hence, the blessing of work is taken for granted, as is the toil of work, while they are at pains to warn the faithful of the dangers of wealth and avarice.

In *Laborem Exercens*, John Paul II notes the underlying acceptance of all professions in the Old Testament.

> The books of the Old Testament contain many references to human work and to the individual professions exercised by man: for example, the doctor, the pharmacist, the craftsman or artist, the blacksmith—we could apply these words to today's foundry-workers—the potter, the farmer, the scholar, the sailor, the builder, the musician, the shepherd, and the fisherman. The words of praise for the work of women are well known.[7]

There are, however, cautions expressed in Scripture. The Book of Sirach, for example, stressed that the gaining of wisdom is important which means that people must make time to stop, pray, think and reflect.[8] Contemplation has priority over activity. Nevertheless, work itself becomes a source of contemplation: "prayer is concerned with what pertains" to the trades. As Weber notes,[9] we can discern here the writer's preference for the work of the scribe and scholar, that is, for intellectual work. But his treatment of other work does not suffer—he simply sees an order that is necessary to facilitate the proper functioning of society. The work of the tradesman is crucial. Without them "a town could not be built" and "there would be no settling, no travelling." For "they give solidity to the created world" just as those who "hold high ranks" provide their contribution to the *polis*. Here we discern the beginning of an appreciation of how all work in general—and entrepreneurial work in particular—gains added value and dignity by lending order to the common good.

Entrepreneurial work is present in this text, albeit implicitly. It appears under the form of the work of the craftsman and potter. It was suggested in the previous chapter that the work of an entrepreneur is like the work of an artist. The sacred text seems to affirm this judgment. Here the artist is a craftsman and potter and he displays many of the elements of the definition developed in the previous chapter. He is "always thinking of new designs"—"setting the heart on a new likeness." He is alert to new possibilities and "stays up perfecting his work" so that his work comes to fruition (production).

The prophet Isaiah condemns the sin of idolatry, but amidst this scathing attack he discloses the skill of the artists, the blacksmith, and wood carver. In the midst of sin, the author of the sacred text is nonetheless able to praise what is good.

Who ever fashioned a god or cast an image without hope of gain?. . . The blacksmith works on it over the fire and beats it into shape with a hammer. He works on it with his strong arm till he is hungry and tired; drinking no water, he is exhausted. The wood carver takes his measurements, outlines the image with chalk, carves it with chisels, following the outline with dividers. He shapes it to human proportions, and gives it a human face, for it to live in a temple. He cut down a cedar, or else took a cypress or an oak which he selected from the trees in the forest, or maybe he planted a cedar and the rain made it grow. *For the common man it is so much fuel; he uses it to warm himself, he also burns it to bake his bread. But this fellow makes a god of it and worships it; he makes an idol of it and bows down before it.*[10]

The end of the work is condemned as idolatrous; but the means—creative knowledge, carving, shaping, and so forth—are not. These skills are praised and they are used by the common man, the faithful man, to earn his living (which, by contrast, is a good end).

The Book of Exodus depicts the skill of the craftsmen as sharing in the Spirit of God himself. God is the source of intelligence, knowledge, and skill.

The LORD said to Moses, "See, I have called by name Bezalel the son of Uri, son of Hur, of the tribe of Judah: and I have filled him with the *Spirit of God*, with ability and *intelligence*, with *knowledge* and all *craftsmanship*, to devise artistic designs, to work in gold, silver, and bronze, in cutting stones for setting, and in carving wood, for work in every craft. And behold, I have appointed with him Oholiab, the son of Ahisamach, of the tribe of Dan; and I have given to all able men ability, that they may make all that I have commanded you: the tent of meeting, and the ark of the testimony, and the mercy seat that is thereon, and all the furnishings of the tent, the table and its utensils, and the pure lampstand with all its utensils, and the altar of incense, and the altar of burnt offering with all its utensils, and the laver and its base, and the finely worked garments, the holy garments for Aaron the priest and the garments of his sons, for their service as priest. . .[11]

The Jerusalem Bible observes: "The spirit of God is regarded as the source of outstanding gifts, in this case of technical skill, which is considered as a share in the divine wisdom."[12]

Then there is the work of the scholar. The scholar needs a spirit of initiative and must be alert to knowledge that exists but is as yet unexploited.

> *It is otherwise with the man who devotes his soul*
> *To reflecting on the Law of the Most High.*
> *He researches into the wisdom of all the Ancients,*
> *He occupies his time with the prophecies.*
> *He preserves the discourses of famous men,*
> *He is at home with the niceties of parables.*
> *He researches into the hidden sense of proverbs,*
> *He ponders the obscurities of parables.*
> *He enters the service of princes,*
> *He is seen in the presence of rulers.*
> *He travels in foreign countries,*
> *He has experienced human good and human evil...*[13]

Alertness and knowledge seem to be the key to the work of the academic. Paying close attention to the wisdom of the ancients and to the prophecies of the past yields new knowledge and insights. Thus, while a scholar may not be employing the means of the production as does an entrepreneur (nor does he have the same interest in money that an entrepreneur has), it is nevertheless true that his work leads to the creation of something new. Advances in knowledge have been made because of his initiative, alertness and dedication.

While in the modern world we would hardly equate the work of the sailor with that of the entrepreneur, in the ancient world sailing was associated with risk and discovery. John Paul II supplies two references here, one to the Psalms and the other to the Book of Wisdom.[14] The latter discusses the sailor from the perspective of idols. Once again, the ingenuity that is needed both to build the ship and to undertake the voyage embodies alertness, risk, and the decision to employ the various factors of production.

> *Or someone else, taking ship to cross the raging sea,*
> *Invokes a log even frailer than the vessel that bears him.*
> *No doubt that ship is the product of a craving for gain,*
> *Its building embodies the wisdom of the shipwright,*
> *But your providence, Father, is what steers it...*[15]

Unlike current times, in which people hardly think twice about sailing (or about flying, to use a more modern example), in the ancient world sailing was undoubtedly a very risky and daring feat. The dangers inherent in such a decision are manifest in the Psalms:

Others, taking ship and going to sea,
Were plying their business across the ocean;
They too saw what Yahweh could do,
What marvels on the deep!

He spoke and raised a gale,
Lashing up towering waves.
Flung to the sky, then plunged to the depths,
They lost their nerve in the ordeal,
Staggering and reeling like drunkards
With all their seamanship adrift.[16]

The final reference supplied by John Paul II in *Laborem Exercens* is the hymn in praise of the virtuous wife in the Book of Proverbs. Various authors have noted the significance of this concluding section of the Book of Proverbs. Typically, commentaries notice the qualities of the woman with respect to her role as homemaker and wife. Below, those elements of the woman's personality that resonate with the description of the entrepreneurial personality are highlighted:

Aleph   A perfect wife—who can find her?
          She is far beyond the price of pearls.

Beth   Her husband's heart has confidence in her,
          From her he will derive no little profit.

Ghimel Advantage and not hurt she brings him
          All the days of her life.

Daleth She is always busy with wool and with flax,
          She does her work with eager hands.

He   She is like a merchant vessel
          Bringing her food from far away.

Waw   She gets up while it is still dark
          Giving her household their food,
          Giving orders to her serving girls.

Zain   She sets her mind on a field, then she buys it;
          With what her hands have earned she plants a vineyard.

Heth   She puts her back into her work
          And shows how strong her arms can be.

Teth   She finds her labour well worth while;
          Her lamp does not go out at night.

Yod   She sets her hands to the distaff,
          Her fingers grasp the spindle.

Kaph   She holds out her hand to the poor,
         She opens her arms to the needy.

Lamed   Snow may come, she has no fears for her household,
         With all her servants warmly clothed.

Mem   She makes her own quilts,
         She is dressed in fine linen and purple.

Nun   Her husband is respected at the city gates,
         Taking his seat among the elders of the land.

Samek   She weaves linen sheets and sells them,
         She supplies the merchant with sashes.

Ain   She is clothed in strength and dignity,
         She can laugh at the days to come.

Pe   When she opens her mouth, she does so wisely;
         On her tongue is kindly instruction.

Sade   She keeps good watch on the conduct of her household,
         No bread of idleness for her.

Qoph   Her sons stand up and proclaim her blessed,
         Her husband, too, sings her praises.

Resh   'Many women have done admirable things,
         But you surpass them all!'

Shin   Charm is deceitful, and beauty empty;
         The woman who is wise is the one to praise.

         Give her a share in what her hands have worked for,
         And let her works tell praises at the city gates.[17]

Chapter 1 identified four elements associated with the entrepreneurial personality: that the entrepreneur is commercially focused, creative and innovative, enjoys taking risks and has high energy levels (along with a need for high achievement). The four qualities noted above are exhibited quite strikingly by this description of the faithful wife. The woman described maintains a high degree of interest in her work, as can be readily seen from her eagerness to carry it out daily. Her work is equated with the work of the merchant: "She is like a merchant vessel," which perhaps is a reference to her bargaining ability at the markets and her skill at transportation. That she has a high need for achievement—high energy levels—is demonstrated by her rising before dawn, and the late night burning of her oil lamp. Undoubtedly, she is a woman who is thoroughly alert and displays that entrepreneurial creativity and innovative flare: "She sets her mind on a field." Then she makes the decision employing the various factors of production: "then she buys it; with what her hands have earned she plants a vineyard." Risk does not daunt her. And as Golis notes, the entrepreneur typically is a person who is not overcome by obstacles; in fact, he is one who relishes them. This is precisely the sense of the text: "Snow may come, she has no fears for her household, with all her servants warmly clothed." Finally, she demonstrates the skill of communication—a most necessary skill for the entrepreneur, as Golis notes above: "When she opens her mouth, she does so wisely: "On her tongue is kindly instruction." In fact, the import of the text is that her work is for others. The communion of persons is her prime concern.

Entrepreneurial Work in the New Testament

The New Testament continues to have an agrarian flavor when we examine work. *Laborem Exercens* provides various references where work is mentioned in the New Testament, similar to his previous examples:

> In his parables on the Kingdom of God, Jesus Christ constantly refers to human work: that of the shepherd, the farmer, the doctor, the sower, the householder, the servant, the steward, the fisherman, the *merchant*, the labourer. He also speaks of the various form of women's work. He compares the apostolate to the manual work of harvesters or fishermen. He refers to the work of scholars too.[18]

The professions listed in the New Testament are similar to those in the Old, with one significant difference being the Incarnation. John Paul II wants to draw attention to the implications of the Incarnation for the world of work. The hidden life of Christ speaks eloquently in its silence. Indeed, it is a source of scandal for some of the people of his time. The pope brings together the orders of creation and Incarnation and highlights Christ's example of work, above and beyond his words on work. Christ's silence—his hidden life and work in Nazareth—has a greater emotional impact than his words on the subject.[19] This citation affirms the creative dimension of work. Man in his work "participates in the activity of God himself, his Creator." Man's work is creative and by it he prolongs and furthers the work of creation. Man is a participant in bringing to perfection God's creative act. But since creation flows from the heart of God, who is a Father and Creator, man in his work becomes a partner with God in his creative work. Man is not only united with the work of creation, he is united to the Person who creates. And this is precisely because man is made in the image and likeness of God.

Secondly, the pope deepens this affirmation via the person of Jesus Christ. He describes the life and work of Christ as the Gospel of Work—a striking phrase that is meant to convey the *good news concerning the reality of work*. Indeed, the pope goes so far as to say that Jesus Christ is the man of work and that Jesus "looks with love upon human work and the many different forms that it takes."[20] It is, therefore, the Incarnation that definitely affirms the dignity of work. Work is a participation in the creative work of the Creator and finds it fulfillment in the work of the Word made flesh, through whom "all things were made."[21] Furthermore, each form of work intimates (or at least has the potential to intimate) to humanity a "particular facet of man's likeness with God." In other words, different forms of work will make present certain aspects of the Godhead.

Two Parables: Principle of Sublation

One form of work that Jesus affirms and uses in parabolic form is the work of the merchant. The parable itself is preceded by another, which is also appropriate for our discussion.

> The kingdom of heaven is like treasure hidden in a field, which a man found and covered up; then in his joy he goes and sells all that he has and buys that field.

> Again, the kingdom of heaven is like a merchant in search of fine pearls, who, on finding one pearl of great value, went and sold all that he had and bought it.[22]

It is not hard to discern here the notions of alertness and discovery. They are the basis for the decision to invest, to risk all by selling everything one owns to buy the field, the pearl. The parable contains a clear spiritual doctrine—the need to search for and find the treasure of eternal life. Thus the work of the merchant is clearly sublated in the parable. Lonergan notes:

> What *sublates goes beyond what is sublated*, introduces something new and distinct, yet far from interfering with the sublated or destroying it, on the contrary needs it, includes it, preserves all its proper features and properties, and carries them forward to a fuller realization within a richer context.[23]

The kingdom of heaven sublates the hidden treasure and the fine pearls; the search for eternal life sublates the search for the pearls and treasure; the happiness of reaching and finding eternal life sublates the temporal happiness of finding the treasure hidden and obtaining pearls of great price. But as Lonergan notes, far from degrading what has been sublated, what sublates needs includes and preserves what it has sublated. The work of the merchant is sublated, not annihilated. In fact, the work of the merchant obtains a new dignity. Understanding the search for eternal life and its importance depends on an understanding and appreciation of the work of the merchant.

Hence, the force of the parable hinges on two things. The goodness of the work of merchants in and of itself is the first of these. Christ affirms the work of merchants. Why would he have used the example if he did not?[24] Second, the parable depends on the recognition of this goodness by those who hear the parable. His audience must have had some knowledge of what constituted the work of a merchant and have had an experience of the goodness of this work. Without these two realities, the truth of the parable remains ineffectual. Those hearing the parable would not be able to move from what is sublated to what sublates—from matter to spirit.

Jeremias says that the ultimate meaning of the parable is dependent on the phrase found in verse 44. It can be variously translated as "in his joy" or "from sheer joy."[25] I have touched upon the sense of discovery in these two parables. But Jeremias directs our attention to the inner experience of joy upon the discovery. He writes:

> Both parables make use of a favourite theme in oriental story-telling. The audience expected that the story of the treasure in the field would be about a splendid palace which the finder built, or a train of slaves with whom he promenades through the bazaar or about the decision of a wise judge that the son of the finder should marry the daughter of the owner of the field. In the story of the pearl it would expect to hear that its discovery was the reward of special piety, or that the pearl would save the life of a merchant who had fallen into the hand of robbers. Jesus, as always, surprises his audience by treating the well-known stories in such a way as to emphasize an aspect quite unexpected by his hearers. The question is, what aspect?
>
> The double parable is generally understood as expressing the demand of Jesus for complete self-surrender. In reality, it is 'completely misunderstood if it is interpreted as an imperious call to heroic action.'

Then he comments on verse 44 and continues.

> When that great joy, surpassing all measure, seizes a man, it carries him away, penetrates his inmost being, subjugates his mind. All else seems valueless compared with that surpassing worth. No price is too good to pay. The unreserved surrender of what is most valuable becomes a matter of course. The decisive thing in the twin parable is not what the two men give up, but the reason for their doing so; the overwhelming experience of the splendour of their discovery. Thus it is with the Kingdom of God. The effect of the joyful news is overpowering; it fills the heart with gladness; it makes life's whole aim consummation of the divine community and produces the most whole-hearted self-sacrifice.[26]

The joy of discovering Jesus Christ—the Kingdom of God—leads a person to an unreserved surrender of himself. Joy forms another part of the entrepreneur's work. The joy of discovering new possibilities leads him to risk his own wealth and employ the factors of production. Thus, the joy of discovery and the surrender of his wealth to a new business decision have the potential to intimate to the entrepreneur the ultimate joy of discovering Christ and surrendering all to him.

The Parable of the Dishonest Steward

Another of Christ's parables implicitly praises the work of merchants. It is the parable of the dishonest steward.

> He also said to the disciples, "There was a rich man who had a steward, and charges were brought to him that this man was wasting his goods. And he called him and said to him, 'What is this that I hear about you? Turn in the account of your stewardship, for you can no longer be steward.' And the steward said to himself, 'What shall I do, since my master is taking the stewardship away from me? I am not strong enough to dig, and I am ashamed to beg. I have decided what to do, so that people may receive me into their houses when I am put out of the stewardship.' So, summoning his master's debtors one by one, he said to the first, 'How much do you owe my master?' He said, 'A hundred measures of oil.' And he said to him, 'Take your bill, and sit down quickly and write fifty.' Then he said to another, 'And how much do you owe?' He said, 'A hundred measures of wheat.' He said to him, 'Take your bill, and write eighty.' The master commended the dishonest steward for his shrewdness; for the sons of this world are more shrewd in dealing with their own generation than the sons of light."[27]

The parable is concerned with shrewdness and seizing opportunities. As John Nolland writes in his commentary on the passage:

> The whole of the action has taken place in connection with the *less than savory nature* of what so often goes on in the world of business and high finance. The ethics are at a pretty low level. But what should attract our attention is that the steward has shrewdly appraised the situation in which he found himself, and acted to save himself. The challenge is for us to have the *shrewdness to recognize and seize the opportunity* that exists in the midst of threat. In the immediate context, the threat and opportunity are those created by the ministry of Jesus.[28]

A Christian should be as shrewd and opportunistic in his relationship with Christ as is the dishonest steward with his master's business. The steward himself may be dishonest, but the *nature of his work* is not. In fact, by praising his shrewdness, Christ admires his opportunism. While the steward abuses the trust his master extends to him, it must be recognized that the nature of the work that is entrusted to him is fundamentally good. The sin of the steward lies in his misuse of his master's business, not the work of business itself.[29]

The details of the parable are important for the purposes of this study. They reveal a rather developed trading and financial system. Nolland highlights some of these in his commentary:

> The most likely basis for the debts is in connection with the leasing of the land producing the crops reflected in the different debt currencies (leasing could be on the basis of a percentage of the crop, or on the basis of an agreed quantity from the yield...). Another possibility would be that loans of the mentioned commodities

are involved. This introduces the complicating factor of interest and questions about the nature of first-century practice against the background of the biblical prohibitions in Deut. 15:7-8; 23:19-20; Exod. 22:25; Lev. 25:36-37. There is a good likelihood that in the first century these verses were not necessarily understood as a prohibition of business loans...[30]

Finally, there is the important reference to risk and return. This is revealed in Nolland's discussion of the debt-reducing activity of the steward.

> The steward is instructing the debtor to reduce by 50 percent the originally specified debt. At a stroke the master has lost half of what he might have expected to receive from this particular business transaction. What exactly is happening? If this is a loan with interest, then it may be important for us to realize that ancient interest rates were very high indeed. Business risks were high, and returns on successful business were correspondingly high. On commodity loans, interest of 50 percent was typical, so much so that a contract idiom emerged...[31]

Like the two parables above, the force of the parable of the unjust steward depends upon the work of the steward and recognition of this work by those hearing the parable. If the import of the parable is that Christians should have the "shrewd-ness to recognize and seize the opportunity that exists" in the person of Christ, then clearly the work and the remedial action of the steward is foundational to the functioning of the parable.[32] The steward, his work and his remedial action—his shrewdness and opportune behavior—is clearly most fitting to highlight the way the believer should act in relation to Christ. Once again we can see the importance of the principle of sublation at work.

The Parable of the Talents

It is, however, the parable of the talents that most strikingly acknowledges Jesus Christ's respect for the work of business. Many of the elements of the parable are conducive to this interpretation. First, there is the emphasis on the "talent," which is a measure of value.[33] Second, the trading activity of the two stewards is important. Christ praises them for the energy, alertness and perseverance they demonstrate in making a truly significant profit (they have doubled the original sum). There is a reference to accountability that is crucial for any business. Then the nuanced criticism of fear: "I was afraid, and I went off and hid your talent in the ground." This fear leads the lazy steward to avoid the risks and obstacles that are a key part of entrepreneurial work. Finally, there is the clear reference to the financial system. The lazy steward at least could have placed the "money with the bankers, and at my coming I should have received what was my own with interest." The parable is found in the Gospel of Matthew.

For it will be as when a man going on a journey called his servants and entrusted to them his property; to one he gave five talents, to another two, to another one, to each according to his ability. Then he went away. He who had received the five talents went at once and traded with them; and he made five talents more. So also, he who had the two talents made two talents more. But he who had received the one talent went and dug in the ground and hid his master's money. Now after a long time the master of those servants came and settled accounts with them. And he who had received the five talents came forward, bringing five talents more, saying, 'Master, you delivered to me five talents; here I have made five talents more.' His master said to him, 'Well done, good and faithful servant; you have been faithful over a little, I will set you over much; enter into the joy of your master.' And he also who had the two talents came forward, saying, 'Master, you delivered to me two talents; here I have made two talents more.' His master said to him, 'Well done, good and faithful servant; you have been faithful over a little, I will set you over much; enter into the joy of your master.' He also who had received the one talent came forward, saying, 'Master, I knew you to be a hard man, reaping where you did not sow, and gathering where you did not winnow; so I was afraid, and I went and hid your talent in the ground. Here you have what is yours.' But his master answered him, 'You wicked and slothful servant! You knew that I reap where I have not sowed, and gather where I have not winnowed? Then you ought to have invested my money with the bankers, and at my coming I should have received what was my own with interest. So take the talent from him, and give it to him who has the ten talents. For to every one who has will more be given, and he will have abundance; but from him who has not, even what he has will be taken away. And cast the worthless servant into the outer darkness; there men will weep and gnash their teeth.'[34]

We can thus affirm unambiguously that Jesus Christ "looks with love upon human work" and that the work of the merchant—the businessman or the entrepreneur—is one of the "different forms" of work that is affirmed. The parable of the talents makes this clear by its reference to money, trading, risk taking and banking. Like the previous parables discussed, these earthly realities are ultimately sublated by Christ's teaching.

On the other hand, as John Paul teaches, each form of work manifests "a particular facet of man's likeness with God." The entrepreneur's alertness and ingenuity, his ability to discover potential opportunities and to make risky decisions, the energy and drive of his personality—all of these traits imitate something of the character of God. In fact, as we will discover in the writings of the Fathers, Christ is sometimes referred to as The Merchantman and his work of salvation is sometimes referred to as a *work of exchange*. The merchant himself and the activity of exchange becomes a metaphor for the person and work of Jesus Christ. And, as has been noted, the experience of entrepreneurial activity, the joy of discovering new possibilities and the surrendering of one's wealth to a new project, can intimate to the entrepreneur something of the joy of discovering Christ and surrendering one's whole being to him.

To be sure, Jesus Christ did not come to evaluate and comment on the different professions or to call attention to a specific profession. Rather, in and through his life of work, he affirmed the goodness of all types of work. In his teaching, particularly his parables, he refers to some of the professions in order to illustrate his spiritual doctrine. Such is the case with the merchant, the entrepreneur. But as we have seen, through Lonergan's principle of sublation, this method of Christ's does not destroy what is sublated, in this case the work of merchants. Rather, it is affirmed. It can be said, therefore, that by his method of teaching Christ implicitly affirms entrepreneurial work. This is the effect of sublation. While raising what is sublated to a new level, it does not destroy what is sublated, but raises it to a new dignity. What sublates needs and raises what is sublated.

The Dangers of Wealth

As with the Old Testament, so it is with the New Testament. Jesus warns of the danger of riches. This danger of temptation is perhaps more serious for those whose work is concerned directly with an interest in money. The dangers of avarice should not be underestimated, as this passage evidences:

> And he told them a parable, saying, "The land of a rich man brought forth plentifully; and he thought to himself, 'What shall I do, for I have nowhere to store my crops?' And he said, 'I will do this: I will pull down my barns, and build larger ones; and there I will store all my grain and my goods. And I will say to my soul, Soul, you have ample goods laid up for many years; take your ease, eat, drink, be merry.' But God said to him, 'Fool! This night your soul is required of you; and the things you have prepared, whose will they be?' So is he who lays up treasure for himself, and is not rich toward God."[35]

The root of the problem with the rich man seems to be the monologue he carries on with himself: the, "he thought to himself" and "I will say to my soul." Certainly, the fact that the "land brought forth plentifully" cannot be the problem. Land, as has been shown, is God's gracious gift. Rather, the rich man is unable to recognize the land (and his human abilities) as a gift precisely because he is in a monologue with himself. If he were more open to God—if he viewed his life and land as a gift—he would have had more regular recourse with Him who granted such gifts. This failure gives rise to the wealthy man's avaricious desires, "Take your ease, eat, drink, be merry."

The behavior of the rich man affects not only his spiritual wellbeing, but has repercussions far beyond his own personal salvation. Charles notes that while the message of the New Testament is clearly spiritual in nature, it nevertheless has profound social implications:

> Given its nature therefore, the New Testament does not deal so extensively with questions of social ethics as did the Old; Christ's mission was religious, his kingdom

spiritual. The Kingdom of God that Christ preached was concerned primarily with the personal spiritual and moral life of man, the way to holiness for its members, but paradoxically it is this orientation which in the long run has the *most profound implications for social life.*[36]

Charles' claim that the mission of Christ is religious and spiritual and not primarily social or political certainly is correct. It might be said that the social is sublated by the primary mission. Pondering the fact that the Romans had taken political control of Palestine in 63 B.C., we search in vain for any reference that documents Christ's desire to overturn this state of affairs. On the contrary, he seems unconcerned with the matter and on one occasion says: "Give back to Caesar what belongs to Caesar—and to God what belongs to God!"[37]

But precisely because the mission is spiritual, it is profoundly communal. The Gospel attempts to reach deep into the heart of man. "It is what comes out of a man that makes him unclean. For it is from within, from men's hearts, that evil intentions emerge: fornication, theft, murder, adultery, avarice, malice, deceit, indecency, envy, slander, pride, folly. All of these evil things come from within and make a man unclean."[38]

It aims at transforming man from within. From this conversion and transformation other persons are transformed. Goodness tends to be effusive. The good news of Jesus Christ flows from one heart to another. Holiness is therefore the message and it is personal and communal. Essentially it is love of God and love of neighbor.[39] Christ's warning to the rich man in the above parable has these two dimensions. In his desire to accumulate wealth, the rich man breaches not only the commandment to love God, but also to love one's neighbor. In his refusal to attend to the needs of his neighbor, the rich man becomes an obstacle to his neighbor—a hindrance to belief. The Book of Proverbs expresses well the importance of avoiding the extremes of both material poverty and material wealth. There is a peculiar spiritual danger present in each scenario.

> *Two things I ask of thee;*
> *deny them not to me before I die:*
> *Remove far from me falsehood and lying;*
> *give me neither poverty nor riches;*
> *feed me with the food that is needful for me,*
> *lest I be full, and deny thee, and say,*
> *"Who is the LORD?" or lest I be poor, and steal,*
> *and profane the name of my God.*[40]

It is clear that Christ's primary concern is with salvation. His mission, his Kingdom, is spiritual. It is this that unites all men. The Kingdom of Christ is not a political reality. Rather, it is a *way of life.* It is spiritual and communal—apt for the nature of man. But this Kingdom will not be indifferent to grave political or social problems. The Church, consistent with her Jewish heritage and to the teaching of

Christ, attempts to come to the aid of the poor and those unjustly treated, without trying to establish a utopian society.[41] Christians who are wealthy have a special obligation to the poor. They are encouraged by the two great commandments—the spiritual law of love—to try to seek ways to render assistance, without however, acting in a way that would diminish the dignity, freedom, and responsibility of the poor.

Entrepreneurial Work in the Early Church

The Law of Love

This spiritual law of love that Christ taught his disciples is evident in the early activity of the Church and it is, according to various authors, the key to the success of the Church.

> For Chadwick the practical application of charity was probably the most important single cause of that success. These works of charity were not isolated instances and restricted to individuals; no Christian was excused from the obligation of contributing to the needs of the poor and the suffering, and the efficiency of the Church's organization was there to give them help where and when it was needed; dioceses were in contact with one another throughout the Empire. Widows and orphans, the sick, infirm and disabled, prisoners and those working in the mines, the care of the poor needing burial, the care of slaves, those affected by natural calamities, and those seeking work; all were the Church's concern.[42]

Similar observations emerge from recent historical-sociological work. In *The Rise of Christianity*, Rodney Stark acknowledges the absolute importance of charity in the early community. Stark posits that the acceleration of Christianity in the ancient world can be explained by the law of love, especially when viewed in the light of epidemics. He notes that many respected works on the rise of Christianity do not pay any attention to epidemics, plagues, and disease, and considers this to be "no small omission" when examining the growth of the Christian faith.

> Indeed, Cyprian, Dionysius, Eusebius, and other church fathers thought the epidemics made major contributions to the Christian cause. I think so too.... had classical society not been disrupted and demoralized by these catastrophes, Christianity might never have become so dominant a faith. To this end, I shall develop three theses. The first of these can be found in the writings of Cyprian, bishop of Carthage. The epidemics swamped the explanatory and comforting capacities of paganism and of Hellenic philosophy. In contrast, Christianity offered a much more satisfactory account of why these terrible times had fallen upon humanity, and it projected a hopeful, even enthusiastic, portrait of the future. The second is to be found in an Easter letter of Dionysius, bishop of Alexandria. Christian values of love and charity had, from the beginning, been translated into norms of social service and community solidarity. When disasters struck, the Christians were better able to

cope, and this resulted in *substantially higher rates of survival*. This meant that in the aftermath of each epidemic, Christians made up a larger percentage of the population even without new converts. Moreover, their noticeably better survival rate would have seemed a "miracle" to Christians and pagans alike, and this ought to have influenced conversion.[43]

The Social Basis of the Early Church

All Christians, regardless of their profession, were called to live this law of love. The early Church, like Christ, was not concerned with any one profession. All Christians, regardless of their state in life, their social class or their profession, were called to love as Christ loves. One struggles, therefore, to find explicit references to merchants and traders. Research in the area of the work of the entrepreneur and businessman has probably gone unnoticed, too, because of the common position taken by most historians and sociologists of the twentieth century that "Christianity was a movement of the dispossessed—a haven for Rome's slaves and impoverished masses."[44] Stark rejects this notion forcefully:

> In recent decades, however, New Testament historians have begun to reject this notion of the social basis of the early Christian movement. E. A. Judge was perhaps the first major scholar of the present generation to raise a vigorous dissent. He began by dismissing the lack of noble Christians as an irrelevancy:
>
>> If the common assertion that Christian groups were constituted from the lower orders of society is meant to imply that they did not draw upon the upper orders of the Roman ranking system, the observation is correct, and pointless. In the eastern Mediterranean it was self-evident that members of the Roman aristocracy would not belong to a local cult association... [Moreover they] amounted to an infinitesimally small fraction of the total population. (1960:52)
>
> After a careful analysis of the ranks and occupations of persons mentioned in the sources, Judge concluded:
>
>> Far from being a socially depressed group, ... the Christians were dominated by a socially pretentious section of the population of big cities. Beyond that they seem to have drawn on a broad constituency, probably representing the household dependents of leading members....
>
>> But the dependent members of city households were by no means the most debased section of society. If lacking freedom, they still enjoyed security, and a moderate prosperity. The peasantry and persons in slavery on the land were the most underprivileged classes. Christianity left them largely untouched. (60)

Moreover, Judge perceptively noted that the "proof text" in 1Cor.1:26-28 had been overinterpreted: Paul did not say his followers included *none* of the wise, mighty, or noble—merely that there were "not many" such persons, which means that there were *some*. Indeed, based on an inscription found in Corinth in 1929 and upon references in Rom. 16:23 and 2Tim. 4:20, many scholars now agree that among the members of the church at Corinth was Erastus, "the city treasurer"

(Furnish 1988:20). And historians now accept that Pomponia Graecina, a woman of the senatorial class, whom Tacitus reported as having been accused of practicing "foreign superstition" in 57 (*Annals* 13.32, 1989 ed.), was a Christian (Sordi 1986). Nor, according to Marta Sordi, was Pomponia an isolated case: "We know from reliable sources that there were Christians among the aristocracy [in Rome] in the second half of the first century (Acilius Glabrio and the Christian Flavians) and that it seems probable that the same can be said for the first half of the same century, before Paul's arrival in Rome." (1986:28)[45]

Stark then notes a variety of scholars who agree with Judge's initial observations. At the conclusion of his summary of authors, he notes, "Kreissig identified the early Christians as drawn from 'urban circles of well-situated artisans, merchants, and members of the liberal professions' (quoted in Meeks 1983:214)."[46]

While being satisfied that the new view of historians is correct, Stark is nevertheless reserved in his conclusions. He says that "*any* claim about the social basis of early Christianity must remain precarious, at least in terms of direct evidence, and it is unlikely that we shall ever have much more than fragments of historical data we already possess."[47]

One of those "fragments" is Tertullian's observation. Charles writes:

> Christians had from the first been forbidden to take any active part in the games, and a number of other occupations were closed to them for fear of compromising their beliefs. Positions of leadership in the military, which involved a suspicion of idolatry or immorality, were denied them. The position changed somewhat as Christianity became more accepted towards the end of the second century. Christian apologists sought to calm the fears of their fellow citizens by stressing how like them Christians were. Tertullian affirmed that 'we frequent your forum, *your market*, your baths, your inns and your fairs. With you we *take ship* and serve as soldiers;' but in all this he stresses that they reject only what touches on immorality or idolatry. Participation *in commerce and trade*, even if innocent of idolatrous purpose, was treated with reserve because of the fear of dishonesty and sharp practice that all business activity aroused. But 'the recognition of the ordinary forms of honest trade and industry as not only a legitimate but an obligatory means of support' is found in Irenaeus and Clement of Alexandria; Tertullian also refers to the Christian frequentation of the markets as one of the signs of their involvement in ordinary life.[48]

That the early Christians had in their ranks persons who showed interest in entrepreneurial matters seems hard to deny. Judge intimates this: "The Christians were dominated by a socially pretentious section of the population of big cities." Businessmen likely were among some of these "pretentious" types. And then we have the evidence that Erastus, a Christian, was "the city treasurer." Regarding other business-minded early Christians, Kreissig, the Marxist historian (whom as Stark notes "recanted the proletarian thesis" after Judge's book appeared[49]), tells us that the early Christians were drawn from "urban circles of well-situated artisans, *merchants*, and members of the liberal professions."[50] Finally, while the suspicion that existed with regard to participation in commerce and trade is worth noting, this fear does not prohibit participation in the profession of business. The fear relates to the possibilities of dishonesty and avarice, which may well corrupt any profession, and not to the profession of business as such.

Entrepreneurial Work in the Fathers of the Church

Private Property

This concern with the dangers of wealth—the fear of avarice—has proven to be a common theme throughout scriptural discussions of wealth management. The concern is only too apparent in the Church Fathers as well. Likewise, agriculture was the predominant business focus of the Roman Empire. The economic setting was similar to that of the time of the Old and New Testaments.[51]

The social and cultural setting became increasingly difficult. These historical factors led the Fathers of the Church to emphasize the fact that private property "has of its very nature a *social mortgage*."[52] With the advent of the empire the "small peasant soldier/farmer as the typical Roman citizen" died.[53]

> Under the Empire the concentration of land in the hands of fewer and fewer accelerated, and as increasing numbers of the displaced peasants and their families left for the cities, the supply of wage workers to till the estates decreased and the owners then turned to slave labour, the conquests of an expanding Empire guaranteeing them their supply.[54]

With the disintegration of the empire in the third and fourth centuries, the state was compelled to ensure that land continued to produce revenues, thus leading to the repression of those who worked the land.[55] With slavery increasing and access to land diminished—it now being in the hands of the elite—the necessary prerequisites for poverty were in place. With the aid of Roman property law these seeds of poverty sprouted.

> The Roman property law centred on the concept of *absolute ownership*, and the action by which that absolutism was asserted; there was an 'unrestricted right of control over a physical thing and whosoever has this right could claim the thing he owns wherever it is and no matter who possesses it.' There were few restrictions on it in public law and for the rest *dominium* or *proprietas* was for practical purposes unrestrained; it included not only the right of using, but also of abusing. He who was in possession had *unlimited power* over him who was not, and gradually distinctions between types of property and their different natures were elided. What remained was the concept of absolute ownership.[56]

Thus a great emphasis on the alleviation of poverty is found in the writings of the Fathers. They set themselves firmly on the side of those who suffer from injustice as opposed to those who perpetrate it.[57] As noted earlier while dealing with entrepreneurial work in the Old Testament, the land was considered as a gift from God to all human beings. Access to it therefore was considered essential if one desired to fulfill the will of God. Thus did the Fathers of the Church, living at a time when this basic condition was being denied, develop the concept of socially responsible ownership. "Man has a right to private property, but that property has of its nature a social mortgage on it. It has to be socially responsible."[58]

But Phan notes that the concern with inequalities does not thereby lead the Fathers to deny the right to private property:

> From the context of their writings, it is clear that the Fathers do not condemn private ownership as such but the abuse of it. Basil, in his *Hom. 6 in illud Lucae "Destruam,"* 7, distinguished between the common destination of the goods created by God for the use of all and the right of property of which he, as well as the other Fathers, recognize the legitimacy. The Fathers, therefore, *do not intend to advocate any form of communism* of earthly goods. Clement of Alexandria, in his *Who is the Rich Man That is Saved?*, sees wealth as an instrument for producing fellowship and sharing. The right to private property thus depends upon the use made of it. There is a right of private property, but it is limited by the needs of our fellowmen, first Christians and then probably others.[59]

The Fathers and the Science of Economics

The social mortgage placed on private property is thus a dominant theme in the Fathers, tinging all of their comments concerning wealth. Dealing with poverty was their chief concern, not the science of economics. As Charles notes:

> Basil and the Fathers had no knowledge of the science of economics as we understand it; it did not exist in their time, so Basil did not look to increasing the wealth of the time in order that there might be more for the needy, but he saw the actual link between injustice in the uses of property and the poverty of the many and was angered by it.[60]

Charles observes that the same can be said of St. John Chrysostom, whose solution to poverty was understood in terms of wealth distribution and not wealth creation. This attitude can appear to us in the twenty-first century as somewhat naïve.

> Here, as with Basil, we may consider his [Chrysostom's] arguments for overcoming the problems of poverty as naïve, concentrating on distribution instead of wealth creation. The same answer holds. Neither he nor his times had any scientific knowledge of economics. He was concerned with the ethics of the situation as he saw it; private ownership of productive goods in an agricultural economy should fulfill its social obligations. At the time it could only do this by fairer distribution of the wealth that existed...[61]

Given these important observations, it is clear that when examining the Fathers more closely with respect to entrepreneurial work, we can expect to find only fleeting references to the topic. Still, amidst their concern with poverty, the rule of love and the danger of wealth, and given the condition of the empire and the state of property law at that time, some of the Church Fathers show a remarkable capacity to appreciate the beauty and importance of entrepreneurial work.

The Fathers and Jesus Christ

Before examining these writings, it seems opportune to highlight the Fathers' preoccupation with Jesus Christ. The Fathers' fascination with him leads them to read and understand all things through the lens of the hypostatic union. When examining created realities, particularly material riches, the Fathers judge them according to Christ. Jesus contains in himself all riches. Everything compared to him is as nothing. The disciple of Christ is faced with two opposing choices: either choose the richness of Christ or choose material riches.

> For as a rule most people call that only useful which is profitable, but we are speaking of that kind of usefulness which is sought in *earthly loss* "that we may *gain Christ*," whose gain is "godliness with contentment." Great, too, is the gain whereby we attain to godliness, which is rich with God, not indeed in *fleeting wealth*, but in *eternal gifts*, and in which rests no uncertain trial but grace constant and unending.[62]

Because of this fascination with Christ, the Fathers tend to spiritualize events and persons. For example, the Fathers often observe the skills that are required for the practice of a profession and then apply these skills to one's pursuit of Christ. It is an example of the principle of sublation spoken of above.

> Whosoever loves fields and merchandise, shall be shut out of the city of Saints. Whosoever does not bear fruit in the vineyard, shall be uprooted and cast out to torment. Whosoever has received money from his Lord, let him return it to its Giver with its increase. Whosoever desires to become a merchant, let, him buy for himself the field and the treasure that is in it. Whosoever receives the good seed, let him purge his land from thorns. Whosoever desires to be a fisherman, let him cast forth his net at every time. Whosoever is training for the conflict, let him keep himself from the world. Whosoever wishes to gain the crown, let him run as a winner in the race. Whosoever wishes to go down into the course to contend, let him learn to (contend) against his adversary. Whosoever wishes to go down to the battle, let him take unto him armour wherewith to fight, and let him purify himself at every time.[63]

With the above three sections in mind, I now present the findings of my research in the following sections. They are presented chronologically by date of death. This list is not meant to be exhaustive, nor does it develop into a coherent theology. It is simply a presentation of and commentary on the pertinent Patristic writings.

Tertullian (A.D. 145–220)

Tertullian argues that all occupations are open to Christians. Christians can be found in the marketplace, other places of commerce, and the risky travels across the oceans.

> We do not forget the debt of gratitude we owe to God, our Lord and Creator; we reject no creature of His hands, though certainly we exercise restraint upon ourselves, lest of any gift of His we make an immoderate or sinful use. *So we sojourn with you in the world, abjuring neither forum, nor shambles, nor bath, nor booth, nor workshop, nor inn, nor weekly market, nor any other places of commerce.* We sail with you, and fight with you, and till the ground with you; and in like manner we unite with you in your traffickings—even in the various arts we make public property of our works for your benefit.[64]

In the midst of a discussion on population he praises the development of the world, which is achieved by work that has a clearly entrepreneurial tone. Commerce is good and the work of those who transform forests into cultivated fields and make deserts yield crops is to be praised. Transforming the earth is part of the vocation of man to subdue the earth.

> The aborigines remain still in their old settlements, and have also enriched other districts with loans of even larger populations. Surely it is obvious enough, if one looks at the whole world, that it is becoming daily better cultivated and more fully peopled than anciently. All places are now accessible, all are well known, all open to commerce; most pleasant farms have obliterated all traces of what were once dreary and dangerous wastes; cultivated fields have subdued forests; flocks and herds have expelled wild beasts; sandy deserts are sown; rocks are planted; marshes are drained; and where once were hardly solitary cottages, there are now large cities. No longer are (savage) islands dreaded, nor their rocky shores feared; everywhere are houses, and inhabitants, and settled government, and civilized life.[65]

Lactantius (A.D. 250–325)

Continuing the theme of Tertullian, Lactantius writes within the perspective of the goodness of creation. The work of the merchant is as natural as the work of the housewife building a fire, baking bread. Just as the farmer diverts the water from the stream to irrigate his fields, so the merchant utilizes the sea to provide people with what they would not otherwise have obtained.

> If any one considers the whole government of the world, he will certainly understand how true is the opinion of the Stoics, who say that the world was made

on our account. For all the things of which the world is composed, and which it produces from itself, are adapted to the use of man. Man, accordingly, uses fire for the purpose of warmth and light, and of softening his food, and for the working of iron; he uses springs for drinking, and for baths; he uses rivers for irrigating the fields, and assigning boundaries to countries; he uses the earth for receiving a variety of fruits, the hills for planting vineyards, the mountains for the use of trees and firewood, the plains for crops of grain; *he uses the sea not only for commerce, and for receiving supplies from distant countries, but also for abundance of every kind of fish.*[66]

Basil the Great (A.D. 329–379)

In his letter to the governor of Neocoesarea, St. Basil is highly complimentary of the person and the business skills of the governor:

For he [Elpidius] did not cease telling me about you, mentioning one by one your *magnanimity*, your exalted sentiments, your mild manners, *your skill in business, intelligence*, dignity tempered by cheerfulness, and eloquence... How can I fail to love such a man? How could I put such restraint upon myself as not loudly to proclaim what I feel?[67]

Basil's writings demonstrate a strong emphasis on the importance of contemplation on the works of God. The search for a strong spiritual life, however, never leads him to deny the importance and appreciation of the struggles of the ordinary Christian and that of the merchant. Clearly, the search for solitude is not a form of escapism, but provides one with an opportunity for spiritual discipline and contact with God.[68] Basil also locates the goodness of entrepreneurial work within a theology of creation. The sea is good in the eyes of God because of its natural functions, but it also facilitates communication and friendship. And for the first time we notice that the work of the merchant serves the common good. It helps to alleviate poverty.

Thus, in the eyes of God, the sea is good, because it makes the under current of moisture in the depths of the earth... Finally the sea is good in the eyes of God, ... because it brings together the most distant parts of the earth, and facilitates the inter-communication of mariners. By this means it gives us the boon of general information, supplies the merchant with his wealth, and easily provides for the necessities of life, allowing the rich to export their superfluities, and blessing the poor with the supply of what they lack.[69]

John Chrysostom (A.D. 344–407)

Concern with avarice dominates Chrysostom's thought, so much so that it is often difficult to discern whether he makes a distinction between the goodness of material, created things and the inordinate desire for material gain.

But if wealth is good, and increases by grasping, the more a man grasps, the better he must be. Is not this plainly a contradiction? *But suppose the wealth is not gained wrongfully. And how is this possible? So destructive a passion is avarice, that to grow rich without injustice is impossible.* This Christ declared, saying, "Make to yourselves friends of the Mammon of unrighteousness."[70]

But there are glimmers of appreciation of entrepreneurial work in his writings. He says one should pursue the Lord as one pursues a marriage or as a merchant pursues wealth. A Christian is advised to imitate the risk-taking attitudes of merchants and their energy levels. If he can reproduce these desires in his spiritual life then he will be able to follow Christ fruitfully. Desire is essential in the spiritual life and one can learn from the earthly desires of the merchant.

For tell me, he that would marry a wife, is he content with wishing? By no means; but he looks out for women to advance his suit, and request friends to keep watch with him, and gets together money. *Again, the merchant is not content with sitting at home and wishing, but he first hires a vessel, then selects sailors and rowers, then takes up money on interest, and is inquisitive about a market and the price* of merchandise. Is it not then strange for men to shew themselves so much in earnest about earthly things, but that when they are to make a *venture for heaven,* they should be content with wishing only?[71]

Tell me now, in the case of any arts, when we wish to attain them, are we content with wishing, or do we also engage with the things themselves? ... *He wishes to become a merchant; he does not merely say, I wish, but he also puts his hand to the work.* Again he wishes to travel abroad, and he does not say, I wish, but he puts his hand to the work. In everything then, wishing alone is not sufficient, but work must also be added; ...[72]

Again the merchant is used, along with the example of the artisan and soldier, to demonstrate the need to be concerned with not only one's personal salvation, but with the salvation of the rest of humanity.

For the *merchant* too, to increase his wealth, crosses the sea; and the *artisan,* to add to his substance, doeth all things. Let us also then *not be satisfied with our own salvation only,* since else we destroy even this. For in a war too, and in an engagement, the *soldier* who is looking to this only how he may save himself by flight, destroys the rest also with himself; much as on the other hand the noble-minded one, and he who stands in arms in defense of the others, with the others preserves himself also.[73]

References to the common good can also be found. This theme was first noticed in the writings of St. Basil, and it begins to inform the definition developed in Chapter 1. This is a rather striking passage. Underlying it is the fact that man is fundamentally a personal and communal being. If man lives only for himself, then he cannot be considered a human being!

For, if in worldly matters no man lives for himself, but artisan, and soldier, and husbandman, and merchant, all of them contribute to the common good, and to their neighbor's advantage; much more ought we to do this in things spiritual. For this is most properly to live: since he at least who is living for himself only, and overlooking all others, is useless, and is not so much as a human being, nor of our race.[74]

Interestingly, the work of a merchant can be helpful in understanding repentance. Here the work of a merchant acts as a form of encouragement to those who have been disloyal to Christ. The merchant is demonstrating that personal trait of overcoming obstacles that was identified in Chapter 1. Chrysostom is concerned with encouragement of the sinner and the rejection of despair.

No merchant, having once suffered shipwreck, and lost his freight, desists from sailing, but again crosses the sea and the billows, and the broad ocean, and recovers his former wealth. We see athletes also who after many falls have gained the wreath of victory; and often, before now, a soldier who has once ran away has turned out a champion, and prevailed over the enemy. Many also of those who have denied Christ owing to the pressure of torture, have fought again, and departed at last with the crown of martyrdom upon their brows. But if each of these had despaired after the first blow, he would not have reaped the subsequent benefits.[75]

Jerome (A.D. 347–419)

After a long reflection on the dangers of travel by sea the saint notes:

What, you ask, is the drift of all this? Surely it is clear enough. For if the merchants of the world undergo such hardships to win a doubtful and passing gain, and if after seeking it through many dangers they only keep it at risk of their lives; what should Christ's merchant do who "selleth all that he hath" that he may acquire the "one pearl of great price;" who with his whole substance buys a field that he may find therein a treasure which neither thief can dig up nor robber carry away?[76]

Compared to the riches one gains by following Christ, the riches of the merchant are "doubtful and passing." Still, by analogy one can see the beauty of the Christian becoming "Christ's merchant" in risking, selling, and acquiring the true treasure. The work of a merchant is not condemned. Rather, his work renders understandable something crucial to the spiritual life: the search for Christ is risky, but the gain is enormous.

Jerome comments on the parable of the talents in Matthew's Gospel. He focuses on the interior struggle of the Christian and the desire of Christ that Christians advance in the life of grace. Interestingly, Jerome likens the spirit of Paul to that of a businessman. Capital is a metaphor for grace.

But our Lord is not satisfied with what we have, but always desires more, He himself shows by saying, 'Wherefore didst thou not give my money to the money-changers, that so when I came I might have received it with usury?' The Apostle Paul understood this, and forgetting those things which were behind, reached forward to those things which were in front, that is, he made daily progress, and did not keep the grace given to him carefully wrapped up in a napkin, but *his spirit, like the capital of a keen man of business, was renewed from day to day*, and if he were not always growing larger, he thought himself growing less.[77]

Augustine (A.D. 354–430)

Augustine is the first, to my knowledge, to use the metaphor of exchange in describing Christ's redemptive activity. In commercial dealings, things are exchanged. In divine dealings, persons are exchanged. Christ exchanges both his life and death for our salvation. Augustine, in developing the metaphor, expounds a clear understanding of the business of the trader:

So then neither could He have death in that which was His own, nor we life in that which was our own; but we have life from that which is His, He death from what is ours. *What an exchange!* What hath He given, and what received? Men who trade enter into commercial intercourse for exchange of things. For ancient commerce was only an exchange of things. A man gave what he had, and received what he had not. For example, he had wheat, but had no barley; another had barley, but no wheat; the former gave the wheat which he had, and received the barley which he had not. How simple it was that the larger quantity should make up for the cheaper sort! So then another man gives barley, to receive wheat; lastly, another gives lead, to receive silver, only he gives much lead against a little silver; another gives wool, to receive a ready-made garment. And who can enumerate all these exchanges? But no one gives life to receive death.[78]

But he makes a clear distinction between moral and immoral trading. This passage is very clear in affirming the legitimacy of trading. Augustine has been speaking of dishonesty and deceit in trading. The trader interjects: surely he is entitled to a reward for his work? Augustine agrees. He has been speaking only of lying and deceit, not of the trade itself.

But a trader saith to me, behold I bring indeed from a distant quarter merchandise unto these places, wherein there are not those things which I have brought, by which means I may gain a living: I ask but as reward for my labour, that I may sell dearer than I have bought: for whence can I live, when it hath been written, "the worker is worthy of his reward"? But he is treating of lying, of false swearing. This is the fault of me, not of trading: for I should not, if I would, be unable to do without this fault. I then, the merchant, do not shift mine own fault to trading: but if I lie, it is I that lie, not the trade.[79]

Finally, as with St. Basil, Christ is referred to as "the Merchantman." The metaphor of exchange is employed once again:

> Examine thoroughly man's estate, convict me if I lie: consider all men whether they are in this world for any other end than to be born, to labour, and to die? This is the merchandize of our country: these things here abound. To such merchandize did that Merchantman descend. And for as much as every merchant gives and receives; gives what he has, and receives what he has not; when he procures any-thing, he gives money, and receives what he buys: so Christ too in this His traffic gave and received. But what received He? That which aboundeth here, to be born, to labour, and to die, And what did He give? To be born again, to rise again, and to reign for ever. O Good Merchant, buy us. Why should I say buy us, when we ought to give Thee thanks that Thou hast bought us? Thou dost deal out our Price to us, we drink Thy Blood; so dost thou deal out to us our Price.[80]

John Cassian (A.D. 360–435)

The following simple reference highlights the fact that the entrepreneurial work needed no justification. It arose out of necessity, out of the geographical placement of the people concerned. It arose, too, from the intelligence of the people. The preamble, which is uplifting, emphasizes the way the early Christians lived and sought after the communion of saints. Obviously, there were saints in the field of business! And these saints were ingenious. Besides their business of trade, they were able to build houses, even though the natural conditions were not at all co-operative. They are surely the forerunners of Venice, Genoa, and other Catholic commercial republics of the Middle Ages.

> When we were living in a monastery in Syria after our first infancy in the faith, and when after we had grown somewhat we had begun to long for some greater grace of perfection, we determined straightway to seek Egypt and penetrating even to the remotest desert of the Thebaid, to visit very many of the saints, whose glory and fame had spread abroad everywhere, with the wish if not to emulate them at any rate to know them. And so we came by a very lengthy voyage to a town of Egypt named Thennesus, whose inhabitants are so surrounded either by the sea or by salt lakes that they devote themselves to *business alone* and get their wealth and substance by *naval commerce* as the land fails them, so that indeed when they want to build houses, there is no soil sufficient for this, unless it is brought by boat from a distance.[81]

Here then we can see the great desire for holiness that existed in the early years of the Church. After an initial conversion, the Christians were looking for a "greater grace of perfection" and they sought it among Christians who were in fact devoted to business. Cassian's primary concern is holiness. And this holi-ness was achieved by these early Christians in and through the work of business. Besides Basil's reference to Christ as the Merchantman and Augustine's use of the metaphor of exchange, there is perhaps no better reference than this one of Cassian's. Following Christ is completely compatible with a life devoted to business.

Leo the Great (A.D. 400–461)

Like Augustine, Leo uses the metaphor of exchange in highlighting Christ's work of salvation. Once again we see that Christ is referred to as "the Merchant." In this sense it is true to say that by referring to Christ as "the Merchant" not only is the work of the merchant accepted and praised, but it is indeed raised to a higher dignity. He speaks here of Christ's words of fear: "Father, if it be possible, let this cup pass from Me" and argues that Christ is really expressing "His desire to heal the affection of our weakness by sharing them, and to check our fear of enduring pain by undergoing it."

> In our nature, therefore, the LORD trembled with our fear, that He might fully clothe our weakness and our frailty with the completeness of His own strength. For He had come into this world a *rich and merciful Merchant* from the skies, and by a *wondrous exchange* had entered into a *bargain of salvation* with us, *receiving ours and giving His*, honour for insults, salvation for pain, life for death: and He Whom more than 12,000 of the angel-hosts might have served for the annihilation of His persecutors, preferred to entertain our fears, rather than employ His own power.[82]

Both the merchant and his work of exchange are sublated. The merchant himself is sublated by Christ, the true Merchant. The exchange of goods is sublated, too. But here it is possible to see the transformation of values that takes place, which is entirely unique to the work of Christ. Christ receives a human nature from us and gives his divinity in return. This exchange takes place in the Incarnation and definitively on the cross. He exchanges his death for the lives of men. The exchange is not patterned after normal exchange, what might be called "good business." Rather, the exchange is totally disproportionate. Man receives something totally unexpected: divine life. Christ, in his passion, death and Resurrection, sublates exchange and transforms it profoundly. It is the work of merchants—the activity of exchange—that can, strangely enough, call to attention this profound reality. Thus, the work of merchants contains and carries within itself, seed-like, a salvific meaning. Christ's death and resurrection is a "work" of exchange. Thus can all work, viewed from this elevated divine viewpoint, become a work of exchange. United to Christ, the Christian offers to God his life and work, and in return God raises that work and life to the divine level. In reality, Leo offers a profound vision of the meaning of human work.

John Damascus (A.D. 675–749)

St. John writes that faith sustains "both human and divine" realities, including the risky work of the merchant. And like all work, the work of the merchant is a gift "brought out of nothing" and must be directed back to God in and through faith.

> But without faith it is impossible to be saved. For it is by faith that all things, both human and spiritual are sustained. For without faith neither does the farmer cut his furrow, nor does the merchant commit his life to the raging waves of the sea on a small piece of wood, nor are marriages contracted nor any other step in life taken. By faith we consider that all things were brought out of nothing into being by God's power. And we direct all things, both divine and human, by faith.[83]

A Summary of Entrepreneurial Work in the Fathers

References to entrepreneurial work are sparse but significant in the writings of the Fathers. The Fathers emphasize that all Christians are called to holiness, which is essentially identification with Jesus Christ. This takes place in and through one's occupation or profession (Cassian). No occupation is incompatible with this calling except those that are immoral (Augustine). Entrepreneurial work is also viewed as sharing in the "subduing of the earth." Thus it is primarily understood within a theology of creation. The entrepreneur is thus called, like all Christians, to transform the world. He is called to perfect the work begun by God. In addition, all the natural resources of the earth and the wealth that is subsequently generated (Basil) are a gift from God. With the gift of faith they should be directed to God as an offering (Damascus). With the Incarnation, Christians now see that they are called to focus all of their desires on the person of Jesus Christ. The Fathers use the metaphor of the merchant and exchange to highlight the intensity and importance of this desire. The entrepreneur's work receives implicit affirmation. The work of the merchant intimates to Christians how they should pursue Christ. The entrepreneur is seen as a key figure in alleviating poverty and contributing to the common good (Basil and Chrysostom). For the Fathers, this is critical. In light of the writings of St. Thomas in the following section, we begin to see that the common good enters into the very definition of entrepreneurial work. The definition developed in Chapter 1 undergoes a significant development and refinement. The work of the merchant is also a useful metaphor in understanding the Christian meaning of repentance (Chrysostom).

The Benedictines

St. Benedict was born in Norcia (Italy) in the year 480 and died in Monte Cassino, after the year 546. He is considered the "author of the most celebrated monastic rule, which bears his name and has made of him a saint and confessor, among the most honored of the Latin Church."[84] It is the Benedictines' combination of manual

and intellectual work that is of particular interest for this study. It is not a comprehensive study of their contribution to the development of spirituality in general or
of their contribution to a spirituality of work. Nor is it a complete commentary on
the Rule of Benedict. Rather, it will seek to highlight how the Benedictines gave
rise to significant developments in the field of science. Through their particular
emphasis on intellectual and manual work, the Benedictines paved the way for a
spirit of invention and discovery, which has benefited society enormously. Can the
Benedictines be considered entrepreneurs or merchants? The question is somewhat
odd, not least because the Benedictines are religious monks and would not consider
themselves to be entrepreneurs or merchants as such, but their work does contain
some of the key elements of the definition developed in Chapter 1. They may be
considered forerunners of later entrepreneurial work. Certainly the Benedictine rule,
with its emphasis on both speculative and practical knowledge, provides a sort of
typology for many forms of human behavior that would emerge in later centuries
including entrepreneurial work.

The Benedictine Rule (between the years 530 and 540) contains seventy-three
chapters and a prologue. Of particular significance is the division of the monk's
day. "The waking hours are divided almost equally between three occupations:
prayer in common, religious reading (*lectio divina*, 48), and manual work of
domestic, craft (57), and horticultural (48) character."[85] Lynn White, Jr., writes in
Dynamo and Virgin Reconsidered that Benedict "is probably the pivotal figure in
the history of labor."

> Greco-Roman society had rested on the backs of slaves. Work was the lot of
> slaves, and any free man who dirtied his hands with it, even in the most casual
> way, demeaned himself... In the classical tradition there is scarcely a hint of the
> dignity of labor. The provision of Benedict, himself an aristocrat, that his monks
> should work in the fields and shops therefore marks a *revolutionary reversal of the
> traditional attitude toward labor*; it is a high peak along the watershed separating
> the modern from the ancient world. For the Benedictine monks regarded *manual
> labor* not as a mere regrettable necessity of their corporate life but rather as an
> *integral and spiritually valuable part of their discipline.*[86]

In addition, the Benedictines have bequeathed to us the dictum *Ora et labora*
(pray and work). Benedict clearly saw the implications of the hidden life of Christ
which were noted in Chapter 1. Not only is manual labor viewed in a new light (it
is no longer the arena of slaves, but of freemen). But Benedict also develops the
concept that work becomes prayer. *Work is worship.*[87]

These two points are vital. Work is not a form of slavery or penance for sin. True,
it is necessary. But it is essentially a free act. Furthermore, work is an expression of
love and worship. Yet it is White's further observations that place the Benedictines
squarely in the company of merchants, traders, and entrepreneurs.

The importance of frugal living and consecrated labor in building up fluid investment-capital and in fostering the rapid expansion of capitalist economy in the regions of Europe and America most deeply affected by the puritan spirit is commonplace of the economic history of early modern times.[88]

Entrepreneurial work is the fruit of both the practical and speculative intellect. The entrepreneur not only conceives and molds his projects through creative knowledge, he actually carries out these thoughts in the practical sphere. In this way his work is akin to an artist's. Benedict's Rule stipulates that the monk's day will be divided into three parts: common prayer, spiritual and intellectual reading, and practical work. White comments that herein lies the revolution for science, discovery and invention:

> Moreover, although St. Benedict had not intended that his monks should be scholars, a great tradition of learning developed in the abbeys following his *Rule*: for the *first time the practical and the theoretical were embodied in the same individuals*. In antiquity learned men did not work, and workers were not learned. Consequently ancient science consisted mostly of observation and abstract thought; experimental methods were rarely used. The craftsmen had accumulated a vast fund of factual knowledge about natural forces and substances, but the social cleavage prevented classical scientists from feeling that stimulus from technology which has been so conspicuous an element in the development of modern experimental science. The monk was the first intellectual to get dirt under his fingernails. He did not immediately launch into scientific investigation, but in his person *he destroyed the old artificial barrier between the empirical and the speculative*, the manual and the liberal arts, and thus helped create a social atmosphere favorable to scientific and technological development.[89]

Thus religion and science are not opposed. Rather, science (invention and discovery) owes its beginning and development to the melding of theoretical and practical knowledge, first accomplished in the holy monks known to us as Benedictines. It is they, through their sense of community, frugality and commitment to intellectual and manual work, who first enabled ideas to become reality.[90] Dougherty comments:

> The Benedictine abbey was to be a self-contained economic organism, like the villa of a Roman landowner, save that the monks were themselves the workers and the old classical contrast between servile work and free leisure no longer held sway. According to the *Rule*, St. Benedict intended the abbot to be the manager of the estate of the monastery... Benedict's monasteries, by their *sanctification of work and poverty, revolutionized the order of social values*... The effects were not long in coming. The disciplined and tireless labor of the monks brought back into cultivation the lands which had been deserted and depopulated during the age of the invasions. As John H. Newman beautifully described the period, "by degrees the woody swamp became a hermitage, a religious house, a farm, an abbey, a village, a seminary, a school of learning and a city."[91]

Benedictine monasteries became places of discovery, creativity and invention. The monks certainly engaged the factors of production. And while they clearly do not have the interest in money and finance that is characteristic of the entrepreneur, a general interest in money is not excluded.

Dougherty points out that the Rule of Benedict differed significantly from other forms of monasticism (particularly the earliest forms of monasticism), which were "born in the African desert as a protest against the whole tradition of the classical culture of the Greek and Roman world."

> Benedict's conception of the monastic life, by contrast, is essentially *social and cooperative*. As the discipline of the common life, his *Rule* differs from older rules in its strongly practical character.[92]

Longenecker points out[93] that the Benedictines, in contrast to Franciscan vows of poverty, chastity, and obedience, pledge to desire and seek a life of stability, obedience and, conversion. The Benedictines also shed new light on the meaning of manual labor. By combining it with theoretical knowledge, through the practice of the Rule of St. Benedict, they were able to advance science, invention and discovery. They therefore have paved the way for many later developments in science. In addition, the Benedictine Rule provides a solid foundation for many modern professions that combine both theoretical and practical knowledge. This would seem to be the case with entrepreneurial work.

Entrepreneurial Work in the Writings of St. Thomas Aquinas[94]

Charles notes that "economic theory as we know it did not exist in the Middle Ages, though the beginning of one emerged in the fifteenth century."[95] Nonetheless, he provides important historical data that helps to clarify Aquinas' concern with the morality of trading:

> [F]rom about 1150 Europe moved from self-sufficiency in food to support industrial expansion as towns attracted the skilled crafts and monopolized industrial production; the move from a domestic and manorial agricultural economy began, a market economy was emerging, and Europe took the first great economic leap forward, the basis of all that followed over the next centuries. It was the central middle ages, and not the Renaissance period that was the age of the rebirth of the European economy.[96]

So while there may have been no coherent economic theory during the Middle Ages, it cannot be maintained that there was an absence of capitalists and capitalism. Aquinas was not a stranger to the world of trade and business, since he lived at a time when trade was flourishing. These two facts provide a helpful background when examining the thought of St. Thomas on entrepreneurship.[97]

The Meaning of Economics in St. Thomas

In general, St. Thomas demonstrates a more balanced view of trade than some of his contemporaries. While Gratian "had condemned trade and its profits," Aquinas "was very cautious in handling the matter, but he was also positive."[98] St. Thomas is "cautious" because of the concern with avarice, and he is "positive" because trade can serve the common good. In *Wealth and Money in the Economic Philosophy of St. Thomas*, Flynn notes that for St. Thomas economics is less about the production of wealth (as is modern economic theory) than it is about virtue.

> It would be a great confusion to identify St. Thomas "economics" with the modern use of the term. The similarity is to a large extent only nominal. The difference is sharply brought out by the following text:
>
> > It (economics) has more to do with men then with the possession of inanimate things such as wheat, wines and other things of the sort; and it should deal more with the virtue by which men live well, than with the virtue by which we procure and multiply those possessions which are called wealth.[99]

Flynn makes it clear that St. Thomas follows Aristotle in his use of the term "economics." It is a term that had "both a wider and a narrower" meaning for Aristotle than it now has.

> It was wider in that it referred to the management of the entire life of the family, to the ordering of the material, intellectual, and moral requirements of domestic society. It was narrower in that it referred to that prudence whose proper care is the regulation of the household alone.[100]

Economics is today understood as the science of the production and distribution of goods and the consequent satisfaction of the demands and needs of the consumer. It is restricted solely to this area. For the ancients, economics dealt with the management of the household, but included not only the satisfaction of its material demands, but also with its intellectual and moral requirements as well. It had a "wider and narrower" meaning, with the "wider" meaning being crucial. Economics for Aquinas has more to do with men than with things and primarily involves management of the household. Economics concerns each of the persons in that household considered in their material, intellectual and moral aspect.

The Purpose of Economics in St. Thomas

Aquinas' thought on the relationship between wealth and economics is influenced largely by Aristotle. Flynn begins his discussion by searching for an appropriate term in the writings of Aristotle which would be the equivalent of the term "economics" and settles on the Greek word *chrematistics*.

> Chrematistics is the art of wealth-getting and is of two kinds, natural and un-
> natural. Natural chrematistics is part of household management... Unnatural
> chrematistics, though so closely allied to the former as to be often mistaken for
> it, is not related to household management. Its aim is the amassing of artificial
> wealth, i.e., money.[101]

Flynn notes that natural chrematistics is not only part of economics (household
management), but is in fact subordinate to it. On the other hand, unnatural chrematistics is part of trade.

> The former is concerned with procuring the means to an end; it procures the
> material needs which are so utilized and ordered as to make possible the full life
> of the family. The latter aims at acquiring material goods considered as an end in
> themselves; here wealth is ordered to nothing higher, for it is sought for its own
> sake and without limit.[102]

This distinction between natural and unnatural trading gives rise to the distinction
between *acquiring* and *using* wealth. In economics (household management) one
acquires wealth for the purpose of using it for the good of one's family. The object
of one's action is maintenance and development of one's family. And this is natural
trading. On the other hand, unnatural trading is concerned solely with *acquiring*
wealth. It concerns itself with the amassing of wealth and is not so concerned with
the use of it. As we shall see, this causes St. Thomas to deem it immoral unless it
is accompanied by the intention to use the wealth acquired for some further end
or good.

The purpose or end of economics is not wealth.[103] Rather, wealth is acquired
to serve the needs of the household and the *polis*. Properly speaking, wealth is
subsidiary to economics and not part of economics. It is these crucial distinctions
that must be borne in mind when interpreting the thought of St. Thomas when he
touches upon the matters of trade and commerce. His concern is with the good of
the family and good of the *polis*. While the work of merchants is good in and of
itself, it does receive additional moral value by its ordering to the common good.
In this St. Thomas reflects the teaching of the Fathers.

The Virtue of Magnificence

In his encyclical letter commemorating the fortieth anniversary of *Rerum
Novarum*, entitled *Quadragesimo Anno*, Pius XI noted the following:

> However, the investment of superfluous income in developing favorable oppor-
> tunities for employment, provided the labor employed produces results which are
> really useful, is to be considered according to the teaching of the Angelic Doctor
> an act of real liberality particularly appropriate to the needs of our time.[104]

Here Pius XI relies on Aquinas' teaching in the *Summa Theologica* which deals with the virtue of magnificence. In question 134, article one, Aquinas notes:

> On the contrary, Human virtue is a participation of Divine power. But magnificence belongs to Divine power, according to Psalm 48:12: "His magnificence and His power is in the clouds." Therefore magnificence is a virtue.

In article two, Aquinas concludes that magnificence is a special virtue after he has discussed the meaning of *facere* in its strict sense and in its broad sense.[105] He gives a succinct definition of magnificence: "I answer that, It belongs to magnificence to do [*facere*] something great, as its name implies [magnificence = *magna facere*—to make great things]."

In his reply to objection two, St. Thomas makes a distinction between magnanimity and magnificence[106] and then comments:

> On the other hand, it belongs to magnificence not only to do something great, doing [*facere*] being taken in the strict sense, but also to tend with the mind to the doing of great things. Hence Tully says [*De Inventione Rhetorica* ii] that "magnificence is the discussing and administering of great and lofty undertakings, with a certain broad and noble purpose of mind, discussion" referring to the inward intention, and administration to the outward accomplishment. Wherefore just as magnanimity intends something great in every matter, it follows that magnificence does the same in every work that can be produced in external matter [*factibili*].

And then his reply to objection three:

> *The intention of magnificence is the production of a great work*. Now works done by men are directed to an end: and no end of human works is so great as the honor of God: wherefore magnificence does a great work especially in reference to the Divine honor. Wherefore the Philosopher says (Ethica Nicomachea iv,2) that "the most commendable expenditure is that which is directed to Divine sacrifices": and this is the chief object of magnificence. For this reason *magnificence is connected with holiness*, since its chief effect is directed to religion or holiness.[107]

Having defined the *nature* of magnificence, Aquinas, in article three, deals with the *matter* of magnificence. This section seems especially appropriate to entrepreneurial work since it concretizes the proposed work by the expenditure of money and clearly entails the notion of risk. He states:

> I answer that, As stated above (A2), *it belongs to magnificence to intend doing some great work*. Now for the doing of a great work, proportionate expenditure is necessary, for great works cannot be produced without great expenditure. Hence *it belongs to magnificence to spend much in order that some great work may be accomplished in becoming manner*. Wherefore the Philosopher says (Ethica Nicomachea iv,2) that "a magnificent man will produce a more magnificent work with equal," i.e. proportionate, "expenditure." Now expenditure is the outlay of

a sum of money; and a man may be hindered from making that outlay *if he love money too much*. Hence *the matter of magnificence may be said to be both this expenditure itself,* which the magnificent man uses to produce a great work, and *also the very money which he employs in going to great expense,* and as well as the love of money, which love the magnificent man moderates, lest he be hindered from spending much.[108]

Accordingly, what makes a man magnificent is not only his decision to expend the monies belonging to him in order to produce a great work, but also that this very decision is occasioned by his ability *to moderate his love of money*. Aquinas seems to suggest that the magnificent man is motivated more by the common good than by his own personal interest or his own well being. This seems to be his meaning as he replies to objection three.

> The magnificent man also makes gifts of presents, as stated in Ethica Nicomachea iv,2, but not under the aspect of gift, but rather under the aspect of expenditure directed to the production of some work, for instance in order to honor someone, or in order to do something which will reflect honor on the whole state: as when he brings to effect what the whole state is striving for.

It is precisely here that Pius XI's application of the Thomistic doctrine is revealed. Pius noted that in modern times this virtue of magnificence could entail the expenditure of money aiding employment opportunities.[109] St. Thomas, as we have just noted, describes the magnificent man as one who outlays a significant amount of money that either honors someone or brings honor to the State. Clearly, Pius believed that nothing would bring more honor to the state than the honoring of the subjects of the state through their employment in productive enterprises.

Finally, Aquinas deals with the question of magnificence in the context of the virtue of fortitude. He notes that it can be considered as part of fortitude:

> Now magnificence agrees with fortitude in the point that as fortitude tends to something arduous and difficult, so also does magnificence: wherefore seemingly it is seated, like fortitude, in the irascible. Yet magnificence falls short of fortitude, in that the arduous thing to which fortitude tends derives its difficulty from a danger that threatens the person, whereas the arduous thing to which magnificence tends, derives its difficulty from the dispossession of one's property, which is of much less account than danger to one's person. Wherefore magnificence is accounted a part of fortitude.

St. Thomas and the Entrepreneur

Thomas speaks directly of the magnificent man and only indirectly of the entrepreneur. The magnificent man may not necessarily be an entrepreneur, and likewise, an entrepreneur may not be a truly magnificent man. A man possessing the virtue of magnificence may not be an entrepreneur at all. He may simply be one who decides to spend a proportionately large amount of money to achieve an honorable goal that could have clear implications for the social order. On the other hand, an entrepreneur may not necessarily be concerned to do something great—to be concerned with the "discussing and administering of great and lofty undertakings." Rather, his activity, which may give rise to the appearance of a great undertaking, may simply be an assertion of self and the manifestation of an inordinate desire for profit. To be a magnificent man, one would need to "intend" a great undertaking, which intention may well be far from the mind and will of the entrepreneur.

This last point raises the question of what would make entrepreneurial activity ethically acceptable according to Thomistic doctrine. Given the above discussion, Thomas would judge entrepreneurial actions through the lens of the virtue of magnificence. Based on his analysis in question 134 of the *Summa*, the following can be stated.

Since all virtue, including magnificence, is a participation in the Divine Power, entrepreneurial work would have to begin with this premise. Sharing in divine power is synonymous with accepting all of created reality—animate and inanimate creatures—as a *gift*. This is, as we have seen, a strong biblical theme. It goes without saying that entrepreneurial work would be concerned with the "discussing and administering of great and lofty undertakings." It involves, as we saw in Chapter 1, the engagement of the factors of production in a work that is large and expensive. This magnificent act, according to St. Thomas, should be *directed to the glory of God*.

Second, the pursuit of these great undertakings would have to be a manifestation of one's *moderate love for money*. It would have to be the result not of a desire to amass wealth, but in fact be a result, in some sense, of one's disregard for money. Perhaps it can be suggested, in line with the distinction St. Thomas makes in his writings, that entrepreneurial activity need be a manifestation of *using* one's wealth, rather than *acquiring* wealth.

Third, there are then *three moral elements* that need to characterize entrepreneurial activity according to the Angelic Doctor. It should be done for the *glory of God*. It should be a reflection of one's *moderate love for money*. It must facilitate the development and maintenance of the *common good*.

The moderation of one's love for money is a critical Thomistic insight. It is related to the risky nature of entrepreneurial activity and the virtue of fortitude. St. Thomas argues that if a man does not moderate his love for money, it would be highly unlikely that he would embark on a great and lofty undertaking. Motivated by an inordinate love for money, the immoderate man opts for a safer form of investment that would ensure returns and the protection of his original sum. No great projects would be undertaken as a result of his love for comfort and fear of risk.[110] It is only the magnificent man, the man with the virtue of fortitude and a moderate love for money, who is capable of undertaking risks that will benefit the common good.

Remarkably, St. Thomas prefigures modern corporate finance theory, but in doing so he draws attention to risk. His focus is not so much on return, as on risk. As we noted above, one of the principles of modern finance theory is the relationship between *risk* and *return*: the higher the risk of a project, the higher the expected return. Likewise, the lower the risk is, the lower the expected return. As a consequence, businessmen and entrepreneurs will seek out and attempt to discover investment opportunities that have potential to either reduce the level of risk given a rate of return or increase return given a level of risk or discover an investment that reduces risk while increasing returns. The process is known as arbitrage.[111]

St. Thomas sheds significant light on the consideration of this process of risk and return by shifting the focus from return to risk. In a sense, we could say that he challenges the predominant pattern of thought. *Entrepreneurs should be judged more by the risks they undertake than by the returns they expect.* It is the risk that is undertaken that is primary in Aquinas' thought, rather than the return. So while it is often customary to equate the entrepreneur with the returns he receives, St. Thomas in fact issues a challenge: to contemplate the risk that entrepreneurs undertake, to contemplate and appreciate the virtues of magnificence and fortitude that they embody in their activity.

The Role of Profit in the Writings of St. Thomas and the Question of Usury

The question remains as to the role of profit in the thought of Thomas. Allied to this question is the issue of usury. These are important questions for the entrepreneur and those involved in business. First, I treat St. Thomas' position on profit. The clear conclusion of the discussion is that profit is morally acceptable, but it does not thereby constitute the sole reason for one's activities. The issue of profit is dealt with in ST 2. 2. Q. 77. Question 77: "Of Cheating, which is committed in buying and selling." It is divided into four articles. The first article: "Whether it is lawful to sell a thing for more than it is worth?" The second article: "Whether a sale is rendered unlawful through a fault in the thing sold?" The third article: "Whether the seller is bound to state the defects of the thing sold?" The fourth article: "Whether in trading, it is lawful to sell a thing at a higher price than what was paid for it?"

Articles one and four are of particular interest. In the first article, Thomas rejects the idea that one may sell a thing to another person for more than it is worth, but clearly allows for profit as it is based on commutative justice.[112] Thomas speaks of the fact that "buying and selling seem to be established for the common advantage of both parties, one of whom requires that which belongs to the other." Thus, the seller requires from the buyer some level of profit as a form of payment for his services and compensation for the risks he has undertaken in providing the thing for sale. In addition, profit ensures—not absolutely, but possibly—that the buyer will enjoy continued access to the thing sold. Profit acts as a form of insurance both to seller and buyer. But the notion of profit does not permit the injustice of selling a thing for more than it is worth or the buying of the thing for less than it is worth. In article four, Aquinas writes:

> On the contrary, Augustine commenting on Psalm 71:15, "Because I have not known learning," (OBJ 1) says: "The greedy tradesman blasphemes over his losses; he lies and perjures himself over the price of his wares. *But these are vices of the man, not of the craft, which can be exercised without these vices.*" *Therefore trading is not in itself unlawful.*
>
> I answer that, A tradesman is one whose business consists in the exchange of things. According to the Philosopher (*Politica* i,3), exchange of things is twofold; one, natural as it were, and necessary, ... The other kind of exchange is either that of money for money, or of any commodity for money, not on account of the necessities of life, but for profit, ... The former kind of exchange is commendable because it supplies a natural need: but the latter is justly deserving of blame, ... it satisfies the greed for gain, which knows no limit and tends to infinity... Nevertheless gain which is the end of trading, though not implying, by its nature, anything virtuous or necessary, does not, in itself, connote anything sinful or contrary to virtue: wherefore *nothing prevents gain from being directed to some necessary or even virtuous end, and thus trading becomes lawful.* Thus, for instance, a man may intend the moderate gain which he seeks to acquire by trading for the upkeep of his household, or for the assistance of the needy: or again, a man may take to trade for some public advantage, for instance, lest his country lack the necessaries of life, and seek gain, not as an end, but as payment for his labor.[113]

There are two types of trading. One is natural and necessary; the other is not. The first form is moral and clearly allows for profit. The second form of trading—perhaps called unnatural trading—is a different matter. It is indifferent, but still can be directed to the common good. In unnatural trading a person is involved in trading activities "not on account of the necessities of life, but for profit." Aquinas notes that unnatural trading is the "kind of exchange, properly speaking," that "regards tradesmen." That is, unnatural trading is "justly deserving of blame" not because of trading (which he has already declared to be lawful in and of itself), but because of the avarice that resides in the tradesman. Thus, unnatural trading receives it object of choice from the end for which it is done. And this can be good, as Thomas notes.[114]

What then can be said concerning usury? For the ancient philosophers—Plato (*Laws*) and Aristotle (*Politics*)—interest was considered "as contrary to the nature of things."[115] Cicero ("*De Officiis*," II, XXV) mentions that Cato compared "it to homicide, as also did Seneca."[116] One could consult Noonan's foundational work on the topic.[117] Consider Charles' brief but excellent analysis, given that the context of the Christian teaching forbidding usury is first, the Old Testament and the poverty of peasants, and second, the ancient view that money was sterile:

The idea that a rich man had the obligation to lend without charge to the poor who were in desperate need was one that was inherited from the Old Testament; it was a basic obligation of human solidarity.[118]

The fact that there was a significant development in commerce and trade during the middle ages did not eliminate the peasant class.

The Church's usury laws were then of the greatest relevance to the peasants and the poor generally, the vast majority of the people at the time; they made good sense in terms of Christian social charity and justice. They were a way of trying to ensure that the goods given by God to all should serve the needs of all.[119]

Hence the laws concerning usury were concerned not with business deals, but with lending from the rich to the poor who were seeking survival.[120] Charles cites Lactantius, Basil, Ambrose, Augustine, and Jerome in support of his argument.[121]

Second, what can be said with respect to the long held belief in the sterility of money?

Money was regarded as sterile in the sense that since it is only the human agent who puts it to use who makes it profitable, it is only that agent who should profit from such increase. A charge cannot be made by the lender, because he no longer owns the money; it is not his efforts that make it fruitful.[122]

But as trade expanded, so too the demand for money, not only as a means of exchange "but as a store or measure of value. It could be used to make more money by investment; *it was capital.*"[123] Can it be said that the Church has changed her teaching on the matter or has the teaching developed? The teaching has developed to say that usury is the practice of lending money at exorbitant rates of interest and this is clearly against the moral law. It is against justice. But with trade expanding in the middle and late middle ages, the science of economics continued to develop, allowing the Church to see that the long-held belief in the sterility of money was incorrect. The Church still wanted to defend the poor, but she also began to recognize that there exists an opportunity cost to money. One could morally lend money at a rate of interest that corresponded to what could have been obtained by the lender in an alternative investment decision had the money not been lent. The teaching underwent a development with a new understanding of the fertility of money.

The Scholastic Period and Economic Thought

Odd Langholm notes the importance of St. Thomas' thought, but also draws attention to numerous authors who have contributed to an understanding of economics, finance and trading in the medieval period. Of Thomas he notes: "Thomas Aquinas is a towering figure in scholastic economics, just as he towers in European intellectual history in general... Nevertheless, to make a single author represent a broad tradition, running through several centuries, badly distorts the historical picture. It makes the tradition look stationary (as though there were no development of economic doctrine) and uniform (as though there was no disagreement and exchange of opinion). It distorts and confuses the picture of Aquinas' own contribution as well."[124] It is perhaps the most systematic study of economic thought that is available to date. His study covers the period 1200–1358 and devotes a chapter to each author or authors who made a significant contribution during this period. Forty-seven theologians are covered. Of them, eighteen were Franciscans, fourteen were Dominicans, nine theologians were of other religious orders, and six were seculars.[125] It is my purpose to highlight three authors. In my judgment, they represent the best of all of those documented by Langholm. Langholm covers a variety of issues pertaining to economics and markets. I restrict myself to the topic of entrepreneurial work.

Thomas of Chobham

Chobham was an Englishman and his *Summa confessorum* appeared around 1215. It is, according to Langholm, the "fullest statement of the case for commerce yet to appear in a theological text."[126] He quotes the *Summa*.

> Commerce is to buy something cheaper for the purpose of selling it dearer. And this is all right for laymen to do, even if they do not add any improvement of the goods which they brought earlier and later sell. For otherwise there would have been great need in many regions, since merchants carry that which is plentiful in one place to another place where the same thing is scarce.[127]

Alexander of Hales

Born in England, Hales joined the Franciscans in 1236. In his *Summa* he replies to pseudo-Chrysostom "that merchants cannot please God." Langholm quotes the *Summa*.

> Also, if someone with his labour brings some object from one region to another region, the object being in no way impaired, it is indeed transferred complete and unaltered as to substance, but not as to place, and therefore, because he can lawfully demand a reward for his labour, the words of Chrysostom are not meant to apply to such a one. Also, if someone purchases an object under such conditions that storing it is accompanied by risk, because it may be damaged or consumed by fire or removed by a thief, if nevertheless under the said circumstances he may intend to profit by the sale of such an object, then surely, by considering the uncertainty about what may happen in the future, and by undertaking the risk of buying such an object, he does not purchase this object in order to make a profit by selling it complete and unaltered, and therefore what Chrysostom says is not meant to apply to such a one neither.[128]

Thus, according to Hales, Chrysostom's words apply to those "whose ultimate end is profit and who do business out of greed in order, without labour and care, to acquire surpluses beyond bound and measure."[129] Langholm comments that Hales gives certain conditions under which commercial activity would be deemed appropriate.

> Business may indeed be done lawfully if it is conducted by a suitable person, such as a layman; and for a necessary or pious cause, such as to provide for oneself and one's family in need or to exercise works of mercy; and in correct manner, namely without falsehood and perjury; and at a suitable time, such as not on a holiday; and in a location where such activity is permitted and appropriate; and by a just estimation of the goods, and by trade, according to how it is usually sold in that city or region in which business is conducted.[130]

John Duns Scotus

Scotus was born in 1265, took the Franciscan habit in 1280, was ordained a priest in 1291, and died in 1308. In the following citation, the common good is mentioned, as is the energy (industry) of the merchant and his alertness to information. Important, too, is Scotus' emphasis on risk and its appropriate reward.

> But he who transports and conserves goods, serves the state honestly and usefully, and therefore he ought to live by his labour. Nor is this all, but anyone can justly sell his industry and solicitude, and great industry is required of one who is to transport goods from country to country, in that he must have information about what a country can supply and what it needs. Therefore, he may justly receive a fee for his industry, over and above the necessary support of himself, and of his family included in this necessity, and thirdly beyond this something corresponding to his risk. For since he transports at his own risk if he is a transporter of good and stores at his own risk if he is a custodian of goods, for such risk he can with tranquillity receive a recompense, and especially if he sometimes through no fault of his own in such service to the community suffers a loss; as, for example, a merchant engaged in transport sometimes loses a ship laden with highly valuable commodities and another one sometimes loses in an accidental fire the most precious things which he stores for the state.[131]

Entrepreneurial Work and the Late Scholastics

If we may date Medieval Scholasticism from 800 A.D. to 1500 A.D., then Late Scholastic thought can be located in the period from 1350 to 1600 A.D.[132] Authors that are helpful in understanding the material with respect to entrepreneurial activity in the Late Scholastic period include: Chafuen,[133] De Roover,[134] Charles,[135] and Jarrett.[136]

In contrast to Langholm, De Roover is more circumspect with regard to Scholastic attitudes to trade and entrepreneurship. Generally speaking, the attitude to merchants and trading activity, as he describes and reviews the writings of this period, could be described as suspicious. However, as he points out in union with Chafuen (who relies on the work of De Roover),[137] two men stand out in particular for their praise and reverence of the work of the entrepreneur—San Bernardino da Siena and Sant'Antonino of Florence.

San Bernardino da Siena and Sant' Antonino

San Bernardino da Siena (1380–1444) joined the order of the Observant Friars in 1403 and was ordained a priest in 1404. Sant'Antonino (1389–1459), who became the Archbishop of Florence in 1445, joined the Dominicans in 1405.[138] De Roover, in his study of the two men, notes important historical details.

> Both San Bernardino and Sant'Antonino were contemporaries of the great Florentine banker, Cosimo de' Medici (1389-1464) and were living at the time that Florence was the principal banking center of Europe and also had silk and woolen industries. Siena had been an important banking center, too, but it was on the decline. Both men were well informed about prevailing business practices. Sant'Antonino, especially, was thoroughly familiar with labor conditions in the Florentine textile industry, whose organization was more capitalistic than one might suppose and had given birth to a working class depending on wages for its livelihood.[139]

It is De Roover's claim that St. Thomas did not offer, or attempt to offer, an economic doctrine. Rather, he says one finds in the writings of the saint "some casual remarks buried here and there among extraneous material and two or three more extensive fragments in his *Summa theologica* and his *Commentaries on the Nicomachean Ethics of Aristotle*."[140] Thus, attempts to "reconstruct the economic thought of Thomas," as some have tried to do, have proven rather difficult.

> A safer procedure is to examine what became of Thomas Aquinas' unrelated ideas in the hands of his immediate successors, the Schoolmen of the fourteenth and fifteenth centuries. The significance of Bernardino of Siena and Antonino of Florence is precisely that they give us a coherent and systematic exposition of scholastic economics and build up the synthesis which remains unfinished in Thomas Aquinas.[141]

As we have seen with the help of Langholm, Thomas was not the only one to have thought about and addressed the ethical issues with respect to trade. Bernardino and Antonino were building not only on the foundation of Thomas, but many others as well. Furthermore, is it true to say that Thomas' engaged in only "casual remarks" when it came to the subject of business and trade? His concern is essentially ethical. But we have noted his comments on the virtue of magnificence and trade. They are not without significance. Perhaps De Roover either did not notice these important writings or simply underestimated their importance. Nevertheless, he has made a fine contribution with respect to the two men under discussion.

De Roover notes that Bernardino follows the thought of John Duns Scotus in mentioning three kinds of merchants.

San Bernardino of Siena (1380-1444), the famous Franciscan theologian and preacher, who was perhaps the ablest economist of the Middle Ages, knows *three categories of merchants* whose services are valuable to the commonweal. The first are the *importers-exporters* (mercantiarum apportatores), who have already been described by John Duns Scotus and who make it their business to import goods from abroad, sometimes at considerable risk, trouble, and expense. Next come the "*storekeepers*" (mercantiarum conservatores), who store goods away and have them available when customers want them. These conservatores are certainly performing warehousing functions; however, it is not clear from the text whether they are storekeepers who buy wholesale and sell retail. (Retailing is not usually mentioned in scholastic treatises until the sixteenth century.) The third category is composed of the mercantiarum immutores seu melioratores, or *manufacturers*, whose job is to transform raw materials into finished products, for example, to make cloth from wool, shoes from leather, or candles from wax. Craftsmen were not regarded as merchants, and it may be that the text refers to master-manufacturers, or industrial entrepreneurs, who possessed some capital and put out materials which they had worked up by artisans dependent upon wages paid by their employers.[142]

De Roover says that Bernardino is "unusually realistic,"[143] since he "stressed the positive qualities which a merchant should possess not only in order to be a good Christian but also a good businessman."[144]

The saint is unusually realistic; he fully realized that managerial ability, far form being common, is a rare quality and that a scarce combination of competence and efficiency goes into the making of a successful businessman. San Bernardino lists four necessary qualifications: diligence or efficiency (*industria*), responsibility (*solicitudo*), labor (*labores*), and willingness to assume risks (*pericula*). First of all, merchants should be efficient, by which he means that they should be well informed about qualities, prices, and costs and be "subtle" in computing risks and assessing profit opportunities, "which indeed very few are capable of doing." Second, businessmen should be responsible and attentive to detail, "which in the conduct of business is most necessary" (*quae in tali exercito plurimum neces- saria est*). Nothing can be achieved without a great deal of trouble and toil. The merchants must be prepared to endure discomforts and to suffer hardships in crossing seas and deserts. They will unavoidably expose their persons as well as their goods to many perils. In spite of the best management, the businessman may be visited by bad luck and suffer a loss. It is, therefore, meet that he should earn enough on successful ventures to keep him in business and compensate him for all his troubles.[145]

Of San Antonino, De Roover writes:

> San Bernardino does not enter into much detail; his treatment of this matter is infe-
> rior to that of his contemporary, San Antonino (1389-1459), archbishop of Florence,
> who was not as good an economist, but had a flair for concrete detail and was well
> informed about conditions in the Florentine woolen and silk industries.[146]

Both men, while praising the work of merchants and traders, never relinquish their responsibility to point out the ethical demands of the profession and the possible and real moral dangers faced by these businesspersons. Of Bernardino, the following can be said:

> What the zealous preacher deplored—here the moralist speaks again—was the
> fact that so many merchants stayed abroad for long periods of time, separated
> from their wives, and defiled themselves by living in carnal sin or even in "filth"
> with infidels as well as with believers.[147]

San Antonino, consistent with his eye for detail, had no trouble highlighting the potential and ever-present moral dangers of the work of merchants.

> He discusses an impressive array of unfair practices which the manufacturers used
> to oppress their workers, such as withholding wages or paying them in truck or
> in clipped and debased coin. In revenge, the workers cheated their employers in
> various ways by poor workmanship, cabbaging, loafing on the job, and other petty
> forms of sabotage. Of course, the saintly archbishop condemned all fraudulent
> practices and stressed the responsibilities of the employees toward their masters.
> What he found especially appalling was the lewdness which prevailed in certain
> workshops among carders, combers, and woolbeaters, whose tedious and dirty
> jobs attracted only the most brutal and uncouth men.[148]

The visible reverence for the work of merchants is balanced by the temptations of their profession. In this the Late Scholastics are consistent with St. Thomas and the Fathers of the Church.

Conclusion

The entrepreneur can (and should) work for the development and maintenance of the common good. This is a consistent feature of the Fathers of the Church, of St. Thomas Aquinas and other Scholastic theologians. St. Thomas' writings on the virtue of magnificence also lead us to refine the entrepreneurial personality. The entrepreneur, in fact, is a man who possesses the virtues of magnificence and fortitude and this leads him to moderate his love of money. It is this moderation that is the source, in the mind of St. Thomas, which leads him to undertake the risks so characteristic of the work of entrepreneurs.

We can thus say that Catholic tradition views entrepreneurial work as alert to information; discovers new possibilities in the marketplace; engages the factors of production in a large enterprise; looks for profit as a compensation for the risks undertaken in engaging the factors of production; is characterized by the creation and sustaining of relationships; and intends to develop and maintain the common good. We can also say that the entrepreneurial personality is commercially focused; is creative; enjoys taking calculated risks; possesses high energy levels; enjoys working with others; possesses the virtues of magnificence and fortitude, which moderates his love for money.

What, however, has the Church taught about entrepreneurship in its modern social teaching? Have there been developments? What importance does the Church place on private initiative in economic and social life? By examining the development of modern Catholic social teaching, which was ushered in by Pope Leo's encyclical, *Rerum Novarum*, the principles in this chapter will be further enforced and enhanced. Chapter 3, therefore, will be vital to the search for an appropriate theology of the entrepreneur.

Notes

1. St. Augustine, Sermons on Selected Lessons of the New Testament, Sermon LXXX (On the words of the Gospel, John 6:9, where the miracle of the five loaves and the two fishes is related), 2, in: Philip Schaff, ed., *Augustine: Sermon on the Mount, Harmony of the Gospels, Homilies on the Gospels*, 14 vols., vol. 6, *Nicene And Post-Nicene Fathers: First Series* (Peabody, MA: Hendrickson Publishers, 1999), 499.

2. Charles, *Christian Social Witness, Vol. 1*, 18.

3. Ibid.

4. Ibid.

5. Ibid., 19. Emphasis added.

6. Ibid., 21.

7. *Laborem Exercens*, 26.

8. Sir. 38:24–28, 32–39, *The Jerusalem Bible*, Alexander Jones, ed. (Garden City, NY: Doubleday & Company, Inc., 1966).

9. Weber in his commentary in *The Jerome Biblical Commentary* says: "It is hardly surprising that Sirach would extol his profession. Although others before and after him were apt to disparage the trades in their quest to show the superiority of the scribe, the author here maintains his usual balance and moderate attitude. The scribe's vocation is superior. Yet craftsmen have an important and necessary place in society. From this passage we gain information about the types of craft practiced in Jerusalem in Sirach's day as well as a lofty concept of the work and activity of a Jewish scribe. No doubt much of what the author writes about the scribe is autobiographical... The work of the craftsman is noble, but in the affairs of government, his lot is to be ruled rather than to rule." See Raymond E. Brown, Joseph A. Fitzmyer, and Roland E. Murphy, eds., *The Jerome Biblical Commentary* (Englewood Cliffs, NJ: Prentice Hall, 1968), 552.

10. Is. 44:10–16 (*The Jerusalem Bible*).

11. Ex. 31:1–10.

12. Jones, *The Jerusalem Bible*, footnote a, 117.

13. Sir. 39:1–5 (*The Jerusalem Bible*).

14. *Laborem Exercens*, 26. The references are: Wis. 14:1–3 and Ps. 107:23–27.

15. Wis. 14:1–3 (*The Jerusalem Bible*).

16. Ps. 107 (108):23–27 (*The Jerusalem Bible*).

17. Prov. 31:10–31 (*The Jerusalem Bible*).

18. *Laborem Exercens*, 26. Emphasis added.

19. *Laborem Exercens*, 26. Emphasis added.

20. *Laborem Exercens*, 26.

21. See Jn. 1:2–14.

22. Matt. 13:44–46.

23. Bernard Lonergan, *Method in Theology* (New York: Herder and Herder, 1972), 241. Emphasis added.

24. Of course, not all actions in the parables are commended (e.g., Matt. 22:1–14, where the King slays his enemies). But the context of Matthew 13:44–46 suggests strongly that the actions of merchants are valued and appreciated.

25. Max Zerwick and Mary Grosvenor, *A Grammatical Analysis of the Greek New Testament*, trans. Mary Grosvenor, Unabridged, 5th, revised ed. (Roma: Editrice Pontificio Istituto Biblico, 1996), 44.

26. Joachim Jeremias, *The Parables of Jesus*, trans. S. H. Hooke, 6th ed. (New York: Charles Scribner's Sons, 1962), 200–201.

27. Lk. 16:1–8.

28. John Nolland, *Word Biblical Commentary: Luke 9.21-18.34*, ed. David A. Hubbard, Glenn W. Barker, and Ralph P. Martin, vol. 35B (Dallas: Word Books, 1993), 803. Emphasis added.

29. St. Jerome comments: "Why, even shopkeepers who are particularly frugal, and slaves who are not wasteful, and the care-takers who made our childhood a burden to us and even thieves when they are particularly clever, we speak of as diligent; and so the conduct of the unjust steward in the Gospel is spoken of as wise." (St. Jerome, Jerome's apology for himself against the Book of Rufinus, Book 1, 24, in: Schaff, *Theodoret, Jerome*, 495).

30. Nolland, *Word Biblical Commentary*, 798.

31. Ibid., 799.

32. Joseph A. Fitzmyer, S.J., *The Gospel According to Luke (X-XXIV): Introduction, Translation, and Notes*, The Anchor Bible (Garden City: Doubleday & Company, 1985), 1098.

33. "A talent was not any kind of coin but a measure of value worth about fifty kilos (one hundred pounds) of silver." (See José María Casciaro, ed., *The Navarre Bible: Saint Matthew's Gospel: Text and Commentaries*, 2d ed. (Dublin: Four Courts Press, 1991), 210. Also, "a talent was more than fifteen years' wages of a labourer." (Ibid., 166.) The entrustment of such a large sum makes it clear, I think, that we are dealing with a work of business that one does not ordinarily find servants involved in.

34. Matt. 25:14–30 (also Luke 19:12–27). St. Athanasius sees the talent as symbolic of grace: "Also in the Gospel, He praises those who increased the grace twofold, both him who made ten talents of five, and him who made four talents of two, as those who had profited, and turned them to good account... For it is not His will that the grace we have received should be unprofitable; but He requires us to take pains to render Him His own fruits, as the blessed Paul saith; 'The fruit of the Spirit is love, joy, and peace.'" (St. Athanasius, Letter VI., 5, in:

Philip Schaff and Henry Wace, eds., *Athanasius: Select Works and Letters*, 14 vols., vol. 4, *Nicene and Post-Nicene Fathers: Second Series* (Peabody: Hendrickson Publishers, 1999), 21.) The talent is symbolic of grace. One should produce the fruits of the Spirit. Athanasius, however, *does not* suggest that the fruits of the Spirit are produced independently of the activity of trading. *Thus one can respond to the grace of God, producing the fruits of the Spirit, in and through one's work of trading.*

35. Lk. 12:16–21.
36. Charles, *Christian Social Witness, Vol. 1*, 28. Emphasis added.
37. Mk. 12:17.
38. Mk. 7:21–23.
39. See Mk. 12:28–34.
40. Prov. 30:7–9.
41. "You have the poor with you always, you will not always have me." (John 12:8) This saying of Christ's is in the context of the anointing at Bethany, but it acts also as a prophecy for every age.
42. Charles, *Christian Social Witness*, vol. 1, 60.
43. Rodney Stark, *The Rise of Christianity: How the Obscure, Marginal Jesus Movement Became the Dominant Religious Force in the Western World in a Few* Centuries (San Francisco: HarperCollins Publishers, 1997), 74–75.
44. Ibid., 29.
45. Ibid., 30–31.
46. Ibid., 31.
47. Ibid., 32–33.
48. Charles, *Christian Social Witness, Vol. 1*, 65–66. Emphasis added.
49. Stark, *Rise of Christianity*, 31.
50. Ibid., 31. Emphasis added.
51. Charles, *Christian Social Witness, Vol. 1*, 84.
52. Ibid., 86. Emphasis added.
53. Ibid., 84.
54. Ibid.
55. Ibid., 85.
56. Ibid., 85–86. Emphasis added.
57. Peter C. Phan, "Social Thought," in *Message of the Fathers of the Church, Vol. 20*, ed. Thomas Halton (Wilmington, DE: Michael Glazier, Inc., 1984), 37, comments on the poverty present in the Empire and the Fathers' response to it: "Only in the last decade of the fourth century, as the social and economic conditions of the Empire considerably worsened, do we find a *more vigorous attack by some of the Fathers not so much on private property as on its excessive accumulation in the hands of the rich*, and some of the Fathers very boldly discuss the abuse of private property. Basil of Caesarea, Gregory of Nazianzus, John Chrysostom, Ambrose of Milan, and Augustine of Hippo, in their writings as in their homilies, *denounce the love of money*, the luxurious lifestyle of the rich, the lack of concern for the poor. *But it is not possible to find in their writings any advocacy of compulsory communal sharing. Property remains private.*" Emphasis added.
58. Charles, *Christian Social Witness, Vol. 1*, 86.
59. Phan, *Social Thought*, 36. Emphasis added.
60. Charles, *Christian Social Witness, Vol. 1*, 88.
61. Ibid., 89.

62. St. Ambrose, On the duties of the clergy, Book II, Chapter VI, 26, in: Philip Schaff and Henry Wace, eds., *Ambrose: Select Works and Letters*, 14 vols., vol. 10, *Nicene And Post-Nicene Fathers: Second Series* (Peabody: Hendrickson Publishers, 1999), 48. Emphasis added.

63. Aphrahat the Persian Sage, Demonstration VI, Of Monks, 1, in: Schaff, *Gregory the Great*, 363–64.

64. Tertullian, Apology, Chapter. XLII, in: Alexander Roberts and James Donaldson, eds., *Latin Christianity: Its Founder, Tertullian I. Apologetic; II. Anti-Marcion; III. Ethical*, 10 vols., vol. 3, *Ante-Nicene Fathers* (Peabody: Hendrickson Publishers, 1999), 49. Emphasis added.

65. Tertullian, A Treatise on the Soul, Chapter XXX (Further Refutation of the Pythagorean Theory. The State of Contemporary Civilization), in: Roberts, *Latin Christianity*, 210.

66. Lactantius, A Treatise on the Anger of God, Chapter XIII (Of the advantage and use of the world and of the seasons), in: Alexander Roberts and James Donaldson, eds., *Lactantius, Venantius, Asterius, Victorinus, Dionysius, Apostolic Teaching and Constitutions, 2 Clement, Early Liturgies*, 10 vols., vol. 7, *Ante-Nicene Fathers* (Peabody: Hendrickson Publishers, 1999), 269–70. Emphasis added.

67. St. Basil the Great, Letter LXIII (To the Governor of Neocoesarea), in: Philip Schaff and Henry Wace, eds., *Basil: Letters and Select Works*, 14 vols., vol. 8, *Nicene And Post-Nicene Fathers: Second Series* (Peabody: Hendrickson Publishers, 1999), 162. Emphasis added.

68. St. Basil the Great, Letter II (Basil to Gregory), 2, in: Ibid., 110. Emphasis added.

69. St. Basil the Great, Nine Homilies on the Hexaemeron, Homily IV (Upon the gathering together of the waters), 7, in: Ibid., 75.

70. St. John Chrysostom, Homilies on First Timothy, Homily XII (1Tim 4:1–3), in: Philip Schaff, ed., *Chrysostom: Homilies on Galatians, Ephesians, Phillipians, Colossians, Thessalonians, Timothy, Titus, and Philemon*, 14 vols., vol. 13, *Nicene And Post-Nicene Fathers: First Series* (Peabody: Hendrickson Publishers, 1999), 447. Emphasis added.

71. St. John Chrysostom, Homilies on First Corinthians, Homily, XIV (1 Cor. 4:17), 5, in: Philip Schaff, ed., *Chrysostom: Homilies on the Epistles of Paul to the Corinthians*, 14 vols., vol. 12, *Nicene And Post-Nicene Fathers: First Series* (Peabody: Hendrickson Publishers, 1999), 79–80. Emphasis added.

72. St. John Chrysotom, Homilies on the Epistle to the Hebrews, Homily XVII (Hebrews 9:24–26), 10, in: Philip Schaff, ed., *Chrysostom: Homilies on the Gospel of Saint John and the Epistle to the Hebrews*, 14 vols., vol. 14, *Nicene And Post-Nicene Fathers: First Series* (Peabody: Hendrickson Publishers, 1999), 446. Emphasis added.

73. St. John Chrysostom, Homilies on the Gospel according to St. Matthew, Homily LIX (Matt. 18:7), 5, in: Philip Schaff, ed., *Chrysostom: Homilies on the Gospel of Saint Matthew*, 14 vols., vol. 10, *Nicene and Post-Nicene Fathers: First Series* (Peabody: Hendrickson Publishers, 1999), 369. Emphasis added.

74. St. John Chrysostom, Homilies on the Gospel according to St. Matthew, Homily LXXVII (Matt. 24:32, 33), 6, in: Ibid., 469.

75. St. John Chrysostom, An Exhortation to Theodore after his Fall, Letter II, 1, in: Philip Schaff, ed., *Chrysostom: On the Priesthood, Ascetic Treatises, Select Homilies and*

Letters, Homilies on the Statues, 14 vols., vol. 9, *Nicene And Post-Nicene Fathers: First Series* (Peabody: Hendrickson Publishers, 1999), 111–12.

76. St. Jerome, Letter CXXV (To Rusticus), 4, in: Philip Schaff and Henry Wace, eds., *Jerome: Letters and Select Works*, 14 vols., vol. 6, *Nicene and Post-Nicene Fathers: Second Series* (Peabody: Hendrickson Publishers, 1999), 245.

77. St. Jerome, Against Jovinianus, Book II, 33, in: Ibid., 413. Emphasis added.

78. St. Augustine, Sermons on Selected Lessons of the New Testament, Sermon XXX (On the words of the Gospel, Matt. 17:19, "Why could not we cast it out"? Etc., and on Prayer), 5, in: Schaff, *Augustin: Sermon on the Mount*, 351.

79. St. Augustine, Expositions on the Book of Psalm, Psalm LXXI, 15, in: Philip Schaff, ed., *Augustine: Expositions of the Book of Psalms*, 14 vols., vol. 8, *Nicene And Post-Nicene Fathers: First Series* (Peabody: Hendrickson Publishers, 1999), 320.

80. St. Augustine, Sermons on Selected Lessons of the New Testament, Sermon LXXX (On the words of the Gospel, John 6:9, where the miracle of the five loaves and the two fishes is related), 2, in: Schaff, *Augustin: Sermon on the Mount*, 499.

81. John Cassian, The Second Part of the Conferences of John Cassian, XI (The First Conference of Abbott Chaeremon), Chapter I (Description of the town of Thennesus), in: Schaff, *Sulpitius Severus, Vincent of Lerins, John Cassian*, 415. Emphasis added.

82. Leo the Great, Sermon LIV (On the Passion, III; Delivered on the Sunday before Easter), 4 (Christ voluntarily bartered His glory for our weakness), in: Philip Schaff and Henry Wace, eds., *Leo the Great, Gregory the Great*, 14 vols., vol. 12, *Nicene And Post-Nicene Fathers: Second Series* (Peabody: Hendrickson Publishers, 1999), 166. Emphasis added.

83. St. John Damascus, An Exact Exposition of the Orthodox Faith, Book IV, Chapter XI (Concerning the Cross and here further concerning Faith), in: Philip Schaff and Henry Wace, eds., *Hilary of Poitiers, John of Damascus*, 14 vols., vol. 9, *Nicene And Post-Nicene Fathers: Second Series* (Peabody: Hendrickson Publishers, 1999), 80.

84. Editorial Staff at The Catholic University of America, ed., *New Catholic Encyclopedia*, First Edition ed., 15 vols., vol. 2 (New York: McGraw-Hill, 1967), 271.

85. Ibid., 284. The numbers in brackets are the relevant chapters of the Rule of Benedict. See 283–84 for a good summary of the Rule.

86. Lynn White Jr., "Dynamo and Virgin Reconsidered," *The American Scholar* 27 (1958): 183–94, 187–88. Emphasis added.

87. See Lynn White Jr., *Medieval Religion and Technology: Collected Essays* (Berkeley: University of California Press, 1978).

88. White, *Dynamo and Virgin Reconsidered*, 188. Emphasis added.

89. Ibid., 188–89. Emphasis added.

90. White points out many of the inventions that came about in subsequent years: the water wheel, the windmill, steam engines, etc. See White, *Dynamo and Virgin*, 189–91.

91. Jude P. Dougherty, "'Intellectuals with dirt under their fingernails': Attitudes toward science and technology and the difference they make," *Communio* 9, no. 3 (1982): 225–37, 230–31. Emphasis added. Dougherty lists an extraordinary array of inventions from the seventh century until the sixteenth century (See Ibid., 233–34).

92. Ibid., 230. Emphasis added.

93. Dwight Longenecker, "What St. Benedict can teach you about business success," *Crisis* 20, no. 3 (2002): 42–46.

94. References to the *Summa Theologica* are from: St. Thomas Aquinas, *Summa Theologica*, trans. Fathers of the English Dominican Province, Revised ed., 5 vols. (Allen, TX: Christian Classics, 1981).

95. Charles, *Christian Social Witness, Vol. 1*, 195.

96. Ibid., 197.

97. Frederick E. Flynn, "Wealth and Money in the Economic Philosophy of St. Thomas" (Doctoral Dissertation, Notre Dame, 1942). Flynn's study is extremely helpful in that he examines all of St. Thomas' writings with respect to business, money and trade. Regarding economics as a science he notes: "The problem of economics as a practical science receives scant treatment in St. Thomas. In fact, the furthest he goes into the question is to mention merely that economics is also a practical science. When speaking elsewhere of economics and politics he points out that 'economics and politics are not accepted here according as they are sciences, but rather according as they are prudences of a sort.' What of the possibility of economics being a speculative science as well? In the *Sentences* St. Thomas says: 'and so there is economics which is a speculative discipline, that is a deliberative discipline, and economics which is practical, that is, a discipline ordained to action.' This is the only place where St. Thomas seems to suggest that economics is a speculative discipline. However, it must be borne in mind that this text comes from the *Sentences* which represents the less mature thought of St. Thomas and in which his terminology had not yet attained the precision of his later works. Thus he may be using the word 'speculative' with a much wider connotation than the same word has, for instance, in the *Summa*. The fact that he uses *considerativus* as a synonym seems to imply merely that he refers to a less thoroughly practical phase in the development of practical thinking. The conclusion would be, then, that *St. Thomas regarded economics as a practical discipline on the scientific or prudential level*. Economics as a practical science is less practical than economics as a prudence. In the former case it indicates a general course of action; in the later case it goes so far as to determine the right course of action regarding particular and unrenewable circumstances. As a prudence, economics regulates actions at closer range; its practical conclusion is unique" (Ibid., 9–10). Emphasis added.

98. Charles, *Christian Social Witness, Vol. 1*, 197–98.

99. Flynn, *Wealth and Money in St. Thomas*, 10. Flynn's reference to Thomas is: St. Thomas, Polit., Lib. I, Lect. 10.

100. Ibid., 1.

101. Flynn, *Wealth and Money in St. Thomas*, 2.

102. Ibid., 2.

103. Flynn notes: "Even more strongly he insists elsewhere that 'the end of economics is not wealth,' for 'wealth can be compared to economics not as the ultimate end but as an instrument.'" Ibid., 10. (The two quotes from St. Thomas are: St. Thomas, *Ethic*, Lib. I, Lect. 1 and *Summa Theol.*, II-II, 50.3, ad 1.)

104. *Quadragesimo Anno*, 51. Emphasis added.

105. The strict sense: "to work something in external matter, for instance to make a house." The broad sense: "to denote any action, whether it passes into external matter, as to burn or cut, or remain in the agent, as to understand or will."

106. The import of his thought appears to be that magnanimity tends to the doing of something great (*ST*, Q. 129, AA.1,2) and relates to all the virtues.

107. Emphasis added. What then does magnanimity consist in? How is it different from magnificence? Thomas answers in Q. 129, A 1: "Now an act may be called great in two ways:

in one way proportionately, in another absolutely. An act may be called great proportionately, even if it consist in the use of some small or ordinary thing, if, for instance, one makes a very good use of it: but an act is simply and absolutely great when it consists in the best use of the greatest thing." So an act of magnificence includes the virtue of magnanimity, while magnanimity does not necessarily include a work of magnificence.

108. Emphasis added.

109. *Quadragesimo Anno*, 51.

110. This point is reminiscent of the Parable of the Talents. The lazy servant hid his talent because of fear. He lacked the virtue of fortitude and thereby refused to take the risk.

111. Thomas' insight applies to all business and investment decisions and not just entrepreneurial acts that are by nature huge and magnificent undertakings. One has only to think of a group of persons who begin with their first business venture or perhaps a single person who attempts to begin a small business. They risk a substantial amount of their capital in pursuit of a new business, which strictly speaking is not entrepreneurial, but is nevertheless significant. For them it is risky, the possible returns are high and their business contributes to the common good. They may not be entrepreneurs in the strict sense, but their activity is somewhat entrepreneurial.

112. Thomas writes: "But, apart from fraud, we may speak of buying and selling in two ways. First, as considered in themselves, and from this point of view, buying and selling seem to be established for the common advantage of both parties, one of whom requires that which belongs to the other, and vice versa, as the Philosopher states (Politica i,3). Now whatever is established for the common advantage, *should not be more of a burden to one party than to another*, and consequently all contracts between them should observe equality of thing and thing. Again, the quality of a thing that comes into human use is measured by the price given for it, for which purpose money was invented, as stated in Ethica Nicomachea v,5. Therefore if either the *price exceed the quantity of the thing's worth, or, conversely, the thing exceed the price, there is no longer the equality of justice*: and consequently, to sell a thing for more than its worth, or to buy it for less than its worth, is in itself unjust and unlawful." Emphasis added.

113. Emphasis added.

114. Thomas gives the example of a man intending a moderate gain "for the upkeep of his household or for the assistance of the needy: or again, a man may take to trade for some public advantage, for instance, lest his country lack the necessities of life, and seek gain, not as an end, but as payment for his labor."

115. Charles G. Herbermann, ed., *The Catholic Encyclopedia: An International Work of Reference on the Constitution, Doctrine, Discipline, and History of the Catholic Church*, 15 vols., vol. 15 (New York: Robert Appleton Company, 1912), 235.

116. Ibid.

117. See John T. Noonan, *The Scholastic Analysis of Usury* (Cambridge: Harvard University Press, 1957).

118. Charles, *Christian Social Witness, Vol. 1*, 200.

119. Ibid.

120. Ibid., 95.

121. Ibid., 95–96.

122. Ibid., 201.

123. Ibid. Emphasis added.

124. Odd Langholm, *Economics in the Medieval Schools: Wealth, Exchange, Value, Money and Usury According to the Paris Theological Tradition 1200-1350.* (Leiden: E.J. Brill, 1992). 12.

125. Langholm, *Economics*, 35.

126. Langholm, *Economics*, 54.

127. Ibid., 54–55.

128. Ibid., 131.

129. Ibid.

130. Ibid., 136.

131. Langholm, *Economics*, 411.

132. Alejandro A. Chafuen, *Christians for Freedom: Late-Scholastic Economics* (San Francisco: Ignatius Press, 1986), 21.

133. Ibid.

134. See Raymond De Roover, "The Scholastic Attitude Toward Trade and Entrepreneurship," *Explorations in Entrepreneurial History* 1, no. 1 (1963): 76–87; Raymond De Roover, ed., *Business, Banking, and Economic Thought in Medieval and Early Modern Europe: Selected Studies of Raymond De Roover* (Chicago: University of Chicago Press, 1974); Raymond De Roover, *San Bernardino of Siena and Sant'Antonino of Florence; The Two Great Economic Thinkers of the Middle Ages* (Boston: Harvard Graduate School of Business Administration, 1967).

135. Charles, *Christian Social Witness, Vol 1*. Chapter ten contains much that is useful.

136. Bede Jarrett, *S. Antonino and Medieval Economics* (St. Louis: B. Herder, 1914).

137. Chafuen, *Christians for Freedom*, 61.

138. De Roover, *San Bernardino of Siena and Sant'Antonino of Florence*, 1–5.

139. Ibid., 7.

140. Ibid.

141. Ibid.

142. De Roover, *Business, Banking, and Economic Thought*, 339. Emphasis added.

143. De Roover, *San Bernardino of Siena and Sant'Antonino of Florence*, 13.

144. De Roover, *Business, Banking, and Economic Thought*, 343.

145. De Roover, *San Bernardino of Siena and Sant'Antonino of Florence*, 13.

146. De Roover, *Business, Banking, and Economic Thought*, 339–40.

147. Ibid., 343.

148. Ibid., 340.

4

Private Initiative in the Social Teaching of the Church: Leo XIII–Paul VI

Only those who do not take a realistic view of the world can fail to see that religion alone has an answer to its problems.

—Etienne Gilson[1]

John Paul II once wrote that *Rerum Novarum* "created a lasting paradigm for the Church."[2] This chapter does not give a systematic account of the development of social teaching from Leo XIII through Paul VI. Rather, it examines the writings of the popes with respect to private initiative in the economic and financial sphere. Where is private initiative referred to and what importance do the popes attach to it? Is private initiative important in the development of society and the promotion of the common good? Is there any development of thought discernible from *Rerum Novarum* onwards? These are important questions for the topic of entrepreneurial work. We need then to examine *Rerum Novarum* and other pre-1981 encyclicals closely in order to understand the paradigm that Leo has bequeathed the Church. It is within the overall context of these documents that we understand the essential nature of private initiative. In continuity with Chapter 2, it becomes apparent that private initiative receives its value, dignity and importance both from the *dignity of the human person* and the *common good*.

Rerum Novarum: Leo XIII (1891)

Gilson notes that various titles have been given to the encyclical *Rerum Novarum*.[3] It is known, he writes, that the encyclical is devoted to a "bettering of the social condition of the working class."[4] Leo XIII, however, had a wider frame of reference. Gilson writes:

> [B]ut the Pope himself has defined it in wider terms as dealing with the rights and duties by which *rich and poor, or capital and labor, are bound together* in the body politic. This is clearly stated in *Rerum Novarum* (art. 1), and no less clearly restated in the encyclical *Graves De Communi* (art. 2). Accordingly, the emphasis should not be placed on either side of the problem, but on both.[5]

No doubt the Church of Leo XIII faced an extraordinary challenge. "A traditional society was passing away and another was beginning to be formed."[6] Perusing the outline of the encyclical, one can readily submit to Gilson's thesis. While it is clear that Leo XIII wanted to address the plight of the "working man," he situated his analysis, discussion and solution to the problem within a wider setting of the obligations of both capital and labor. Indeed, not only is the condition of labor understood in this wider setting, but the whole encyclical is concerned with the still wider context of the role played by both Church and State in fostering of the common good. This is, I believe, the sense in which it is possible to say that *Rerum Novarum* has "created a lasting paradigm for the Church."[7]

Rerum Novarum: Statement of the Social Problem and the Rejection of Class Struggle (1-2)

After a brief summary of the changes taking place in society at the time of writing, Leo comments in paragraph two:

> But all agree, and there can be no question whatever, that some remedy must be found, and quickly found, for the misery and wretchedness which press so heavily this moment on the large majority of the very poor.

The "misery and wretchedness" was not the result of one cause. Rather, the social dislocation was caused by a number of critical factors. Habiger lists five reasons for the social upheaval: The rise of personal freedom (occasioned by the French Revolution), the influence of England in fostering the Industrial Revolution, the resulting shift in population to the cities, the rise in mechanical transport (which lead to new empires) and the rise in nationalism and imperialism.[8] The second reason—the Industrial Revolution—was clearly critical.[9] Murphy comments that the actual condition of workers in the nineteenth century "gave rise to the socialist option."[10] It is his understanding that the socialists viewed workers as a new class, while the Church viewed workers as the *new poor*. The distinction is important. Murphy then observes:

> The Christian social movement in the nineteenth century was not born as a phi-losophy or ideology, a movement or a political party. Rather, it was the Church's response to specific problems it faced in various countries as it tried to minister to the new poor. Only after a certain amount of experience had accumulated did the Church grasp the deeper implications of what was happening.[11]

Leo, for his part, does not use the phrase "new class." He prefers, as the above citation indicates, to use the phrase the "very poor." Murphy is surely correct in observing that the Church took some time in grasping the implications of the indus-trial revolution.[12] And yet Leo's use of the term *infirmus* (*poor*), rather than *classis* (class), is not without significance. The text strongly suggests that Leo wanted to avoid any hint of a suggestion that the Church was becoming involved in a class struggle. After commenting on the rapaciousness of a few men (the rich) and the effect that they have on the vast majority of men, he states:

> To remedy these evils the *socialists*, working on the poor man's envy of the rich, endeavor to destroy private property, and maintain that individual possessions should become the common property of all...[13]

Without rejecting the historical fact that two classes were in fact developing, Leo XIII was not about to submit to a socialist interpretation of history—the pit-ting of one group against another.[14] Rather, the Church would base her response on the *dignity of the person*. It was this, and this alone, that would determine her response. Thus, if the Church was going to speak out on behalf of one sector of society, it would be precisely because the rights of those persons were being denied them or at least being endangered. In the time of Leo, the working class was to be defended, not because it was the working class as such, but rather because it was materially poor and could be and was, in fact, being manipulated by the class known as capital. Leo notes the *efficacy* of Christianity—a theme he develops in sections 13–45.

Rerum Novarum: The Rejection of Socialism—Private Property, Human Nature and the Family (Section 3-12)

The socialist doctrine, expressing itself in the rejection of private property and its transferal to the state, is rejected initially on practical grounds. Leo XIII says that the proposal to socialize property is "so clearly futile for all practical purposes" and that if it were implemented "the working man himself would be among the first to suffer." Then he moves into more philosophical ground, stating that *posses-sion is the reason for action*. "It is surely undeniable that, when a man engages in remunerative labor, the very reason and motive of his work is to obtain property, and to hold it as his own possession."[15]

Thus socialists strike at the interest of the laborer. By denying the right to private property, "they deprive him of the liberty of disposing of his wages," thus thwarting any attempt at possessing what he needs for the fulfillment of his life.[16] But more fundamentally, Leo argues that the socialists' claim is *against justice*. His argument is based on natural law. "It is the mind, or the reason, which is the chief thing in us who are human beings; it is this which makes a human being human, and distinguishes him essentially and completely from the brute."[17]

It is on account of *reason* that "it must be within his right to have things not merely for temporary and momentary use, as other living beings have them, but in stable and permanent possession."[18] Allied to reason is *freedom*. Man, unlike the rest of the animal world, is "master of his own acts."[19] He "governs himself" with reason "under the eternal law of God."[20] Thus when man acts, he acts intelligently and with freedom and is entitled to the fruits of his work.[21] This activity is entirely in accord with the divine plan.[22] Hence, the State should not abolish private property. On the contrary it should promote private property with vigor. "The law, therefore, should favor ownership, and its policy should be to induce as many as possible to become owners."[23]

Leo returns to the question of private property in paragraph 35. Here, it is a question of the State protecting the "sacred and inviolable" right to private property. The discussion takes place not amidst an attack on socialism, but rather on the importance of private property for the common good. It thus seems appropriate to discuss this important paragraph here. In order to solve "this great labor question," a question that is fundamental to the common good, the right to private property must be defended. Leo gives three reasons. First, property will be more equitably divided. He writes: "If working people can be encouraged to look forward to obtaining a share in the land, the result will be that the gulf between vast wealth and deep poverty will be bridged over, and the two orders will be brought nearer together."[24] Second, private property will lead to greater wealth. "Men always work harder and more readily when they work on that which is their own; nay they learn to love the very soil which yields in response to the labor of their hands, not only food to eat, but an abundance of the good things for themselves and those that are dear to them."[25] Third, private property leads to national stability and devotion to one's country. Emigration is less likely. Leo thus provides three important benefits of private property. Finally, besides defending the right to private property, which the State must assiduously uphold, he gives some fiscal advice to the State. One crucial way of defending the right is for the State to ensure that citizens are not overtaxed.[26]

Having considered socialism in the light of human nature and private property, *Rerum Novarum* now submits socialism to the truth of the family. Here again it is found wanting. Private property enables a father to provide for his family and besides, the family is "anterior both in idea and in fact to the gathering of men into a commonwealth."[27] Thus by paragraph twelve, Leo has rejected socialism out of hand. Private property and, by implication, private initiative, is the means by which the common good can be advanced. Socialism will lead to its disintegration. Accordingly, Leo XIII, in defending the right to private property on both practical and philosophical grounds, provides the Church with a fundamental social principle that will be defended, maintained and developed in the social teaching that succeeds him.

Rerum Novarum: The Counter Proposal of Leo XIII and the Birth of the Social Doctrine of the Church

The Church's Role in Society (13-24)

Murphy[28] and Gilson[29] agree that Leo XIII was a realist. Leo's great strength lay in the fact that he was both a realist and a Christian. Men are endowed with different gifts; this is part of nature. It would be absurd to deny this fact or attempt to annihilate it. "There naturally exist," writes Leo, "among mankind innumerable differences of the most important kind; people differ in capability, in diligence, in health, and in strength; and unequal fortune is a necessary result of inequality in condition."[30] And these differences, far from causing a problem, are actually advantageous to society and to individuals.[31]

Realism, however, admits the truth that despite these gifts of nature, suffering exists. Man's labor is both a blessing and toil. "To suffer and to endure," he writes, "is the lot of humanity."[32]

> If any there are who pretend differently—who hold out to a hard-pressed people freedom from pain and trouble, undisturbed repose, and constant enjoyment—they cheat the people and impose upon them, and their lying promises will only make the evil worse than before.[33]

But Leo was a Christian. The Gospel is light for a darkened world. It is a light for the mind and heart and directs the steps of believers along their journey of life. The light of faith accordingly reaches into the moral life of the believer.[34] Leo's Christian-realism undoubtedly makes *Rerum Novarum* attractive. Christianity, reflecting the light of her master, bathes and soothes humanity. The Gospel does not disparage human beings, human nature or the world. Rather, it enlightens their existence, shedding light on its meaning and raising it to a new dignity.

This Christian-realism gives rise to the fundamental contribution of *Rerum Novarum*. John Paul II teaches, as we have noted, that Leo XIII "created a lasting paradigm for the Church." That "lasting paradigm" is supernatural faith penetrating and enlightening the meaning of the temporal order. Commenting on the fact that Leo was aware that "peace is built on the foundation of justice,"[35] John Paul II says: "[W]hat was essential to the encyclical was precisely its proclamation of the fundamental conditions of justice in the economic and social situation of the time."[36]

The "lasting paradigm" that Leo bequeathed to the Church was indeed the fact that with the light of faith, the Church "has something to say about specific human situations, both individual and communal, national and international."[37] Not that the Church had remained silent on social issues before. On the contrary, as we have seen in Chapter 2, the Church has always attempted to address social questions in the light of faith. But rather, the "new things" of the world demanded a more thorough response. The "new things" were the occasion, not the cause,[38] of the birth of what we now call the social teaching of the Church.[39]

The paradigm created by Leo XIII is thus essentially the Gospel and its direct consequences in a new, complex society. Charles takes notes of the new situation, which clearly demanded a response unlike any before, when he writes:

> [B]ut the modern industrialized world was changing with alarming rapidity. There was no precedent for the situation. The social question was of vast complexity and immediate urgency. It affected all aspects of social, political and economic life in the industrializing nations of the old world.[40]

It is Leo XIII, the Christian-realist, to whom we are indebted for the birth and subsequent development of what is now known as the social doctrine of the Church.

The Role of the State in Society (25-35)

Leo clearly recognizes that in order to attain justice in social life, the work of the Church will be insufficient. The role of the State is crucial. *Rerum Novarum* teaches that "The first duty" of the State "should be to make sure that the laws and institutions, the general character and administration of the commonwealth, shall be such as to produce of themselves public well-being and private prosperity."[41] Likewise, the State prospers from the flourishing of her citizens. "Morality, well-regulated family life," "respect for religion and justice," "the moderation and equal distribution of public burdens," "progress of the arts and of trade," "the abundant yield of the land," in short "everything which makes the citizens better and happier" contributes to the prosperity of the State.[42] Murphy comments: "This echoes book nineteen of the *City of God*, in which Augustine sets forth as the two aims of every state the happiness of its citizens and the harmonious achievement of peace."[43]

Leo XIII is also insistent that the State must pursue justice for all based on the equal dignity of each human person. "This includes the work of distributive justice by which the state provides those goods that are for the advantage of the whole of society. It includes the respect and fostering of those principles, symbols, and values by which a nation forms its own identity through its culture, thus guaranteeing its own future." [44]

Rerum Novarum also holds that the State should "not absorb the individual or the family; both should be allowed free and untrammeled action as far as is consistent with the common good and the interests of others."[45] One can discern here an implicit reference to freedom to act with private initiative in the economic sphere. But it is just that—an implicit and subtle reference. Moreover, Leo insists, the State has the duty to protect the rights of citizens especially the right to private property. The State, he argues, also has a duty to respect the right to practice religion, the right to education and to rest. In addition, the State needs to ensure that citizens are subject to appropriate and proper hours of work, that children are not exploited in the workplace and that citizens are paid a just wage and have freedom of association. Under the topic of a just wage, *Rerum Novarum* attempts to outline the meaning of work. The simple contractual notion of work is insufficient (i.e., wages determined by supply and demand). For work is concerned with "procuring what is necessary for the purposes of life, and most of all for self-preservation."[46] Thus work, according to Leo, has two "notes" or "characteristics." It is *personal* and *necessary*.[47]

The Relationship between Employer and Employee— Communal Dimensions of Work (36-44)

The encyclical now addresses "the question of the hour": the condition of the working man.[48] As noted above, the issue is not addressed from the perspective of class, but rather from the more holistic theme of the equality of individuals and now, as Leo reveals his mind, the communal nature of man. He avoids entering into the dangerous waters of the class struggle, while nevertheless admitting that social and economic changes have produced two classes (orders).

In paragraph 36, Leo reflects on the communal dimension of work. Leo's main focus is the bringing together of the two orders (classes). Associations, both of employers and workmen, have the ability to draw together the two orders by means of "opportune assistance to those in need." He then focuses exclusively on the associations of workmen. It is here that he unveils the communal dimension of work, based as it is on the social/communal dimension of man. He bases his assertion on the natural impulse of man to be united with his fellow man and offers some scriptural texts. He merely introduces the topic and does not develop any clear theological arguments. His observations are, however, interesting when viewed in light of later Church teaching in social matters.

> The experience of his own weakness urges man to call in help from without. We read in the pages of Holy Writ: "It is better that two should be together than one; for they have the advantage of their society. If one fall he shall be supported by the other. Woe to him that is alone, for when he falleth he hath none to lift him up" [Eccles. 4:9,10]. And further: "A brother that is helped by his brother is like a strong city" [Prov. 18:19]. It is this natural impulse which unites men in civil society; and it is this also which makes them band themselves together in associations of citizen with citizen; associations which, it is true, cannot be called societies in the complete sense of the word, but which are societies nevertheless.[49]

Private Initiative and *Rerum Novarum*

Having briefly considered the encyclical, two points emerge for this thesis. First, in defending so vigorously the right to private property, Leo XIII has acknowledged the importance of possession in helping man to attain his human fulfillment. Private property is clearly related to the right of working and the right to dispose of one's wealth as one sees fit. Private property is intimately related to private initiative. In order to preserve the right to private property, one must respect the right to private initiative—one is not possible without the other. The right to private property, therefore, presumes the right to initiative. One obtains property in and through human action. But it is clearly possession that is foremost in the mind of Leo, engrossed as he was in the struggle against socialism (and capitalism). It is Pius XI who will move the discussion from possession to action in *Quadragesimo Anno.*

Second, Leo highlights three important responsibilities of the State: the protection of the rights of citizens, creating conditions that allow citizens to achieve their natural ends, and the fostering of the common good. Leo's defense of the right to private property applies to each of these responsibilities of the State. This we have seen in the discussion. Of particular note, however, is the importance of private property in relation to the common good. Defending the right to private property ensures that property will be more equitably divided, that greater wealth will be generated in society, and national stability and harmony will follow. As we have noted and will continue to observe, private property (and as a consequence, private initiative) receives its importance from the common good.

Pius XI: *Quadragesimo Anno—*
"On Reconstructing the Social Order"

Pope Pius XI in 1931 faced a different situation than did Leo XIII. O'Brien comments:

> In 1931 Pius faced a very different situation. World War I had shattered liberal confidence. Parliamentary democracy seemed almost helpless in the face of the mass movements of fascism and communism. And the economy of the Western world lay in the ruins of a worldwide depression. The church, better organized and more united than ever before, might be able to offer a credible alternative to a failed capitalism and a fearsome socialism.[50]

Yet for all the differences, *Rerum Novarum* and *Quadragesimo Anno* form a substantial unity. Certainly Pius XI is more prescriptive than Leo XIII in his suggestions and recommendations for the economy. But of seventy-seven references in the text of Pius' encyclical, thirty-eight refer to *Rerum Novarum*, ten to other writings of Leo and twenty-eight to scripture. *Rerum Novarum* is shorter—around two-third's the size of *Quadragesimo Anno*—with only thirty-nine references. Surprisingly, twenty-eight of the references are to scripture.

Private Property: Individual and Social Character

We have observed *Rerum Novarum's* insistence on the "sacred and inviolable right" to private property. It was also noted that Leo, in line with traditional Catholic thought, made the distinction between the right of possession of property (and money) and its use. One has the right to possess property, but one should consider this property "as common to all."[51] Pius, in *Quadragesimo Anno*, now fully enunciates this principle as it applies to private property.

> Like human nature itself, and like all manifestations and institutions of human life, property, too, manifests a double aspect, an individual and social phase. Man is at once and equally an individual and a social being. The same is true of the various institutions of human life, and especially of property... Thus it is a matter of course for St. Thomas Aquinas that property belongs fully to the owner, but that nevertheless this does not exclude a certain common ownership among mankind.... Thomas Aquinas made a clear distinction between the administration of goods, which is exclusively in the hands of the owner, and the use of the goods, which is always shared by others, that is, individual administration and social use. This thought of Thomas Aquinas adapted and developed by Leo XIII, we now find elaborated in its full consequences by Pius XI.[52]

Thus the right to private property is not denied, but it is refined in light of Aquinas' doctrine of the distinction between ownership and use.[53]

The Virtue of Magnificence

Nell-Breuning suggests that Pius "resurrected" the duty of magnanimity from the Middle Ages where it was associated with feudalism. However, in the form that Pius gave it, it is hardly archaic, but rather takes on the form of a capitalistic virtue.

> We see, however, that Pius XI revives it not in it feudal form, but rather modernized throughout. The *magnificentia* of Pius XI is a *genuinely capitalistic virtue*, indeed, the Pope makes it the *virtue of the entrepreneur*, not in the sense that all present-day employers practice this virtue, but meaning that it is *the virtue proper of the capitalistic employer.*[54]

The "resurrection" of *magnificentia* is perfected by Pius' modern intonation. Nell-Breuning lists the twofold demands of the virtue. It is clear that the entrepreneur must participate in the cross if he wishes to share in the resurrection.

> His demand is twofold: (1) that large incomes be invested in enterprises offering the opportunity of employment and wages; therefore in enterprises that not merely keep hands busy, but offer an opportunity to those employed to earn a living; (2) that the capital be not invested according to a misunderstood principle of profit that asks merely for interest irrespective of whether it be obtained

morally or immorally. Only that entrepreneur practices the virtue of liberality who in his activity gives first thought to service and second thought to gain, who in his enterprise and in his means of production employs his workingmen for the creation of goods of true worth. . .[55]

The Meaning of Work

In *Rerum Novarum* Leo XIII wrote that work had two characteristics—it was *necessary* and *personal*. Pius introduces the social character of work.

> The obvious truth is that in labor, especially wage labor, as in ownership, there is a social as well as personal or individual aspect to be considered. For unless human society forms a truly social and organic body; unless labor be protected in the social and juridical order; unless the various forms of human endeavor, dependent one upon the other, are united in mutual harmony and mutual support; unless, above all, intellect, capital and labor are brought together in a common effort, man's toil cannot produce due fruit. Hence, if the social and individual character of labor be overlooked, it can be neither equitably appraised nor properly recompensed according to strict justice.[56]

The movement from *Rerum Novarum* to *Quadragesimo Anno* is from work seen as personal and necessary to work viewed as personal and social. This last point clearly has ramifications for the relationship between capital and labor. And while Leo XIII noted that the one cannot do without the other, Pius states why this is actually the case. *Work is profoundly social* and therefore men cannot do without each other. Man is a personal and social being. Some fifty years after Pius, John Paul II, in the introduction of *Laborem Exercens*, will write that working "within a community of persons" constitutes the "very nature" of man's work on earth.

Free Competition and Capitalism

Pius had already made some comment on the relationship between economic activity and moral discipline.[57] Now he suggests, in the midst of what can appear to be a severe critique of free competition, that *social justice* and *social charity* must guide economic behavior.[58] Taken out of context, his remarks could seem to be a direct rebuff of free competition. But in fact, they are really a commentary on those who create an idol out of self-direction and free competition. His distinction is important, particularly when we consider John Paul II's acceptance of market economies as the most effective way to serve the common good. Like Pius, John Paul II offers guarded praise of free markets, but with language that is a little less confrontational! They belonged to different eras. Pius' statement in its full context reads:

> Just as the unity of human society cannot be built upon "class" conflict, so the proper ordering of economic affairs cannot be left to the free play of rugged

competition. From this source as from a polluted spring have proceeded all the errors of the "individualistic" school. This school, forgetful or ignorant of the social and moral aspect of economic activities, regarded these as completely free and immune from any intervention by public authority, for they would have in the market place and in unregulated competition a principle of self-direction more suitable for guiding them than any created intellect which might intervene. Free competition, however, though justified and quite useful within certain limits, cannot be an adequate controlling principle in economic affairs.[59]

The "adequate controlling principle" is not free competition, but social justice. Pius returns to this theme again in paragraphs 101–110 as he considers the changes in economic life since the publication of *Rerum Novarum*. It is his claim that the capitalist system "has penetrated everywhere"[60] and this has been accompanied not only by unrestrained free competition, but other evils as well.

In the first place, then, it is patent that in our days not alone is wealth accumulated, but immense power and despotic economic domination is concentrated in the hands of a few...[61]

Still, he notes that "it is clear that the system as such is not to be condemned."[62] The system is to be guided by justice so that the right order between capital and labor is observed.[63]

The Principle of Subsidiarity

Pius XI reveals this principle of the social order (for the first time, it seems, in an encyclical) in the section of the encyclical headed *The Reconstruction of the Social Order*. Referring to the principle he says that "it is a fundamental principle of social philosophy, fixed and unchangeable."[64] Thus, despite the fact that it had never been articulated before, the suggestion seems to be that *it has always been assumed in the life of the Church* and, one would imagine, in the polis. Leo's insistence on the right to private property and the means by which this property is obtained seems to have echoed in the ears of Pius. Perhaps, too, Paul's words found a welcome resting place and have emerged, albeit unconsciously, in Pius' teaching. Paul did write to the Thessalonians an exhortation to work—a command which seems to have all the authority of Christ behind it.[65]

Paul's command urges personal and institutional responsibility. One should do what one can and ought to do. Nobody should relieve another from the joyful and at times painful duty to work. There is to be no shirking of responsibility. But perhaps Pius is simply doing what he says he is doing, recognizing and developing a tenet of social philosophy. What is clear is that the principle is "fixed and unchangeable."

In *Quadragesimo Anno* the accent is now on *action*. With *Rerum Novarum*, as we have seen, the accent was undoubtedly on *possession*. So there is a clear development of thought between the two documents, with Pius building on the groundwork of Leo. He acknowledges this in his preamble before articulating the principle. Leo had made "a happy beginning."[66] But to ensure the stability of this new beginning, to achieve "what has not yet been accomplished" and to facilitate the passage of "still richer and brighter blessings" for mankind, Pius says two things are necessary: "the reform of institutions and the correction of morals."[67] The principle of subsidiarity belongs to the former.

Pius is clearly aware of the dangers of individualism.[68] The "signs of the times" in 1931 was an increase in rampant individualism with the result that there was a loss of organic social life. Thus what remained were the individual and the state. Gone were those intermediary bodies that supplied social cohesion. On account of individualism, writes Pius, "as we called it, things have come to such a pass that the highly developed social life, which once flourished in a variety of prosperous and interdependent institutions, has been damaged and all but ruined, leaving virtually only individuals and the State, with no little harm to the latter."[69] In light of Pius' preamble on individualism, it is my understanding that the formulation of the principle of subsidiarity is motivated by three concerns, with the first two really forming a cohesive unity.[70]

First, the pontiff is concerned with *the disappearance of a highly developed social life* expressed by intermediary bodies that are normally the fruit of personal and voluntary initiative. The disappearance was caused by individualism or selfishness. People had not the time, nor the concern, to bother themselves with those social institutions that provided invaluable social harmony and development. This is clearly Pius' argument from the text of the encyclical itself.

Second, as a result of this disappearance, i.e., with the decline of a "supporting social structure," the State was "now encumbered with all burdens once borne by the disbanded associations."[71] Accordingly, *the State began to reach into areas of personal and social life that was not its particular domain.*

Third, the principle is a protection against socialism, against the wresting of private initiative from the individual and the placing of this initiative in the hands of the State. This occurs clearly in planned economies.

Commenting on the first two points, Nell-Breuning notes that with the climate of individualism prevailing, the State begins to assume monstrous proportions. What at first promised liberation in fact delivers tyranny:

> These individuals, powerless in their isolation, find themselves confronted with the all-powerful absolute and centralized state that tolerates no other gods and claims divine authority, omniscience, and omnipotence for itself... No one ever recognized better than Emmanuel Ketteler that the atomist-individual spirit which, in the form of Liberalism, was in his day at the height of its power, must logically lead to unlimited state authority.[72]

Individualism is detained in a prison of its own making. What had promised liberation from authority actually becomes an enslavement to a new tyrannical structure—the

State. Pius' brief discussion of individualism before articulating the principle is crucial to understanding the principle of subsidiarity.

In paragraph seventy-nine of the encyclical we read "... that one should not withdraw from individuals and commit to the community what they can accomplish by their own enterprise and industry."[73] Here he addresses the question of socialism—the withdrawal from individuals of what rightfully belongs to them: their own personal initiative and industry.

And thus Pius affirms the importance of private initiative in the economic sphere. He continues, this time addressing the question of individualism.

> So, too, it is an injustice and at the same time a grave evil and a disturbance of right order to transfer to the larger and higher collectivity functions which can be performed and provided for by lesser and subordinate bodies. Inasmuch as every social activity should, by its very nature, prove a help to members of the body social, it should never destroy or absorb them.[74]

That the principle covers not only economic realities but all social realities is clear from the text. But Pius, in paragraph eighty, seems focused on the economic sphere.

> The State authorities should leave to other bodies the care and expediting of business and activities of lesser moment, which otherwise become for it a source of great distraction.

The result will be that the State will perform its functions with greater freedom and effectiveness. Pius now names the principle explicitly.

> Let those in power, therefore, be convinced that the more faithfully this principle of "subsidiarity" is followed and a hierarchical order prevails among the various organizations, the more excellent will be the authority and efficiency of society, and the happier and more prosperous the condition of the commonwealth.[75]

The importance of the principle of subsidiarity becomes clear. On the one hand, Pius enunciates the principle as a defense against, and an attack on, socialism. No one should withdraw from individuals and transfer to the State what rightfully belongs to individuals. Private initiative is essential, in economic matters and other activities, particularly the family. But clearly, as can be observed, Pius was also deeply concerned with radical individualism and the role that it was playing in dismantling intricate social structures vital for the survival and development of the common good. In this way he was urging not only the State to examine its ever-expanding and damaging role, but perhaps more importantly, he was challenging each citizen to see that, in fact, it was his responsibility to promote those intermediary bodies so essential to society.

The State had moved beyond its jurisdiction precisely because individual citizens had narrowed their jurisdiction. Their eyes were now fixed on the "self" and not the wider society. Not only was Pius asking the State to make a sincere examination of conscience; individuals were being asked to do the same. Wasn't it true to say that individualism was playing its part in contributing to an all-pervasive State? Negligence of social responsibilities was being fostered by a philosophy that was promoting only individual concerns and not social responsibility. Paradoxically, this philosophy did not lead to the liberation of the "self," but to its entombment.

The principle of subsidiarity thus has this twofold purpose. First it defends the role of the individual against collectivist tendencies. It promotes the principal of private initiative and this is crucial for the work of the entrepreneur and for the life of society. Without this personal initiative, the generation of wealth, income and employment is impossible and the common good suffers. This principle defends private initiative "always" as John Paul II notes, *"with a view to the common good."*[76] Second, it promotes the role of the State as a helper (*subsidium*) and not as a usurper. Under this second aspect, individuals are encouraged to respond to the call that is theirs by virtue of their social being and status. Indeed they are challenged in two ways. First, the principle of subsidiarity challenges them to see the ramifications of radical individualism. Second, subsidiarity challenges them to assume the responsibilities that are theirs by virtue of their humanity and only to seek the assistance of the State in the fulfillment of these responsibilities. In this way Pius is attempting to renew society through structures that are evidently social, but not structures of the State, per se. These structures are to proceed from the personal initiative of citizens, are for the good of the ordinary citizen and receive the support of the State in their functioning.

Pius XI says that the principle is "fixed and unchangeable." It defends the individual from State excesses, it encourages the State to play an auxiliary role and it challenges persons to discover and meet their social responsibilities. It calls them forth to service. Without subsidiarity, communion would be rendered impossible.

Hence we can ask: Is it possible that the principle of subsidiarity, by calling the State to moderate its behavior, but more importantly by calling forth the individual citizen to live up to his social nature and vocation, becomes the foundational principle to a more just and Christian world? Can we not surmise that this principle is foundational to social love, to what John Paul II calls the principle of solidarity, of communion? To "love the little platoon we belong to in society." Is this not the key to developing a *communion of persons* in public life and within a corporation?

The principle of subsidiarity, then, protects the legitimate right that each individual has to act with freedom in the social and economic sphere. The State should be wary of suffocating personal initiative. But the freedom of the individual is ordered to the social good of others and to society in general. Man is a personal and social being. The principle of subsidiarity confirms that personal initiative receives its value and importance from the human person himself and the common good. This is the ultimate human reason for the defense and promotion of the work of the entrepreneur. It is essential to the meaning of his calling.

Pius XII and the Principle of Private Initiative

Upon his election to the Papacy on 2 March 1939, Eugenio Pacelli took the name of Pius XII. Like Benedict XV, his pontificate would be influenced greatly by war. Nonetheless, Pius' contributions to the social question are significant. They come to us in the form of his addresses, either by radio or to select groups. Here I do not attempt to give a systematic account of his social teaching, but will focus on his addresses that are significant in terms of private initiative and the work of the entrepreneur.[77]

The Anniversary of *Rerum Novarum*, 1 June 1941

On June 1, 1941, Pius broadcast a radio message to the workers of the world. The occasion was the fiftieth anniversary of *Rerum Novarum* for which thousands of Italian workers had gathered in St. Peter's Square. It was noted above that Pius XI refined somewhat Leo XIII's understanding of the right to private property, placing it in the context of the *use* of property. One has a right to private property, but this does not prohibit its use by others. Property, according to Pius XI, has a personal and social character. Pius XII now confirms Pius XI and perhaps develops the relationship between private property and its use a little more. Rather than speaking of the right to private property first, as Leo XIII and Pius XI do, Pius XII prefers to speak of the fundamental right to make use of the material goods of the earth. Only then does he speak of the right to private property. The right to private property is thus based on this later right and serves it.

> Every man, as a living being gifted with reason, has in fact from nature the *fundamental right to make use of the material goods of the earth*, while it is left to the will of man and to the juridical statutes of nations to regulate in greater detail the actuation of this right.[78]

It is within this fundamental right to make use of the material goods of the earth that the right to private property arises. It "demands also private property."[79] But the right must be regulated by man himself precisely because the material goods of the earth belong to all.[80] It is within this fundamental right to make use of the material goods of the earth that Pius speaks of, "the free reciprocal commerce of goods by interchange and gift."[81] It, too, is subject to the oversight of the State precisely for the same reason that private property is; it must serve the fundamental right that all people have to make use of the material goods of the earth. Pius sees this right as fundamental because man is called to perfect and fulfill his "material and spiritual life."[82] He affirms the principle of subsidiarity, without referring to it by name,[83] confirms the right to work, and the importance of the family.[84]

Social Function of Banking, 25 April 1950, and
Vocation of Businessmen, 27 April 1950

In 1950, Pius gave two addresses that have significance for this study. The first was to bankers, the second to businessmen. His address to Italian bankers on 25 April 1950 is interesting for its articulation of the meaning of professional work. Pius' teaches that professional work is a means of serving God and a means of sanctification (of the person). In addition, work is seen as necessary and social.[85] With regard to the social dimension of work, Pius observes that "one's work ought to contribute to the common good; it should testify to the sense of responsibility of each for the well-being of all."[86] These four elements of work seem to constitute, in some sense, the beginning, not the development, of a spirituality of work.

Of particular interest is the intimate connection that Pius sees between work as a service to God and to the common good. "Conscientiousness, honesty, exactitude," he writes, are qualities of work that become even "more inseparable from work when it is considered as the service of God, and become, in this way, profitable for the welfare of the community."[87] From this address he appears to be developing a vision of work where there is in fact a *profound unity* between personal virtue, service of God and neighbor. The human (personal and social) and divine dimensions of work are indeed inseparable in the mind of Pius. This brief passage, therefore, seems to build on the understanding of work that Leo XIII articulated (work as personal and necessary) and that Pius XI further developed (work as personal and social).

In commenting further on the social dimension of work, he appears to anticipate the writings of John Paul II. In *Centesimus Annus*, John Paul II sees the establishment of the communion of persons as a fundamental characteristic of work. Pius writes:

> How is it that an organization such as yours is a real community, and not a mere existence in common, unless it is that all of you, from the first to the last, are conscious of working with Christian loyalty for the good of all?[88]

Pius speaks of Christian loyalty as the means of achieving this real community. For John Paul II it is the gift of self. In two Christmas addresses, Pius once again anticipates John Paul II. This time he anticipates the thoughts contained in *Laborem Exercens*. In his 1952 Christmas address, Pius mentions the priority of man over things, a theme intimately tied to the subjective meaning of work. This topic is developed remarkably in *Laborem Exercens*. Pius writes: "Every plan or program must be inspired by the principle that man as subject, guardian and promoter of human values is more important than mere things, is more important than practical applications or scientific progress."[89] He returns to this theme, briefly, in his Christmas address of 1955, and also speaks of the creative and redemptive meanings of work. Pius writes:

There is now being asked the question whether the creative power of work truly constitutes the steady support of man independently of other values not purely technical, and if, consequently, it deserves to be, as it were, worshipped by modern man. Certainly not, for no power whatsoever or other activity of an economic nature can be so regarded. Even in the technical era, the human person, created by God and redeemed by Christ, remains elevated in its being and in its dignity, and therefore its creative power and its work have very much higher permanence. Thus firmly established, human work is also a profound moral force, and the human race or workers is a society which not only produces things, but also glorifies God. Man can consider his work as a true instrument of his sanctification because by working he makes perfect in himself the image of God, fulfills his duty, and the right to gain for himself and his dependents the necessary sustenance, and makes himself a useful unit of society."[90]

To return to Pius' address on the 25 April 1950, the pope distinguishes in this address between avarice and the legitimate acquiring of wealth and does so by means of the parable of the talents as found in the Gospel. Commenting on the good and faithful servant in contrast to that of the lazy servant he draws some conclusions for his audience of bankers. This address and the address of 24 October 1951 (see below) show an acute awareness of the value of money. It appears that this is the first time that a pope has acknowledged its value. The Church has clearly defended the right to private property and private action in the teachings of Leo XIII and Pius XI. By implication, the Church has affirmed the value of money. This amounts to implicit approval of the value of money. Pius makes it explicit.

Does not the social function of the bank consist in making it possible for the individual to render his money fruitful, even if only in small degree, instead of dissipating it, or leaving it sleep without any profit, either to himself or to others? That is why the services which a bank can render are so numerous: to facilitate and encourage savings; to preserve savings for the future, at the same time rendering them productive in the present; to enable savings to share in useful enterprises which could not be launched without them; to make as simple and easy as possible the regulation of accounts, exchanges, commerce between the State and private organisms and, in a word, the entire economic life of the people; . . .[91]

Given two days after the above address, on 27 April 1950, Pius addressed himself to representatives of the Chambers of Commerce from all over the world. The address was entitled: *Vocation of Businessmen*. His concern is to help businesspeople see the importance of crowning their "technical and juridical work by a serious moral consideration of the role and responsibilities of commerce."[92] He begins his address in a very positive way. "It is not without impressive significance that mythology gave wings to Mercury (pagan god of commerce). Should we not see in that the symbol of the liberty that commerce needs to go and come across the borders of its own country?"[93]

He first upholds the importance of private initiative in the economic sphere, rejecting socialism, and then considers the importance of the merchant.

> Further, you will not obtain the goal you wish, which is the general prosperity, without putting into full effect the individual exercise of commerce for the service of society's material well-being. The merchant, one will say, should be skilled without doubt. But he must add to these strictly professional qualities a high concept of the ideal of his profession. As a businessman, he must consider also himself a servant of the community.[94]

Pius thus repeats the teaching of Leo XIII and Pius XI that there *can be no general prosperity without individual, private initiative*. Furthermore, this goal of material well-being is worthwhile since it contributes to the common good, which is, as we have seen in Chapter 2, fundamental to the definition of the entrepreneur. But Pius does introduce something new. He raises the important question of *ideals in professional work*. And the sublime ideal that he places before businessmen is that of service. The calling of a businessman in his desire to provide material prosperity for the community is to be a servant of the community. His work, if it is imbued with this ideal, is real Christian work.

But the vocation of businessmen is not easy. Pius continues speaking of the "difficult calling of a merchant" and warns businessmen not "to betray" their "vocation" by focusing solely on profit. Theirs is a vocation that "aims and strives to circulate worldly goods, destined by God for the advantage of all."[95] Finally, he concludes his address drawing upon Matt. 13:45, the parable of the treasure. His purpose here is to encourage business people to seek *true riches*, to buy the Kingdom of Heaven at the "price of all his goods"[96] and to transmit this faith to their children.

Function of Banking, 24 October 1951

On this day Pius addressed delegates attending the International Congress on Credit Questions. He sees the work of bankers as crucial to the social question. "You mark the border," he tells the bankers, "or, to be more exact, the crossroads where capital, ideas and labor encounter each other."[97] He is serious in his claim that bankers make it possible for capital and labor to encounter each other, and thus provide a solution to the social problem.

> After what We have said, it seems superfluous to speak of the immediate result of the meeting of capital and ideas. In proportion to the importance of the capital and the practical value of the idea, the labor crisis will be more or less slowed up. The conscientious and hard-working laborer will find employment more easily; the growth of production will progressively, though perhaps slowly, lead toward an economic balance; the many inconveniences and disorders, deplorably resulting from strikes, will be lessened for the greater good of a healthy domestic, social and moral life.[98]

Pius also shows an acute awareness of the particular character of the work of bankers and the importance of their work in the promotion of the common good. "A young inventor," he tells them, "a man with initiative, a benefactor of humanity comes to you for a loan. You must study him in order not to put the trusting lender into the hands of a utopian or crook, in order to avoid the risk of sending away a deserving borrower capable of giving immense services but merely lacking the necessary funds for carrying them out."[99]

But it is his *appreciation of the value of money* (once again) that is most striking in this address. One of the characteristics of the entrepreneurial personality that was noted in Chapter 1, was commercial focus, or as Golis has it, an interest in money.[100] Pius recognizes the importance and validity of this quality. His words are worth citing in full for this very reason. They echo his previous address of 25 April 1950 cited above.

How much capital is lost through waste and luxury, through selfish and dull enjoyment, or accumulates and lies dormant without being turned to profit! There will always be egoists and self-seekers; there will always be misers and those who are short-sightedly timid. Their number could be considerably reduced if one could interest those who have money in using their funds wisely and profitably, be they great or small. It is largely due to this lack of interest that money lies dormant. You can remedy this to a great extent by making ordinary depositors collaborators, either as bond or share-holders, in undertakings whose launching and thriving would be of great benefit to the community, such as industrial activities, agricultural production, public works, or the construction of houses for workers, educational or cultural institutions, welfare or social service.[101]

The Catholic Employer, 5 June 1955

Pius XII addressed the Italian Association of Christian Employers in June of 1955. The employers had gathered in Naples to discuss the continued impoverishment of the southern regions of Italy. What role could private enterprise play in developing resources to overcome poverty? Pius addressed four hundred representatives from different parts of Europe and Canada when they traveled to Rome. The address is very significant in that it makes explicit a principle underlying the importance of private initiative. Leo XIII and Pius XI had indeed noted the crucial role of private initiative in developing the common good—Leo, under the guise of private property (possession), and Pius XI within the context of action. But Pius XII focuses on a principle that gives rise to private initiative, apart from its necessary orientation to the common good. Perhaps Pius XII is making explicit what is assumed by both pontiffs? Pius XII notes that private initiative is based upon the human person, the most important element in the economy. In this he appears to once again anticipate John Paul II in *Centesimus Annus*.

One of the essential points of Christian social doctrine has always been the affirmation of the primary importance of private enterprise as compared to the subsidiary function of state enterprise. This is not to deny the usefulness and the necessity, in some cases, of government intervention, but rather to bring out this truth: that *the human person represents not only the purpose of the economy, but is its most important element.*[102]

Then, in what further highlights the social nature of the entrepreneurial vocation, Pius makes some comments, which may at first sight appear to have a socialistic tone, but which in fact are a challenge to direct private initiative toward the common good. The suggestion seems to be that the development of the common good will be facilitated by entrepreneurs acting with both private initiative and mutual cooperation. *Entrepreneurs should act with initiative, but this does not mean they should act independently (of one another).*

> The words of the Gospel naturally come to mind: "Which of you wishing to build a tower, does not sit down first and calculate the outlays that are necessary, whether he has the means to complete it?" (Luke 14:28). Here, indeed, it is not merely a question of investing capital, of perhaps running great financial risks, but especially of putting into action a social idea, a concept of economy, of its laws, of its aims and of its limits. It is a question of directing a whole movement of progress according to a well-defined plan.[103]

Pius suggests strongly that *private initiative is a right* that must be respected. His comments are made in the context of affirming that the economic goal that individuals and the State aspire to "hinges on a true uplifting of the people, and therefore on the acquisition of their legitimate economic, social and cultural autonomy."[104]

> Therefore, from the very beginning it is necessary to admit fully the rights of others, their just needs and their profound aspirations and to be willing to satisfy them adequately.[105]

Finally, Pius returns to that unity between personal and social virtue, and the supernatural divine dimension of work that we observed above. But this address is definitely more developed and in a way anticipates the Second Vatican Council's teaching on lay spirituality. Pius has already shown his appreciation for the particular skills of the merchant and thus has no intention of interfering with the secular character of the laity. He affirms, therefore, that the teaching of the Church in social matters is on the level of principles. In order for the teaching to be effective, it must find a welcome home in leaders of corporations. It will be businessmen, not popes or priests, who will be the primary witnesses to the truth of the Gospel in the world of business. The Church, in her social teaching, will guide her children by principles and will form them with the Gospel. It will be the task of the laity to assimilate these truths and put them into practice. The witness of businessmen to Christ will take place in their workplace and it will be the fruit of an intense interior life, union with Christ, fostered by word and sacrament.

The teaching of the Church, which gives a clear formula of Catholic principles, runs the risk of being neither well understood nor applied *unless it finds in the responsible head of a firm not a resigned and passive reception, but the fullness of an intense interior life, nourished by the sacramental sources of grace.* It seems to Us that Christian social thought should be profoundly organic. Far from being built up solely by starting from abstract pronouncements, it ought to correspond with constant fidelity to the intentions of Divine Providence as they are manifested in the life of every Christian and in the life of the community to which he belongs.[106]

As with all Christians, this noble vocation and task calls for interior effort.

The creative act of God that has launched the world into space never ceases to kindly live with astonishing abundance and variety. In the individual as in society, the aspiration for betterment and for natural and supernatural perfection calls for a continuous overcoming of self and often also for a painful detachment. To follow this rising path and to guide others to it calls for hard work.[107]

The Small Business Manager, 20 January 1956

Here for the first time in Papal teaching the entrepreneur is mentioned explicitly. Pius was speaking to the *First National Congress of Small Industry.* Pius teaches that the entrepreneur is indispensable to society and he articulates the qualities that a business leader should have. Once again he appears to anticipate John Paul II, both in his call for a business to be a *communion of persons,* and in his recognition of the transcendent nature of the human person, a truth that gives rise to private initiative in the economic realm (as we have already seen above). With regard to the latter, Pius teaches that private initiative:

[C]orresponds not only to the needs of our present situation, but likewise to the teachings of the Church, which thus puts into action in its social implications a higher and more fundamental doctrine; namely, of the transcendent vocation of the human being, and his personal responsibility before God and his fellows.[108]

As regards the entrepreneur Pius writes:

Among the motives that justified the holding of your convention, you have given the first place to "a vindication of the indispensable functions of the private entrepreneur." The latter exhibits in an eminent degree the spirit of free enterprise to which we owe the remarkable progress that has been made especially during the past fifty years, and notably in the field of industry.[109]

Pius affirms the fact that private enterprise must be oriented to the common good, thus confirming, without saying so explicitly, that *there is no such person as a purely private, purely individualistic entrepreneur.*

It is in the midst of defining the meaning of true leadership in the business community that Pius speaks of trust and unity between employer and employee. As regards leadership, he notes that particularly in smaller enterprises a man must possess "the most varied intellectual gifts" which should be "united to a strong and versatile character, and in whom above all, there is a sense of morality that is sincere and magnanimous."[110] "An intense desire for true social progress"[111] should characterize the employer, as should a desire for unity with one's employees.[112]

> Let Us say at once that the employer himself is the deciding factor in this: he is the principal source of the spirit which animates his employees. If he is noticeably careful to place the interests of all concerned above his own private interests, he will have little difficulty in maintaining the same spirit among his subordinates.[113]

The employer is thus the principal source of unity and trust in a firm. When he places the interests of his employees above that of his own he does not forfeit his authority, but rather reinforces it! Pius teaches that employees "will readily understand that their superior ... has no intention of profiting unjustly at their expense, or of exploiting their labour excessively."[114]

> On the other hand, they will see that, by providing them and their families with the means of livelihood, he is likewise affording them an opportunity to perfect their own individual capacities, to engage in work that is useful and profitable, and to contribute according to their abilities to the service of the community as well as their own economic and moral improvement.[115]

This attitude of service helps promote "an atmosphere of alacrity, of spontaneity, of willing cooperation in the improvement of their common labours."[116] Finally, although the term is not used, the sentiments suggest that the firm will move toward a *communion of persons*. "When a factory or a workshop has created such a spirit, labour will regain all its significance and nobility; it will become more truly human and will bring men nearer to God."[117]

Business and the Common Good, 17 February 1956

This address was given to the Italian Federation of Commerce. It contains no less than five crucial elements with respect to the entrepreneur. First, Pius acknowledges the suspicion that can often surround the work of businessmen. "People," he writes, "sometimes question his usefulness to the community; they attempt to do without his services; they suspect that he is trying to derive enormous profits from his economic function."[118] For Pius, the businessman is not simply a middleman (although this may form part of his work) between producer and consumer. Rather, he is "a stimulating force in the economy."[119] The significance and value of business activity is not just in its satisfaction of wants and needs. Pius takes note of its ability to arouse within the human person energies and gifts that might not otherwise be realized. In other words, the business world, the economic and financial sphere, is an avenue (one among many) whereby human persons can achieve fulfillment. The business world is an avenue only. It provides the opportunity and possibilities for human fulfillment, but does not ensure it. Only human persons responding in freedom to their personal and social responsibilities can ensure this important goal. In the following citation he notes four benefits of business activity (or what he calls the "exchange of products"). Needs are satisfied, new methods for satisfying these needs are discovered, hidden energies are aroused and the spirit of enterprise is fostered.

> Every exchange of products, in fact, quite apart from satisfying definite needs and desires, makes it possible to put new means into operation, arouses latent and sometimes unexpected energies, and stimulates the spirit of enterprise and invention. This instinct, which is innate in mankind, of creating, improving, and making progress explains commercial activities as much and more than the mere desire for gain. The businessman needs a thorough and well-balanced professional training; he must have a mind always quick to understand and follow up economic trends as they develop, in order to handle his business with success and to foresee the reactions of the masses of the people as well as their mental attitudes. These last considerations are frequently of great importance in the interplay of exchange.[120]

Second, Pius focuses on the moral qualities of entrepreners. The later part of the above quotation touches upon the entrepreneurial personality and his work of alertness. In fact, the entrepreneur and the entrepreneurial personality possess and require "sound moral qualities."

> He must have courage in a period of crisis; he must be tenacious in overcoming public apathy and misunderstanding; he must possess a spirit of optimism in revising his formulas and methods of action, and in estimating and making the best use of the probabilities of a successful outcome. These are the qualities which will enable you to be of service to the nation; with them you are entitled to the esteem and good opinion of the whole community.[121]

Third, although Pius does not mention the term explicitly, the thrust of his comments with respect to the relationship between the state and the individual suggests strongly that the principle of subsidiarity is what concerns him. He mentions that the activity of businessmen should "not be barred by too many obstacles" and that taxes should not be "too numerous and too heavy."[122] He addresses the modern movement to provide social security in the form of employment, health and medical cover and workers' compensation. He acknowledges the movement, says it is "justified," but has his reservations.

> It is important, however, that the anxious desire for security should not prevail over the businessman's readiness to risk his resource to such an extent as to dry

up every creative impulse; nor impose on enterprise operating conditions that are too burdensome; nor discourage those who devote their time and energy to commercial transactions. Unhappily, it is an all-too-human tendency to seek out the way of minimum effort, to avoid obligations, and to exempt oneself from the duty of self-reliance in order to fall back upon the support of society and to live at the expense of one's fellows.[123]

Hence the State "ought not to try to take the place of private enterprise, so long as the latter functions usefully and successfully."[124]

Fourth, Pius states clearly the right to private initiative and grounds it in the common good.

... you [businessmen] may claim with every right the liberty necessary to fulfill your function genuinely and effectively.[125]

This right, which is concerned with "freedom of action," serves not only the interests of the entrepreneur, and at times a specific or definite class of society, but it helps "promote the advantage of the whole country."[126]

Lastly, in his address of 17 February 1956 Pius situates freedom in the economic sphere within the wider context of man's freedom. The theme is only introduced. It is not in any way developed. Still, it is important; it places activity in the economic and business world under the mantle of morality, only this time within the category of freedom. Once again, this appears to be a new insight. It is one, among many, that we have been able to notice in the writings and teachings of this truly great Pontiff. He introduces this last consideration with a reflection on the particular temptations of the entrepreneur. "Temptations," he teaches, "of course, are not wanting, if we consider the weakness of human nature; temptations to employ procedures that are not quite honest, to realize unlawful profits, to sacrifice moral dignity to the allurements of material goods."[127] These three temptations can be accentuated by the rapid technical progress of the world and an expanding economy. Nevertheless, these allurements can be offset and "balanced by an even more lively desire for spiritual development."[128] In addition, "a compelling desire to alleviate the sufferings and miseries of one's neighbor," the promotion of the common good, should accompany the desire of one's work and spiritual development.[129] So it is only after these preliminary comments on the material and spiritual aspects of the entrepreneur's work that Pius considers man's freedom. "Freedom of economic activity cannot be justified and maintained *except on condition that it serves a higher freedom*, and has the ability, when need arises, to renounce a part of itself, in order not to fall short of the moral imperative."[130]

Freedom in economic activity is thus subservient to man's freedom. The right to act with the spirit of enterprise in economic activity should enable the entrepreneur to develop spiritually, to become free within himself. Freedom to act in the social order, therefore, has the potential to help the entrepreneur reach human fulfillment through the exercise of his freedom. This possibility is suggested by the nature of his work. As we have seen with the parables of Christ in Chapter 2, his work as an entrepreneur has the potential to intuit to him the need to act with freedom in his search for Christ. Searching for earthly treasure can give rise to the search for heavenly treasure. Putting money (*talents*) to good use can suggest the use of one's gifts in service of man and God. And so there exists the possibility of a profound unity in one's professional life. The desire to be successful in business can be accompanied by the desire to be in union with Christ. It is, however, only a promising possibility. Entrepreneurial work also has the potential to suffocate one's spiritual desires. Succumbing to the temptations noted by Pius extinguishes the light of freedom and can lead to slavery. Keeping before his eyes the need for his own spiritual development and the importance of serving the common good, however, will protect the entrepreneur's freedom. Seeing himself as a servant will realize and fulfill his freedom. Second, acting with a "compelling desire to allevi-ate the sufferings and miseries of one's neighbor" will help facilitate the freedom of other men and women.

Economics and Man, 9 September 1956

In 1956, Pius addressed the First Congress of the International Association of Economists. In the latter part of his address he once again reflects on the impor-tance of freedom. His first comments deal with the vision of man as understood by Marxism. Marxism not only commits the error of socializing the means of pro-duction, "but, by a no less fatal error, it pretends to see men only as an economic medium, and makes the whole structure of human society depend on production yield."[131] Man thus becomes a means to an end—economic well-being. His tran-scendental value is lost amidst purely social and economic concerns. "Beyond the physical needs of man and the interests which they govern, beyond his inclusion in social production reports, it is necessary to envisage the activity—a really free, personal and communal activity—of man, the subject of economy."[132]

His comments in this address on the importance of private initiative are once again inspired by the truth of the freedom of the human person. And it is human freedom that is the base of a society "of understanding and sincere mutual love." Pius returns, therefore, to a previous theme and suggests that it is only when the human person exercises his freedom in pursuing social and personal responsibili-ties that he fulfills himself as a person.

> It is also one of the happy traits of the present epoch that it accentuates the feeling of interdependence among the members of the social body, and leads them on to recognize that the human person reaches his true dimensions only on condi-tion that he recognizes his social and personal responsibilities and that human problems—or simply economic ones—will find their solution only through the medium of understanding and sincere mutual love.[133]

Small Business in Today's Economy, 8 October 1956

Pius took the opportunity to further reflect on the importance of business when he addressed the *Catholic Associations of Small and Medium-sized Businesses.* He speaks, as with previous popes, on the dignity of the worker (employee), but seems to suggest that certain benefits result from allowing workers and employees to share in the ownership of the company they work for.

> It is certain that the worker and the employee who know that they are directly involved in the successful operation of a business, because a part of their wealth is invested and fructifying therein, will feel themselves more intimately obliged to contribute to it through their efforts and even their sacrifices. In that way, they feel themselves more fully men, trustees of a greater share of responsibility; they will realize that others are beholden to them, and thus they will apply themselves with greater courage to their daily task, in spite of its often harsh and tedious character.[134]

Once again, the above passage and the one that I cite below have echoes of John Paul II's social teaching. In *Laborem Exercens*, paragraph 15, the Holy Father writes:

> But here it must be emphasized, in general terms, that the person who works desires *not only* due *remuneration* for his work; he also wishes that, within the production process, provision be made for him to be able to *know* that in his work, even on something that is owned in common, he is working *"for himself."* This awareness is extinguished within him in a system of excessive bureaucratic centralization, which makes the worker feel that he is just a cog in a huge machine moved from above, that he is for more reasons than one a mere production instrument rather than a true subject of work with an initiative of his own.

Apart from the question of employees sharing the ownership of a company, there is the crucial issue of employee participation. Does an employee simply turn up on time, work disinterestedly and become thereby a passive participant in his company? Or might it not be otherwise? The pontiffs suggest the latter. John Paul II speaks of man working "for himself"—i.e., for his own dignity, while Pius speaks of workers "feeling more themselves men," becoming "trustees" of a company and thereby working with more courage. Pius and John Paul II are clearly on the same page. But perhaps Pius is a little more descriptive and evocative.

> But, once again, will the head of the business deny his subordinates what he esteems so highly himself? Will he limit the role of his daily cooperators to that of simple executants, who cannot turn their own experience to account as they would like, and who remain wholly passive with regard to the decisions which govern their own activity.[135]

Of importance, too, is Pius' use of the term *solidarity*. He speaks of the need for enterprises to practice solidarity within their organization, but also among themselves—something we have taken note of previously. The theme of solidarity figures prominently in the work of Pope John Paul II. Here Pius simply introduces the term as he did in *Summi Pontificatus*.

> May the principle of solidarity assert itself more positively, then, not only within each of your businesses, but also between similar enterprises, so as to avoid a waste of energy, useless expenses, and particularly to bring together in a compact unit the scattered elements of a considerable economic potential which, by its present division, is deprived of an effective energy in proportion to its true value.[136]

Private Initiative in the Teaching of Pope John XXIII:
Mater et Magistra

Mater et Magistra was issued seventy years after the publication of *Rerum Novarum*. Its commonly accepted English title is *On Recent Developments of the Social Question in the Light of the Christian Teaching*. In Part 1, John XXIII provides the reader with a summary and short analysis of *Rerum Novarum*, *Quadragesimo Anno* and Pius XII's radio broadcast of 1941. It is part two that contains teaching most applicable for this thesis. John XXIII reaffirms the primary importance of private initiative in economic matters, repeats the teaching of Pius XI with regard to subsidiarity and does not exclude State intervention when necessary. "At the outset it should be affirmed that in economic affairs first place is to be given to the private initiative of individual men, who, either working by themselves, or with others in one fashion or another, pursue their common interests."[137]

Public authorities are called upon to play a more active role in reducing imbalances in economic affairs. But their activities should "not only avoid restricting the freedom of private citizens, but also increase it, so long as the basic rights of each individual person are preserved inviolate."[138]

> Experience, in fact, shows that where private initiative of individuals is lacking, political tyranny prevails. Moreover, much stagnation occurs in various sectors of the economy, and hence all sorts of consumer goods and services, closely connected with needs of the body and more especially of the spirit, are in short supply. Beyond doubt, the attainment of such goods and services provides remarkable opportunity and stimulus for individuals to exercise initiative and industry.[139]

The pope also reaffirms the critical nature of human dignity in the workforce. Even if private initiative is fostered and consumer goods abound, progress cannot be affirmed if injustice is done to the worker.

Consequently, if the organization and structure of economic life be such that the human dignity of workers is compromised, or their sense of responsibility is weakened, or their freedom of action is removed, then we judge such an economic order to be unjust, even though it produces a vast amount of goods whose distribution conforms to the norms of justice and equity.[140]

Why? Pope John supplies the answer in a pithy section toward the end of the encyclical.

What the Catholic Church teaches and declares regarding the social life and relationships of men is beyond question for all time valid. The cardinal point of this teaching is that *individual men are necessarily the foundation, cause, and end of all social institutions.* We are referring to human beings, insofar as they are social by nature, and raised to an order of existence that transcends and subdues nature.[141]

Perhaps this statement summarizes succinctly the foundation of the Church's social doctrine. In the following chapter we will note that this is, in fact, a predominant and foundational theme of *Gaudium et Spes*. The Fathers of Vatican II took this theme, developed its subjective dimensions and placed it in the context of Jesus Christ, the true Adam.[142]

Reminiscent of Pius XII, John XXIII teaches that corporations should pursue unity and fellowship while conducting their enterprises. This will be based on the active participation of employees. Pope John avoids prescriptive measures since this is not the Church's field of expertise, but recognizes the principle, based as it is, on the centrality of man and his dignity.[143]

Finally, John XXIII views work from the theological category of creation. With Leo XIII and Pius XI, work was considered as *necessary, personal* and *social*, while Pius XII began to reflect on the possibility of a *spirituality of work* (without in any way developing it). John XXIII, therefore, introduces for the first time the *theme of creation*, which becomes a predominant theme in *Gaudium et Spes* and in *Laborem Exercens*. His discussion is minimal, but still significant in terms of observing development in the field of work.[144]

Private Initiative in the Social Teaching of Pope Paul VI

In 1967, Pope Paul VI issued the encyclical letter *Populorum Progressio*. Its subject matter is quite different from that of *Rerum Novarum* and *Quadragesimo Anno* and other social encyclicals and social teachings. Written clearly within the tradition of *Rerum Novarum* and subsequent encyclicals, Paul VI considers that "the social question has become worldwide." [145] The subject matter becomes development. It is now not so much the question of capital and labor, as the acute problem of "hunger, misery, endemic diseases, and ignorance."[146]

Not only is the subject matter a little different than previous documents, the method of approach appears to be different. In light of *Gaudium et Spes*, Paul VI approaches the wider social question from the standpoint of a Christian vision of development. As with *Gaudium et Spes*, this approach considers man in light of his divine vocation and not just in terms of human nature, as is the case with previous social teachings. This itself, as will be seen in Chapter 4, is crucial in the development of social doctrine.

Paul VI teaches that development "cannot be limited to mere economic growth," but must be "integral, that is, it has to promote the good of every man and of the whole man."[147] When read in light of *Gaudium et Spes*, this encyclical does not add substantially to the development of social doctrine in terms of Christian action. Paul VI simply confirms the insights of *Gaudium et Spes*. He notes man's call to human fulfillment and the call to "further perfection" by reason of man's "union with Christ."[148] With Christ, "the source of life, man attains to new fulfillment of himself, to a transcendent humanism which gives him his greatest possible perfection: this is the highest goal of personal development."[149] In no way does the pope attempt to develop the teaching of *Gaudium et Spes*, he simply states that development should be understood as Christian development.

Neither does Pope Paul VI say anything new with respect to private initiative. Paul has only a very simple statement: as man's "self-mastery increases, he develops a taste for research and discovery, an ability to take a *calculated risk, boldness in enterprises,* generosity in what he does, and a sense of responsibility."[150]

Octogesima Adveniens was written by Paul VI to Cardinal Maurice Roy on the occasion of the eightieth anniversary of *Rerum Novarum*. It is an apostolic letter that does not purport to advance the social teaching of the Church. Rather, it simply documents new social problems, without offering any specific solutions. This is left to each Christian community.[151] Nothing is said with respect to private initiative. One might have expected that the Pontiff would have emphasized it when discussing employment, but he preferred to place greater trust in policies of investment and organization of production. This represents a more centralized view of economic activity than we have seen in previous social teachings.

Conclusion

Faced with the technological and industrial advances of the nineteenth century, the Church, through Leo XIII, offered her response. She faced two challenges and one temptation. Capitalism seemed to divide the human race into two groups. It especially threatened the dignity of the worker. Socialism promised liberation from the scourges of capitalism, but the Church thought otherwise. Loss of freedom, through the denial of the right to private property, would ultimately lead to poverty. The hoped-for liberation promised by Marx was, in fact, an illusion. In *Rerum Novarum*, Leo XIII met both challenges brilliantly. He first addressed the solution proposed by the Socialists and defended the right to private property. He then took up the "question of the hour"—the plight of workers. In the process he was able to avoid the temptation to judge the social question through the lens of class struggle. Instead, he defended the dignity of the worker (and the capitalist). The question was one of human dignity and poverty and not one of class struggle.

This defense of human dignity, by recourse to human nature and reason, along with the concept of the common good, has provided a lasting paradigm for the development of the Church's social teaching. In terms of private initiative, we can observe two fundamental principles. Private initiative is based on the freedom and transcendence of the human person. For this clear insight we have Pius XII to thank. Free activity in the economic sphere flows from the freedom of the human person. Second, this free economic and financial activity is ordered and finds its end in the common good. For this we have Pius XI to thank with his articulation of the principle of subsidiarity. Subsidiarity is ordered toward solidarity.

In the eighty years from Leo XIII to Paul VI, we can observe remarkable continuity and even more remarkable development. Leo defended the right to private property; Pius XI defended private action (and Pius XII defended this right); Pius XII began to see business and entrepreneurial activity as a service to the community; and Pius XII and John XXIII began to articulate the need for communion in the workplace. Amidst these crucial developments, we have observed a developing theology of work. Work is first understood as necessary and personal with Leo. Pius XI takes note of its social character, while Pius XII begins to reflect on the spiritual character of work in relation to its sanctifying power and its ability to give glory to God.

With *Gaudium et Spes* these developments are further fostered. All human activity is now understood in relation to the Incarnation, the Paschal Mystery and the call to Trinitarian communion. The work of entrepreneurs and businesspersons, as with all other professions and forms of human activity, receives its ultimate meaning from the life, death and resurrection of Christ. It is to *Gaudium et Spes* that we now turn.

Notes

1. Etienne Gilson, ed., *The Church Speaks to the Modern World: The Social Teachings of Leo XIII* (New York: Image Books, 1954), 200.

2. *Centesimus Annus*, 5.

3. Pope Leo XIII. Encyclical Letter *Rerum Novarum* in: O'Brien, *Catholic Social Thought*, 14–39. Most English translations are known as *On the Condition of Labor*. The Latin text is found in: The Catholic University of America Press, ed., *Two Basic Social Encyclicals On The Conditions Of Workers (Leo XIII) and Forty Years After On Reconstructing Social Order (Pius XI): Latin Text with English Translation (Approved By The Holy See)* (New York: Benziger Brothers, Inc, 1943), 2–81.

4. Gilson, *The Church Speaks*, 200.

5. Ibid. Emphasis added.

6. *Centesimus Annus*, 4. The encyclical *Centesimus Annus* devotes sections 4–11 to "Characteristics of *Rerum Novarum*."

7. *Centesimus Annus*, 5.

8. See Mathew Habiger, *Papal Teaching on Private Property: 1891-1981* (Lanham, MD: University Press of America, 1990), 4.

9. Ibid., 4–5.

10. Murphy, *In the Beginning*, 8.

11. Ibid.

12. Murphy, *In the Beginning*, 8.

13. *Rerum Novarum*, 3.

14. *Ibid.*, 15.

15. *Rerum Novarum*, 4.

16. Ibid.

17. Ibid., 5.

18. Ibid.

19. Ibid., 6.

20. Ibid.

21. Ibid., 7.

22. Ibid.

23. Ibid.

24. Ibid., 35.

25. Ibid.

26. *Rerum Novarum*, 35.

27. Ibid., 10.

28. Murphy, *In the Beginning*, 17.

29. Gilson, *The Church Speaks*, 200.

30. *Rerum Novarum*, 14.

31. Ibid.

32. Ibid.

33. Ibid.

34. Ibid., 13.

35. Ibid.

36. Ibid.

37. Ibid.

38. This phrase I attribute to Prof. Kenneth L. Schmitz. He made it in a completely different context, but seems entirely appropriate in the above context.

39. *Centesimus Annus*, 5.

40. Charles, *Christian Social Witness Vol. 2*, 4.

41. Ibid., 26.

42. Ibid.

43. Murphy, *In the Beginning*, 19.

44. Ibid., 20.

45. Ibid., 28.

46. Ibid., 34.

47. Ibid.

48. *Rerum Novarum*, 44.

49. Ibid., 37.

50. O'Brien, *Catholic Social Thought*, 40.

51. *Rerum Novarum*, 19.

52. Nell-Breuning, *Reorganization of the Social Economy*, 96.

53. Kohler, in a less complimentary tone, argues that Pius was correcting the "non-Thomistic understanding of private property that was set forth in *Rerum Novarum*. Ironically, the notions that informed the 1891 encyclical were based on the theories of John Locke, which had been incorporated into neo-scholastic thought by the nineteenth-century Jesuit theologian Taparelli d'Azeglio." (Kohler, *In Praise of Little Platoons*, 39).

54. Nell-Breuning, *Reorganization of the Social Economy*, 115. Emphasis added.

55. Ibid.

56. *Quadragesimo Anno*, 69.

57. Ibid., 43.

58. Pius used the term "social justice" eight times in the encyclical and it first appears in social teaching with Pius' use. (See Kohler, *In Praise of Little Platoons*, 39.)

59. *Quadragesimo Anno*, 88.

60. Ibid., 103.

61. Ibid., 105.

62. Ibid., 101. He writes: "Surely it is not vicious of its very nature..."

63. Ibid. The right order is where capital respects the human dignity of the workers.

64. *Quadragesimo Anno*, 79.

65. 2 Th. 3:10–13.

66. *Quadragesimo Anno*, 77.

67. Ibid.

68. Ibid., 78. See Nell-Breuning, *Reorganization of the Social Economy*, 201, for an excellent discussion of individualism.

69. Ibid.

70. A closer reading of the encyclical suggests that the principle of subsidiarity is concerned not only with socialism, but with individualism.

71. *Quadregesimo Annno*, 78.

72. Nell-Breuning, *Reorganization of Social Economy*, 202.

73. *Quadragesimo Anno*, 79.

74. Ibid.

75. Ibid., 80.

76. *Centesimus Annus*, 48. Emphasis added.

77. A complete list of Pius XII addresses, on all topics, can be found in: Vincent A. Yzermans, ed., *The Major Addresses of Pope Pius XII*, 2 vols., vol. 2: Christmas Messages (St. Paul: The North Central Publishing Company, 1961), 262–300. This book prints in full the Christmas addresses of the Pontiff. Christmas addresses that deal with the social question (and not necessarily the issue of private initiative) are the 1941, 1942, 1952, 1955 and 1957 addresses. I refer only to the 1952 and 1955 addresses. They appear to foreshadow some of the key thoughts in *Laborem Exercens*. In addition to his Christmas addresses, Pius had numerous addresses to groups of people, some of them broadcast on radio. When referring to these addresses I refer to the title of the address and then the date of the address. In the footnotes the reference that is used can be found. The title of the address that I use is the commonly accepted one as found in: Yzermans, *The Major Addresses, Vol. 2*, 262–300.

78. Vincent A. Yzermans, ed., *The Major Addresses of Pope Pius XII*, 2 vols., vol. 1: Selected Addresses (St. Paul: The North Central Publishing Company, 1961), 30. Emphasis added.

79. Ibid., 31.

80. Ibid.

81. Ibid.

82. Ibid.

83. Ibid.

84. Ibid., 32–36.

85. Vincent A. Yzermans, ed., *The Unwearied Advocate: Public Addresses of His Holiness Pope Pius XII*, 3 vols., vol. 3 (St. Cloud: Vincent A. Yzermans, 1954), 79.

86. Ibid.

87. Ibid.

88. Ibid.

89. Yzermans, *The Major Addresses, Vol. 2*, 165.

90. Ibid., 207–8.

91. Yzermans, *The Unwearied Advocate, Vol. 3*, 80.

92. Ibid.

93. Ibid., 81.

94. Ibid.

95. Ibid.

96. Ibid., 82.

97. Pope Pius XII, "Function of Bankers," *The Catholic Mind* LII, no. 1094 (1951): 121–22, 121.

98. Ibid., 122.

99. Ibid.

100. Golis, *Enterprise and Venture Capital*, 3.

101. Pope Pius XII, *Function of Bankers*, 121.

102. Yzermans, *The Major Addresses, Vol. 1*, 338. Emphasis added.

103. Ibid., 338–39.

104. Ibid., 339.

105. Ibid.

106. Ibid., 340.

107. Ibid.

108. Pope Pius XII, "The Small Business Manager," *The Pope Speaks* 3, no. 1 (1956): 49–52, 50.

109. Ibid.

110. Ibid., 51.

111. Ibid. The pope raises the issue of bad will in the business profession. "Many people show no lack of goodwill, but it must be observed at times that an overwhelming attachment to economic advantages tends more or less to blind men to a perception of the want of equity and justice in certain living conditions. Your Christian instincts will aid you to overcome this obstacle and to exercise your authority in a manner conformable to the ideals set forth in the Gospel."

112. "Unity with one's employees" would appear to be another way of expressing communion with other human beings. John Paul II uses the phrase *communion of persons*.

113. Pope Pius XII, *The Small Business Manager*, 51.

114. Ibid.

115. Ibid.

116. Ibid.

117. Ibid.

118. Pope Pius XII, "Business and the Common Good," *The Pope Speaks* 3, no. 1 (1956): 45–49, 45.

119. Ibid., 46.

120. Ibid., 46–47.

121. Ibid., 47.

122. Ibid.

123. Ibid.

124. Ibid., 48.

125. Ibid.

126. Ibid.

127. Ibid.

128. Ibid.

129. Ibid.

130. Ibid. Emphasis added.

131. Pope Pius XII, "Economics and Man," *The Pope Speaks* 3, no. 3 (1956): 241–45, 243.

132. Ibid.

133. Ibid.

134. Pope Pius XII, "Small Business in Today's Economy," *The Pope Speaks* 3, no. 4 (1957): 405–9, 407.

135. Ibid..

136. Pope Pius XII, "Small Business in Today's Economy," 408.

137. John XXIII. Encyclical Letter *Mater et Magistra* in: O'Brien, *Catholic Social Thought*, 84–128, paragraph 51.

138. Ibid., 55.

139. Ibid., 57.

140. Ibid., 83.

141. Ibid., 218–19. Emphasis added.

142. *Gaudium et Spes*, 35.

143. *Mater et Magistra*, 91–92. Emphasis added.

144. Ibid., 144.

145. Paul VI. Encyclical Letter *Populorum Progressio* in: O'Brien, *Catholic Social Thought*, 240–62, paragraph 3.

146. Ibid., 1.

147. Ibid., 14.

148. Ibid., 16.

149. Ibid.

150. Ibid., 25.

151. *Populorum Progressio*, 4.

5

Human Action, Work, and Enterprise:
The Second Vatican Council

In fact, what is an ecumenical Council if not the renewal of this encounter with the face of the risen Christ, glorious and immortal king, shining radiantly on the whole Church, for the well-being, joy, and splendor of humanity.

—Pope John XXIII[1]

In calling the Second Vatican Council, Pope John XXIII set the Church on a path of renewal, including renewing her relationship with the world through a dialogue with the modern world. But what is the nature of dialogue as understood by the Council? What does the Church bring to the dialogue? What content does the Church present to the other partner in dialogue? How does this renewal affect the entrepreneur and his activity? What are the key elements of the Council's teaching with respect to the laity and how might this doctrine apply to the entrepreneur.

The Renewal of Vatican II: The Path of Dialogue

In proclaiming the deposit of faith, Christians need to be sensitive to the customs and language of the time. For Pope John, this was crucial, which is why Vatican II was, to his mind, supposed to be pastoral, helping the Church to carry out her mission of service. Goddfredo Zanchi notes that it is "attention to modern life" that "lay at the root of the pastoral character of the Council."[2] Hence, the unchanging deposit of faith needed to be sensitive to new methods of inquiry and the language of the modern age. The dialogue that Christians carry on with their peers is a direct consequence of their experience of Jesus Christ. Communicating faith is not something added or superimposed on the Christian vocation. On the contrary, communicability is "an intrinsic characteristic" of the light of faith.

Francis Martin attempts such a dialogue in *The Feminist Questions*.[3] He notes two important principles laid down by *Gaudium et Spes*. The first is the role of human experience. The second is the role played by divine revelation. The *encounter* between these two principles produces new knowledge.

> Applied practically to the theological enterprise, these principles imply a sort of correlative method by which what is learned in and through the joy, hope, grief, and anguish of human experience is brought into contact with what has been already acquired, but imperfectly understood, through divine revelation. From this interactive process, new knowledge is gained, making possible a genuine development of doctrine. It is often a lengthy process, painstaking and even tumultuous, but amid human weakness, the Holy Spirit leads the church more deeply into all truth.[4]

The process is difficult, perhaps ambiguous at times, but nevertheless faithful to workings of the Spirit and the Tradition of the Church. According to Martin, Aquinas' words clarify what takes place in this "correlative method." "Those who use the work of the philosophers in sacred doctrine by bringing that work of the human mind into the service of faith, do not mix water with wine, but rather change water into wine."[5]

Thus the dialogue willed by John XXIII is profoundly spiritual. It arises from the very nature of faith itself and leads to new insights with respect to the deposit of faith. It is not unknown to the Church, as Aquinas demonstrates, but perhaps it had been obscured with the passage of time. Vatican II, under the inspiration of the Holy Spirit, retrieves and represents this important theological principle for the benefit of the Church herself and of modern man.

For this reason it is possible to speak of a "shift in the dominant theological metaphor"[6] which the Church uses in describing her relationship with the world. Michael Schuck, in *That They Be One*, contrasts the *dialogical metaphor* employed by the Second Vatican Council with the metaphors of sheepfold and cosmological design.[7]

What lay behind this shift in papal thought is nothing less than a renewed appreciation of the role of the third person of the Blessed Trinity. God is present and active everywhere. The world is his field of action. Thus it is the Spirit, the *experience* of faith and the *goodness* of the world that is operative in the metaphor shift. The chief characteristics of the laity, as understood by Vatican II, are their reception of baptism and their secular character. The world, therefore, is the place of encounter with God. It is there that the vast majority of Christians, the laity, are called by God. It is there that God can be discovered amidst one's daily life and duties. In other words, God is active within his Church, by means of word and sacrament, and he is active in the world through his Spirit. This latter truth enables a renewed appreciation of the work of the Spirit, not only in the lives of Christians in the world, but of all men and women.

Christ, the New Man: Christian Humanism

The world, then, is the place of encounter with God. It is also the setting by which Christians share intimately the "joy and hope, the grief and anguish of the men of our time."[8] This rapport enables them to share the Gospel of Jesus Christ with others. The world is thus a *sacred setting* for the transmission of faith. Each Christian shares, by virtue of baptism, a sacred calling—vocation—to live and spread his Christian faith in the world.

As observed, *Rerum Novarum* and *Quadragesimo Anno* approach the social question predominantly from the perspective of human nature and human reason. *Gaudium et Spes* changes the emphasis. It approaches the social question from the perspective of the human person and his vocation. This can be seen in the chapter headed: "The Dignity of the Human Person." It is the hinge of the document around which everything else revolves. It presents man in light of creation, sin, the incarnation and the Paschal Mystery. After paying particular attention to the phenomena of modern-day atheism in paragraphs nineteen through twenty-one, the Council turns its attention to the person of Jesus Christ, the new man.

The Incarnation

Reflecting on the human person, the Council states:

> In reality it is only in the mystery of the Word made flesh that the mystery of man truly becomes clear. For Adam, the first man, was a type of him who was to come, Christ the Lord. Christ the new Adam, in the very revelation of the mystery of the Father and his love, *fully reveals man to himself* and brings to light his most high calling.[9]

Here the Council is retrieving the early tradition of the Church with respect to Christology and giving it a modern intonation.[10] Adam was formed from the dust with a view to Christ. Adam is at once both a man and a *figure* (type) of Christ. Thus, in order to discover who man is, it is necessary to contemplate not so much Adam (the type), but Christ, the man who was to be. He is the *definitive human being*. By means of typology, the orders of creation and incarnation are brought together into a profound symphony. Creation is ordered to the incarnation of the Son of God. This is the universal testimony of the sacred text. All of creation, especially man, is made through the Word.

The Letter to the Ephesians highlights the absolute unity that exists between the creation of the world and the incarnation of the second person of the Blessed Trinity. God, in his infinite wisdom, first chose man (loved him) in Christ, and only then created him.

> Blessed be the God and Father of our Lord Jesus Christ, who has blessed us in Christ with every spiritual blessing in the heavenly places, even as *he chose us in him before the foundation of the world*, that we should be holy and blameless before him. *He destined us in love to be his sons through Jesus Christ*...[11]

While creation is attributed to the Father, all of creation is nevertheless made through the Word. In this sense we can say that all of creation has a "Word-Structure." Creation was intended with a view to Christ and therefore reaches its fullest meaning in Christ.

> He is the image of the invisible God, the first-born of all creation; for *in him all things were created*, in heaven and on earth, visible and invisible, whether thrones or dominions or principalities or authorities—all things were created *through him and for him*.[12]

Commenting on these realities, Raniero Cantalamessa says Jesus "is described by St. Paul as the 'last Adam' (*eschatos*), that is to say 'the definitive human being,' of whom the first Adam was a kind of sketch and imperfect realization."[13] Christ, therefore, does not "confine himself to becoming human." Rather, he "also reveals what human nature is; with him, the model itself appears, since he is himself the true and perfect 'image of God' (Col. 1:15)."[14] This attentiveness to Christ and the Word of God reveals that man not only possesses a human nature, but that he is called to perfect that nature (person) with the grace of God. Thus while from the first Adam we can catch a clouded glimpse of what human nature is, it is only in light of the last Adam that we can gain some insight into the vocational dimension of man.

Cantalamessa then discusses the fact that for the Fathers this distinction was made via reference to Genesis 1:26. The sacred text speaks of the fact that man is made both in the image and likeness of God.

> Human beings are by nature or birth "in the image" of God, but become 'in his likeness' only during their lives by an effort to be like God, by obedience... "In obedience," says one of the ancient Desert Fathers, "likeness to God is brought about, and not the mere being in his image."[15]

From a slightly different perspective, Joseph Ratzinger notes that the incarnation is the completion—perfection—of what was begun with the original creation of man.

The Rubicon of becoming man, of "hominization," was first crossed by the step from animal to *logos*, from mere life to mind. Man came into existence out of the "clay" at the moment when a creature was no longer merely "there" but, over and above just being there and filling his needs, was aware of the whole. *But this step, through which "logos," understanding, mind, first came into the world, is only completed when the logos itself, the whole creative meaning, and man merge into each other.*[16]

Christ, in and through his incarnation, reveals to man that he is *not only of the dust,* but that he is *of heaven*. Contemplating the first Adam reveals the earthly origins of man, while contemplating the last Adam discloses the divine origin and destiny of man. Christ reveals the true vocation of the human person. Man is truly "from" and "for." In this he finds his truest identity and vocation.

The Paschal Mystery

That man is "from" and "for" is revealed definitively in the Paschal Mystery—the Passion, Death, Resurrection and Ascension of Christ. John's Gospel speaks of the last Adam just prior to his Passion. "And during supper, when the devil had already put it into the heart of Judas Iscariot, Simon's son, to betray him, Jesus, knowing that the Father had given all things into his hands, and that he had come *from God* and was *going to God...*"[17] The Paschal Mystery is thus the definitive affirmation that the last Adam—and thus every human person—is "from" God and "for" God. And not only is each human person called to be "for" God, but after the example of the last Adam, "for" others. Ratzinger emphasizes the *horizontal* dimension of the passion of Christ. That is, the outpouring of love for sinful man, the embracing of "the scattered man-monads" (substances) by Jesus Christ in his act of love on the cross. But the passion has a *vertical* dimension as well. The passion is equally an outpouring of love for the Father.

It is precisely in the love-act of the Paschal Mystery that Christ reveals the Fatherhood of God and his own Sonship. The movement, therefore, of *Gaudium et Spes* is from Creation to Incarnation, finding its fulfillment in the Paschal Mystery. Man is fully revealed to himself by the last and true man, Jesus Christ, in his bloody passion.

> As an innocent lamb he merited life for us by his blood which he freely shed. In him God reconciled us to himself and to one another... By suffering for us he not only gave us an example so that we might follow in his footsteps, *but he also opened up a way*. If we follow this path, life and death are made holy and acquire a new meaning.[18]

The Paschal Mystery is not only to be imitated. In fact it transforms man's entire being, conforming him to the "definitive human being," Christ Jesus. It is from this new ontological configuration to Christ that man is called to make his life one of self-sacrificing love, in union with Christ's life. Through word and sacrament, the very mystery of Christ's Passover enters into the very being of the human person.

The Communion of Persons: *Gaudium et Spes*, 24

It is then from Christ's incarnation and Paschal Mystery that man obtains access to the three Divine Persons. "The Christian man *receives* the 'first-fruits of the Spirit'" and thereby becomes capable of discharging the new law of love. Man is called to communion with God and with the brethren, precisely because God himself is a communion of Persons. Each of the persons of the Godhead does not share the divine nature, but is the divine nature. *The divine persons are really distinct from one another*. God is not solitary, but in fact is Father, Son and Spirit. The three persons are distinct from one another in their relations of origin. *The divine persons are relative to one another*. The real distinction of the persons from one another resides solely in the relationships which relate them to one another and which express themselves to us in their missions.[19] *Gaudium et Spes* begins to suggest the implications of Trinitarian faith for anthropology.

> But God did not create man as a solitary. From the beginning "male and female he created them" (Gen. 1:27). This partnership of man and woman constitutes the first form of communion between persons. For by his innermost nature man is a social being; and if he does not enter into relations with others he can neither live nor develop his gifts.[20]

Man, conformed to Christ in baptism, enters into the very life of the Trinity and their intimate relations.[21] The *Catechism* teaches: "The personal relation of the Son to the Father is something that man cannot conceive of nor angelic powers even dimly see: and yet, the Spirit of the Son grants a participation in that very relation to us who believe that Jesus is the Christ and that we are born of God."[22]

The revelation that God is a communion of life and love informs our understanding of how man is made in the image and likeness of God. This is not something that would have been open to human reason alone.[23] Reason is man's attempt to discover God, depending "upon sense perception and experience and which advances by the light of the intellect alone."[24] But revelation is God's gift of disclosing himself. "This initiative," as John Paul II has restated forcefully in *Fides et Ratio*, "is utterly gratuitous, moving from God to men and women in order to bring them to salvation."[25] And this knowledge which man has of God—precisely through God's free initiative—does not destroy, replace or demean the dignity of human reason, but perfects it. "As the source of love, God desires to make himself known; and the knowledge which the human being has of God perfects all that the human mind can know of the meaning of life."[26]

The revelation of the Trinitarian life of God, through the incarnation and Paschal Mystery of the Son of God, reveals to man that he is not only an individual substance with a rational nature, but that in point of fact man's very being is profoundly relational. Revelation opens vistas closed to human reason. Man through his experience of social interaction realizes, in some fashion, that his nature is social. It is Revelation, however, that brings this intuition to fulfillment. With the light of faith, man is able to comprehend that he is made in the image and likeness of the Divine Persons. Furthermore, man is called not only to share the divine life of the Three Persons, but is also called to form a communion of persons on earth and so *make present* the Blessed Trinity on earth.

Freedom, Self-Gift, and Communion

The free-loving act of Jesus Christ on Calvary calls forth a response from man. It engages his freedom. It calls forth the paradox of human freedom. To be truly free—to truly find himself, man must deny himself and give of himself to others. "Whoever seeks to gain his life will lose it, but whoever loses his life will preserve it."[27] This biblical text is, in fact, the interpretative tool for the statement in *Gaudium et Spes*, 24 that man "can fully discover his true self only in a sincere giving of himself." Communion is thus based on man being made in the image and likeness of God himself and is established in and through freedom. Man is free and he is called to use this freedom in the service of others. By this denial of self and affirmation of others, man is able to establish (with the grace of God) communion with others and thus make present—that is, suggest to other men and women—the life of the Blessed Trinity.

The *Source* and *Summit* of Human Activity: The Paschal Mystery and Communion

Jesus Christ is thus the new and final Adam and through his Paschal Mystery he definitively reveals who man is, his origin and destiny. At the same time it is possible to discern the meaning of human action. It flows from the intimacy of the human person. The Council, having examined man in light of the mystery of the incarnation and Paschal Mystery, proceeds to show how man's activity flows from the truth of man's being. Man is called to use his freedom, to die to himself, to live for others, and thereby form communion. The *source* of activity is thus the Paschal Mystery—Christ's supreme work. The *summit* of man's activity is communion with God and man.

It is clear, therefore, that *Gaudium et Spes* has reoriented the Church by means of Christian humanism. This humanism is the fruit of the Incarnation and Paschal Mystery, which finds it fulfillment in communion. How are these principles applied in the area of human activity? This is the question that is addressed in Chapter 3 of Part 1. Then in Chapter 3 of Part 2 the Constitution considers *Economic and Social Life*. These two questions are examined here.

The Value of Human Activity

In Chapter 3 of Part 1, the Council affirms the value of human activity. In itself it accords with the will of God.

> Man was created in God's image and was commanded to conquer the earth with all it contains and to rule the world in justice and holiness: he was to acknowledge God as maker of all things and relate himself and the totality of creation to him, so that through the dominion of all things by man the name of God would be majestic in all the earth.[28]

In particular, this "holds good also for our *daily work*."[29] Daily work is a service both to family and the common good and is a "prolongation of the work of the creator." [30] Then the text, faithful to its previous analysis, locates work in the divine calling that man receives from God to *fulfill* or *perfect himself*. Human activity thus "proceeds from man" and it is ordered to him.[31] Work has not only an objective meaning, but a subjective one also.

> When he works, not only does he transform matter and society, but he fulfills himself. He learns, he develops his faculties, and he emerges from and transcends himself. Rightly understood, this kind of growth is more precious than any kind of wealth that can be amassed.[32]

All human activity is governed by a norm.

> Hence then is the norm for human activity—to harmonize with the authentic interests of the human race, in accordance with God's will and design, and to enable men as individuals and as members of society to pursue and fulfill their total vocation.[33]

Since the vocation of man is definitively revealed by Jesus Christ, this norm of all human activities is *perfected by love*—redemptive love. The world is transformed by love, not just in important matters, but love "must be exercised above all in the ordinary circumstances of daily life."[34] Christ affirms the norm of human activity and perfects it. "He reveals to us that 'God is love' and at the same time teaches that the fundamental law of human perfection, and consequently of the transformation of the world, is the new commandment of love."[35]

Economic Activity: Spirit of Enterprise and the Entrepreneur

All this holds true for economic activity. In Chapter 3 of Part 2 the Council teaches: "In the sphere of economics and social life, too, the dignity and entire vocation of the human person as well as the welfare of society as a whole have to be respected and fostered."[36] The source and summit of human activity applies with equal force in the economic sphere. Entrepreneurs must strive to imitate the mystery of Christ's dying and rising in their daily work and thus strive to create communion in their place of work.

There is no explicit reference to the entrepreneur in *Gaudium et Spes* or in the other decrees of Vatican II. But there is a clear understanding of the importance of the spirit of enterprise. While it is true that the entrepreneur is not referred to directly by the Vatican Council, it is nevertheless true to say that he receives implicit approval.

Regarding human activity in the economic sphere, the Council makes three important observations. Regarding the spirit of enterprise and its importance for the common good and thus for the human person, the Council teaches:

> Today, more than ever before there is an increase in the production of agricultural and industrial goods and in the number of services available, and this is as it should be in view of the population expansion and growing human aspirations. Therefore we must encourage technical progress and the *spirit of enterprise*, we must foster the *eagerness for creativity and improvement*, and we must promote adaptation of production methods and all serious efforts of people engaged in production—in other words of all elements which contribute to economic progress. The ultimate and basic purpose of economic production does not consist merely in the increase of goods produced, nor in profit nor prestige; it is directed to the service of man, of man, that is, in his totality taking account his material needs and the requirements of his intellectual, moral, spiritual, and religious life.[37]

As can be seen, the conciliar text contains some of the crucial elements that constitute the refined definition of entrepreneurial work and personality established by the end of Chapter 2. The spirit of enterprise relates to the entrepreneur himself—to his personality. Recalling Chapter 2: the entrepreneur is commercially focused, is creative, takes calculated risks and possesses high energy levels. Now these qualities issue forth in his entrepreneurial activity. His work is characterized by alertness to information, leading to the discovery of new possibilities in the marketplace and thus to the engagement of the factors of production. Or as *Gaudium et Spes* puts it, the spirit of enterprise leads to an eagerness to *create* and *expand enterprises*. And all of this is at the service of the common good—the service of man. Hence, there is no inherent contradiction between the spirit of enterprise and the common good.

Second, the Council observes that a spirit of enterprise should not belong to a select few. It is not," the Council teaches, "to be left to the judgment of a few individuals or groups possessing too much economic power, nor of the political community alone, nor of a few strong nations."[38] Finally, *Gaudium et Spes* encourages the active participation of all who make up a corporation. In this way, communion will be fostered among the men and women who constitute such a corporation.[39]

The Call to Holiness of Vatican II and the Entrepreneur

Thus the entrepreneur, through the promotion of the spirit of enterprise, is recognized by Vatican II. He is an important player in economic and social life. Without him the development and maintenance of the common good would be severely hampered. Like all Christians, he too is called to holiness because of his conformity to Christ through the sacraments of initiation. He is called to respond to the grace of the Paschal Mystery, which has been mediated to him by means of word and sacrament. His response is one of imitation. As it is with the source of his activity, so it is with the summit of his activity. The entrepreneur is called to communion with the Most Holy Trinity—i.e., worship, adoration and thanksgiving—and he is called to communion with the brethren.

The Call to Holiness: Love and Secular Character

The entrepreneur shares a common Christian vocation to holiness with Christians in entirely different social, economic and cultural circumstances. The Second Vatican Council teaches: "It is therefore quite clear that all Christians in any state or walk of life are called to the fullness of Christian life and to the perfection of love, and by this holiness a more human manner of life is fostered also in earthly society."[40]

Diversity in form and task does not lessen the call to sanctity. Christ needs witnesses in all walks of life. The forms and tasks of life are many but *holiness is one*—that sanctity which is cultivated by all who act under God's Spirit and, obeying the Father's voice and adoring God the Father in spirit and in truth, follow Christ, poor, humble and cross-bearing, that they may deserve to be partakers of his glory. Each one, however, *according to his own gifts and duties* must steadfastly advance along the way of a living faith, which arouses hope and works through love.[41]

As David Schindler has pointed out, there is not a host of lay spiritualities, but *a* lay spirituality.[42] It is characterized by two elements. The first of these is love. Each Christian is called to the perfection of love.[43] Charity is fostered by Christian practices: an attentive hearing and listening to the Word of God, participation in the sacraments of Penance and Eucharist, personal prayer, sacrifice and Christian service. These practices are one and the same for all Christians. The second element that makes up this lay spirituality is the secular character of the laity.[44] The laity are called to be holy in the world. God calls them in the midst of their daily life and work and *does not ask them to leave it*, as is the case with religious and to a lesser extent priests. The phrase "secular character" does not infer that the laity are not spiritual. Rather, it refers to their vocation to discover the kingdom of God in and through their daily activities, i.e., in the world and not apart from it. *Lumen Gentium* teaches, therefore, four aspects of secularity. First, the laity are to seek the kingdom of God, not so much by engaging in ecclesiastical affairs (although this may happen from time to time), but rather they seek and find Christ by engaging in temporal affairs and directing them to God. Through baptism the laity have the kingdom of God within themselves. This reality, along with their own goodwill, enables them to offer and direct temporal realities to God, in accordance with his design and will. Second, and related intimately to the first aspect, the Council teaches that the laity are called by God in the world. God, in creating the world, has no desire to take them out of the world. Thus third, the laity receives the vocation to remain in the world and sanctify it—to take the human material of daily life and raise it, make it holy. Last, through their Christian lives of holiness in the middle of the world, the laity manifests Christ to others.

These appear as the four critical aspects of the secular character of the laity, and therefore holds true for the entrepreneur. God dwells in his very being and calls him not to abandon his post, but rather to sanctify his life and work. Part of his Christian vocation is to seek the kingdom of God by engaging in his entrepreneurial activities. This is where God calls him and by responding to this call, he manifests Christ to others. Laymen and laywomen are called to the fullness of love in the world and not apart from it. They are to tread the narrow path of holiness in the world. Yet there are many "narrow paths." As the Council teaches, "not everyone marches along the same path."[45] Mothers, academics, engineers, doctors, manual workers, etc., are all called to the perfection of love in the world. Their paths are all narrow, but they must necessarily be different because of varying factors. Circumstances differ, so too abilities, and of course the characteristics of people's work differ.

The entrepreneur finds himself embedded, at least in his work life, in the world of business and enterprise. This is his world, and the narrow path that he walks is a call to perfection that engages these human realities. His work, as we have discovered, has certain characteristics that distinguish his activity from other men and women. He is called by Christ to sanctify this particular work and thereby manifest Jesus Christ to others. As with other Christians, it will be a manifestation achieved first by example and then by word. It will be a manifestation of a witness. This witness will, however, take a particular form. What facet of man's likeness to God, then, does the work of the entrepreneur suggest to the men and women of the world? There are three facets. They are not meant to be definitive. In light of the definition developed by the end of Chapter 2, I tentatively suggest that the entrepreneur in his person and work intimates to us something of God's creativity, of his work of redemption and his existence as a communion of persons.

God's Creativity and the Entrepreneur

The entrepreneur is creative. God is a Father who is a Creator. The entrepreneur has the potential to reveal, suggest and remind us of the creative activity of God himself. Man's creative activity is, however, creative only in a secondary sense. It is only God who creates out of nothing. But while man does not create things out of nothing, he nevertheless participates in God's creative activity. "The universe," as the *Catechism of the Catholic Church* teaches, "was created 'in a state of journeying' (*in statu viae*) toward an ultimate perfection yet to be attained, to which God has destined it."[46] It is man's vocation to perfect the creation—to bring it to fulfillment in accordance with the will of God. While God creates the world out of nothing and guides it by his providence, he nevertheless desires the cooperation of man in bringing his creation to fulfillment. Man, therefore, in his creative cooperation, participates in God's providence.

In *Loving the Church*, Christoph Schönborn, provides a masterful account of the relationship between God's providence and government with that of human freedom.

> It is God's joy when his creatures display their own activity. *God's providence shows its perfection when it produces "provident beings."* The Creator shines brightest in the *creative creature*. The Creator is not magnified when his creatures are belittled. Against such a false "exaltation" of God, Thomas says: "To detract from the perfection of creatures is to detract from the perfection of the power of God... To deny things their proper activity is to disparage the goodness of God."[47]

The entrepreneur, with his creative work, becomes a provident being. This is especially demonstrated in his works of magnificence ordered toward the common good. Therefore, God the Creator is made present—shines brightly—in the person and work of the entrepreneur. He leads them to a deeper awareness of the creative and glorious activity of God. He magnifies the Lord in his very person and work and is thus deeply involved in the practice of Christian humanism.

The Work of Redemption and the Entrepreneur

As we saw in the writings of the Fathers, Christ is seen as "The Merchantman." The risky activity of the entrepreneur can intimate to us something of the risky work of Christ wrought in the redemption. The merchant and his activity of exchange is taken and used as a metaphor for the work of redemption. Christ is The Merchantman who exchanges his death for our life, his blood for our forgiveness. The risky work of the entrepreneur, which facilitates an exchange between merchant and buyer, has the potential to intimate to us the risky work of Christ's Redemption. Christ undertook his work of exchange in obedience to his Father's will and out of love for man. So too, the entrepreneur, in obedience to the gifts he has been given, decides to risk his own personal wealth—to give of himself—not only for personal gain, but also for the benefit of others. In this activity he has the potential to intimate to us something of the Paschal Mystery, whereby Christ gave up his life for ours.

Communion of Persons and the Entrepreneur

Gaudium et Spes highlights the importance of communion and the common good when speaking of the Church's activity in the world. These two elements relate directly to points five and six in the definition of entrepreneurial work and personality found at the end of Chapter 2. It appears that the entrepreneur, involved as he is in work that requires the creation of and sustaining of relationships, and work that is directly concerned with the development and maintenance of the common good, finds himself immersed in realities that are, in fact, profoundly Christological and Trinitarian. His work requires communion with others and is directly concerned with the common good and, thus, the good of the person. His work is a work that is profoundly suitable to the fulfillment of the Christian vocation to holiness.

Relationships created and developed in the workplace are ordinary, but also profound. It is easy to take for granted the experiences of unity and communion with other human beings in the work environment. The role of the entrepreneur in enabling these profound experiences of communion should not be discounted or go unappreciated. His work is vital for initiating the development of social communion. Whether communion—agape love—becomes a reality, will of course, be dependent upon the spiritual lives of the participants. Communion, as we have noted, is dependent on self-gift. But it would seem hard to deny that the entrepreneur provides the avenue or occasion for communion. Due to his initiative, creativity, risk taking and energy, man is given an opportunity to experience unity in the economic and social sphere.

Entrepreneurial Work: Temptation and Sin

The Council's emphasizes the common good and the communion of persons as activities that should characterize the Church's—the Christian's—work in the world. The entrepreneur's work seems uniquely suited to the accomplishment of these noble goals. Yet the entrepreneur is subject to the same temptations as other Christians. The entrepreneur has to struggle valiantly to see that a work of magnificence becomes a work for the common good and not a monument to his own vanity. He will have to struggle against the temptation to use those who are entrusted to his care, to see to it that he creates and sustains relationships based on love and not on indifference or malice. In other words, it will be his task to ensure that those human elements of entrepreneurial work, so apt for Christian activity, are indeed brought to perfection in and through the grace of the Paschal Mystery. Entrepreneurial activity, as with all human activity, must be purified and redeemed from sin and set on the road to perfection. It will also be his struggle, as is the case with all Christians, to become conscious of his work as a participation in the creative work of the Creator.

Conclusion

The Church in the modern world is *Gaudium et Spes*—a joy and hope. This is her call and mission given to her by the Lord Jesus Christ. With Christian humanism, the Vatican Council has opened the way for the call to holiness. The entrepreneur, like all other Christians, is called to walk this joyous and demanding narrow way. In the process, he reveals to other men and women of the twenty-first century the creative, redemptive and communal activity of God himself.

We can see, then, that Vatican II adds a great deal to the Catholic view of the entrepreneur, allowing the Church to expand its appreciation of entrepreneurship beyond what is found, implicitly and explicitly, in the teachings of Leo XIII, Pius XI, Pius XII, and John XXIII. It is, however, in the writings of John Paul II that many of these insights are combined and integrated.

Notes

1. Pope John XXIII, quoted in: Mario Benigni and Goffredo Zanchi, *John XXIII: The Official Biography*, trans. Elvira DiFabio (Boston: Pauline Books & Media, 2001), 388.
2. Ibid. The Official Biography of John XXIII is divided into three parts. Benigni wrote the first two, while Zanchi wrote the third section (the section cited here).
3. The dialogue in *The Feminist Question* is between revelation and feminism. It is a dialogue conducted in the academic setting. However, it is essentially the same as a dialogue that is carried on between a Christian and one of his peers in an ordinary human setting (work, leisure, etc.).
4. Francis Martin, *The Feminist Question: Feminist Theology in the Light of Christian Tradition* (Grand Rapids, MI: William B. Eerdmans Publishing Company, 1994), xii.
5. Ibid., xiii. The reference is: *Commentary on the De Trinitate of Boethius* 2,4,ad5, in St. Thomas Aquinas, *Faith, Reason and Theology:Questions I-IV of his Commentary on the De Trinitate of Boethius*, Medieval Sources in Translation, 32, trans. A. Maurer (Toronto: Pontifical Institute of Medieval Studies, 1987), 50.
6. Michael J. Schuck, *That They Be One: The Social Teaching of the Papal Encyclicals 1740-1989* (Washington, DC: Georgetown University Press, 1991), 134.
7. Ibid.
8. *Gaudium et Spes*, 1.
9. Ibid., 22. Emphasis added.
10. Ratzinger in his commentary on paragraph twenty-two says that "we are probably justified in saying that here for *the first time in an official document of the magisterium*, a new type of completely Christocentric theology appears. On the basis of Christ this dares to present theology as anthropology and only becomes radically theological by including man in discourse about God by way of Christ, thus manifesting the deepest unity of theology." (See Ratzinger, "The Dignity of the Human Person," in: Herbert Vorgrimler, ed., *Commentary of the Documents of Vatican II*, vol. V, *Pastoral Constitution on the Church in the Modern World* (New York: Herder and Herder, 1969), 159. Emphasis added.
11. Eph. 1:3–10.
12. Col. 1:15–16.
13. Cantalamessa, *Jesus Christ: The Holy One of God*, 34.
14. Ibid., 35.
15. Ibid. (The Desert Father is Diadochus of Photice. The reference is: *Ascetic Discourses*, 4 (SCh 5 bis, pp. 108f).
16. Joseph Cardinal Ratzinger, *Introduction to Christianity*, trans. J. R. Foster (San Francisco: Communio Books Ignatius Press, 1990), 176. Emphasis added.
17. John 13:2–3.
18. *Gaudium et Spes*, 22. Emphasis added.
19. See CCC 253–55.
20. *Gaudium et Spes*, 12.

21. Referring to the sacrament of Baptism the Church teaches: "Baptism not only purifies from all sins, but also makes the neophyte 'a new creature,' an adopted son of God, who has become a 'partaker of the divine nature,' member of Christ and co-heir, and temple of the Holy Spirit" (CCC 1265). Man is thus intimately related to the three Divine Persons. He is an adopted son of the Father, co-heir with Christ and a temple of the Holy Spirit.

22. CCC 2780.

23. Vatican Council I teaches: "Our holy mother, the Church, holds and teaches that God, the first principle and last end of all things, can be known with certainty from the created world by the natural light of human reason." (See CCC 36) If reason can demonstrate God's existence, according to Vatican I, and his originating causality, it will follow that there is a likeness of God in creation, but not of the Trinity. See CCC 31, 32, 33, where the proofs for the existence of God are said not to be proofs in the sense of the natural sciences, "but rather in the sense of 'converging and convincing arguments,' which allow us to attain certainty about the truth." "These 'ways' of approaching God from creation have a twofold point of departure: the physical world and the human person." (CCC 31).

24. *Fides et Ratio*, 9.

25. Ibid., 7.

26. Ibid.

27. Luke 17:33.

28. *Gaudium et Spes*, 34.

29. Ibid. Emphasis added.

30. Ibid.

31. Ibid., 35.

32. Ibid.

33. Ibid.

34. Ibid., 38.

35. Ibid.

36. Ibid., 63.

37. *Gaudium et Spes*, 64. Emphasis added.

38. Ibid., 65.

39. *Gaudium et Spes* does not suggest that communion is the result of active participation. This is my interpretation and conclusion. Communion must begin with a recognition of the dignity of each person and a respect for their God given abilities. Active participation clearly suggests this. From such a foundation one can then work toward communion.

40. *Lumen Gentium*, 40.

41. Ibid., 41. Emphasis added.

42. David L. Schindler, *Heart of the World, Center of the Church: Communio Ecclesiology, Liberalism and Liberation* (Grand Rapids, MI: William B. Eerdmans Publishing Company, 1996), 91–92.

43. *Lumen Gentium*, 42.

44. Ibid., 31.

45. *Lumen Gentium*, 32.

46. CCC 302.

47. Christoph Schönborn, *Loving the Church: Spiritual Exercises Preached in the Presence of Pope John Paul II*, trans. John Saward (San Francisco: Ignatius Press, 1998), 54–55. Emphasis added. The references to St. Thomas are: See *ST* 1a 103, 6; *Summa contra Gentiles* 3, 69. The *Catechism of the Catholic Church* treats of God's providence and human freedom in: CCC 306–8.

6

Human Work: First Insights from John Paul II

Man is born to labor as a bird to fly.[1]

—Pope Pius XI

The sight of an eagle soaring the skies is truly exhilarating and yet we know that the bird's flight is not without effort. The theme of joy and toil in the life of a human person at work weaves its way throughout the text of John Paul II's first social encyclical. Work, says the pontiff, is the key to the Social Question.[2] Basing his reflections on biblical revelation and the universal experience of men and women throughout the ages, the pope notes that work is at once both a joy—a blessing from God—and a toil. The sacred text of Genesis gives the true essence of work. Work is a blessing received from the Creator, whereby man participates in the activity of God himself and yet, because of the Fall, work has become a toil. It is now a blessing with ambiguity—work is a joy that exhausts!

John Paul II places *Laborem Exercens* within the whole of the Church's social teaching, and even more so, within the framework of *Rerum Novarum*, but it is the first encyclical devoted exclusively to the question of the meaning of human work and even more so of man in the context of his work. What is John Paul II's understanding of work and how will it—how should it—affect the theological meaning of the work of the entrepreneur and businesspersons? John Paul bequeathed three fundamental ideas concerning human work, all of which impact the work of the entrepreneur and businesspersons. Work has an objective meaning, work has a subjective meaning, and work contains a spiritual meaning—it shares in the creative and redemptive activity of the Blessed Trinity. This chapter examines each of these important themes.

Work and Man

John Paul's theological teaching is focused on the truth concerning man. This theme is central to his social teaching. This is clearly so in *Laborem Exercens*. In the introductory paragraph of *Laborem Exercens*, he writes concerning the communion of persons: "Thus work bears a particular mark of man and of humanity, the mark of a person operating within a community of persons."[3] He also notes that the encyclical is devoted to the meaning of work, but more fundamentally to man himself. Therefore, while *Laborem Exercens* examines work in all its aspects, what John Paul is really concerned with is man. The experience (and study) of work will disclose something of the mystery of man. It is with these thoughts that we can properly approach the study of his first social encyclical.

In the introduction, John Paul II makes it clear that the present encyclical has an organic connection with past social encyclicals, yet nevertheless attempts (because of changes in the modern world) to discover "the new meanings of human work."[4] Placed before the introduction is a preamble (or introductory paragraph), which is an excellent interpretative guide as to how the encyclical should be read. The pope pays attention first to the natural view of work when he writes that work helps man earn his daily bread, it contributes to the advance of science and technology, while at the same time elevating culture. Second, he understands work in its relationship to the Creator and his creation. Man, as the image and likeness, of God is "called to work" (*vocatur*)."[5] Man is a creature who is created and called "to subdue the earth."[6] This subduing is fundamentally different from the activity of the rest of the animal creation for it "bears the particular mark of man and of humanity, the mark of a person operating within a community of persons." And it is this mark, the mark of operating within and establishing a community of persons that "decides its interior characteristics; in a sense it constitutes its very nature."[7] Work gains its fullest meaning when, like man himself, it is viewed within the category of creation and redemption. Within the first category, the pope develops the objective and subjective meaning of work (sections two and three). Then he moves in section five to a consideration of the redemptive meaning of work.

The Objective Meaning of Work

In the encyclical it is possible to discern two senses in which work is objective. The first can be termed *Objective work (1)* and relates to the "transitive" activity of work, while the second—termed *Objective work (2)*—deals with the fact that work reflects or mirrors the creative work of God himself. This second sense of objective work could be called "objective theological work."

Objective Work (1)

John Finnis, in *Fundamental Themes of John Paul II's Laborem Exercens*, comments on the fact that work "has two aspects, two dimensions, two *rationes*."[8]

> In one aspect, work is (I) *directed toward an external object*, e.g., some part of the world's natural resources, and (II) *transforms* that external object with another external object, e.g., some machine created by someone else's work in the past, and (III) results in another external object, the *finished product*. All this is the objective aspect of work.[9]

And work is "any activity by man, whether manual or intellectual"[10] and it represents "a fundamental dimension of man's existence on earth."[11] Who can avoid it? No one—for work is part and parcel of man's existence whether he is remunerated for it or not. Work is necessary. So work (*labor*) is a "transitive" activity, writes John Paul II, "that is to say an activity beginning in the human subject and directed toward an external object." This is the first sense of work as objective.[12]

All that is said here is true of entrepreneurial work. Entrepreneurial work has it own flavor, its specific aspects that delineate it from other forms of work as we saw in Chapter 1. But it, like all other forms of work, is a transitive activity. It sets out or proceeds from (1) the human person, (2) is directed to an object, (3) transforms that object with another external object and (4) results in something new—a finished product (a changed state of affairs).

Objective Work (2)

This transitive activity forms part of the vocation of man to "be fruitful and multiply, and fill the earth and subdue it." For man is made "in the image of God"[13] and the mandate that he receives from God is meant to be a reflection of the action of God himself. The Holy Father teaches:

> Man is the image of God partly through the mandate received from his Creator to subdue, to dominate, the earth. In carrying out this mandate, man, every human being, reflects the very action of the Creator of the universe.[14]

Work, in its outward manifestation, is like a sacrament. It is an outward sign of an invisible reality. Man, by the very fact of working, i.e., taking the material creation, transforming it and making something new. Objective work (1), makes present the work of the Creator. He receives the vocation, in and through his work, to remind people of the existence and action of the Creator. Thus work itself, because it is done by the human person, made in the image and likeness of God, has the innate capacity to reflect the activity of God himself.

> *Human work* proceeds directly from persons created in the image of God and called to prolong the work of creation by subduing the earth, both with and for one another.[15]

Why people may not be moved to recognize the Creator through the activity of working men and women obviously constitutes a very grave question. But if work is like a sacrament, then it may simply be a question of a lack of faith. It may also be, as John Paul hints at in section five of the encyclical, related to the *non-observance of the Sabbath rest*. Failure to rest implies hyperactivity and a lack of contemplation.

This objective theological value of work is thus a direct consequence of the doctrine of creation. The pope makes this explicit in paragraph twelve of the encyclical. Thus man discovers that his work is a gift—a mystery—placed, as it is, within the context of the gift and mystery of creation itself.

> In every phase of the development of his work, man comes up against the leading role of the gift made by "nature," that is to say, in the final analysis, by the Creator. *At the beginning of man's work is the mystery of creation.* This affirmation, already indicated as my starting point, is the guiding thread of this document, and will be further developed in the last part of these reflections.[16]

Finnis notes that this governing image "provides the basis for the two leading ideas" in the encyclical.[17]

> A. All forms of property are ultimately for the good of all human beings, because all are either natural resources, i.e., a sheer gift from the Creator, or are (or are at least radically dependent upon) the product (s) of other men's creative activity, and are thus a kind of inheritance into which I enter (i.e., a quasi-gift);
>
> B. By work, the human person fulfills, develops or realizes himself, i.e., we share in God's creation of us, even when the work is humble in its "objective character."[18]

The implication of Finnis' first leading idea is that entrepreneurial work, as with all human activity, must be viewed within the category of the gift. If this is correctly understood, one readily acknowledges that private property is a right that serves the common good. In addition, the notion of the gift extends beyond the raw gifts of nature, to the inheritance of other men's creativity. These two aspects of the gift that John Paul II develops, and which Finnis underlines, are important for the theological meaning of entrepreneurial work.

Entrepreneurial Work and the Gift of the Creator

In *Laborem Exercens*, John Paul is insistent that this type of work—and indeed all work—can only be properly understood and put into practice in the context of the gift of creation. The entrepreneur's creativity is thus a gift and it, too, is subject to the ordering intended by God. It must be viewed through the lens of the mystery of creation and the mystery of work.

> As man, through his work, becomes more and more the master of the earth, and as he confirms his dominion over the visible world, again through his work, he nevertheless remains in every case and at every phase of this process *within the Creator's original ordering.* And this ordering remains necessarily and indissolubly linked with the fact that man was created, as male and female, "in the image of God." This process is, at the same time, universal: it embraces all human beings, every generation, every phase of economic and cultural development, and at the same time it is a process that takes place within each human being, in each conscious human subject.[19]

Man's work has a definite theological objectivity and if he freely submits to this reality, the name of God is respected and spread throughout all the earth. Human work will intimate the very action and existence of God.

David Schindler observes that human creativity, and thus entrepreneurial work, must be understood within the context of divine creativity.

> Thus the Pope says that human creativity, and the "dominion" over the earth that is tied thereto (and thus by further implication the primitive meaning of "*acting person*," "economic *initiative*," and "the virtues associated with the act of *enterprise*."), are all basic to the human being, in the sense that they reveal the human being in its character as image of God. He then goes on to say that this creativity and "dominion" remain "in every case and at every phase within the Creator's original ordering." ... human freedom is *receptive* freedom before it is *creative* freedom—or, better, is a freedom that becomes authentically creative only by being anteriorly receptive.[20]

The creativity of the entrepreneur is not therefore autonomous. Rather, it is a creativity that is first a gift from God received in and through Jesus Christ. Second, creativity must be exercised conscious of this gift. The entrepreneur is called to order his creative work to the glory of God. The entrepreneur is called to work with a profound spirit of gratitude and humility for this gift. His entrepreneurial work thus becomes a participation in the providence of God.

The "Personalist" Argument: Application to Entrepreneurial Work

This spirit of humility and gratitude must extend to previous generations of men and women who have bequeathed the fruits of their labor. *Laborem Exercens* discusses the historical heritage of human labor in section three devoted to the conflict between labor and capital. It will help him develop the personalist argument: the *priority of labor over capital*.[21]

He first defines capital as natural resources and the "means by which man appropriates natural resources and transforms them."[22] And it is these means that "are the result of the historical heritage of human labor."[23] Hence "it is man that has gradually developed them: man's experience and intellect [*experientia atque ingenium*]."[24] Thus the personalist argument:

> This truth, which is part of the abiding heritage of the Church's teaching, must always be emphasized with reference to the question of the labor system and with regard to the whole socioeconomic system. We must emphasize and give prominence to the *primacy of man* in the production process, *the primacy of man over things*. Everything contained in the concept of capital in the strict sense is only a collection of things. Man, as the subject of work, and independently of the work that he does—man alone is a person. This truth has important and decisive consequences.[25]

Thus "a man can easily see that *through his work he enters into two inheritances*."[26] But it is the latter inheritance, the inheritance of "what others have already developed,"[27] that especially leads to the development of the personalist argument: the priority of labor over capital.[28] It is not, of course, the pitting of labor against capital—something Leo XIII firmly rejected—but rather, the recognition that without man, capital could never be discovered or activated. The priority of labor means the priority of the human person, both management and workers, over things [*capita*].

In his work, therefore, man enters not only into the inheritance of past generations, but also the present. This thought is not explicitly brought out in this section of the text, but would seem to be implied by all that has preceded it.

> In working, man also "enters in to the labor of others." Guided both by our intelligence and by the faith that draws light from the word of God, we have no difficulty in accepting this image of the sphere and process of man's labor. It is a *consistent image, one that is humanistic as well as theological*.[29]

For the entrepreneur, the personalist argument is crucial. Humble and gracious before the gift of nature, he is called—arguably—to an even deeper sense of humility and gratitude before the historical and present inheritance of human labor. But then this attitude is facilitated, as observed in Chapter 1, by the characteristics of his work. Entrepreneurial work is characterized by the creating and sustaining of relationships. This is a particular aspect of the work of the entrepreneur that lends itself to a particular understanding of the personalist argument. Indeed, the successful entrepreneur must have that ability to work with others. It is part of his personal temperament. In addition, he enjoys and is good at communication.

Thus, at the center of the entrepreneur's work are human persons and it is this truth that he is disposed toward. He is naturally inclined, not only toward discovery, risk, and return, but to recognize the potential of others, engage them in the production process and thereby lead them to human fulfillment by way of communion with others in the workplace. It will be the recognition of the personalist argument and continual conversion to it that provides the entrepreneur with the full meaning of his work and indeed will be a source of conversion away from materialism and economism to a true Christian humanism. He is called to see and live the primacy of man over things. Does this mean that all entrepreneurs recognize the personalist principle and act accordingly? Given the reality of sin, the answer must be no. But *Laborem Exercens* is a call to conversion.

It is, therefore, the *personalist argument* that is at the basis of the claim of John Paul II that the essential mark or interior characteristic of work is the community of persons.[30] Man works out of necessity. His first concern—his *primary* concern—is to earn his daily bread and so provide for himself, his dependents, etc. In this activity he realizes that he must work in union with others to achieve this goal and in the process discovers the *principal* structure of work—unity with others. The *primary* aspect of work is the necessity to earn one's daily bread. The *principal* aspect of work is its unifying character. Clearly, one cannot be had without the other, but the latter is deemed to be more essential for man. Work unites people and it is this characteristic that appears to be the *essence* of work. This mark, the community of persons, "decides its interior characteristics; in a sense it constitutes its very nature."[31] Like the personalist principle, the entrepreneur, indeed all men, are called to acknowledge this truth and to see in it a source of conversion.

The Subjective Meaning of Work

Having established the significance of the personalist argument, we can now turn to the second leading idea in *Laborem Exercens*—the subjective nature of work. It is situated within a theology of creation, to be sure, but also within the teaching of Vatican II and the philosophy of Karol Wojtyla.

Subjective Work and Theology: *The Gospel of Work*

Laborem Exercens' analysis of work's subjective dimension begins in the following manner:

Man has to subdue the earth and dominate it, because as the "image of God" he is a person, that is to say, a subjective being capable of acting in a planned and rational way, capable of deciding about himself, and with a tendency to self-realization. *As a person, man is therefore the subject of work.* As a person he works. He performs various actions belonging to the work process. Independently of their objective content, these actions must all serve to realize his humanity, to fulfill the calling to be a person that is his by reason of his very humanity.[32]

The dominion that man is called to exercise concerns not only the material creation, but also himself. Man is called to perfect the world, but more fundamentally himself.

> This dominion, in a certain sense, refers to the subjective dimension even more than to the objective one: this dimension conditions *the very ethical nature of work*. In fact there is no doubt that human work has an ethical value of its own, which clearly and directly remains linked to the fact that the one who carries it out is a person, a conscious and free subject, that is to say, a subject that decides about himself. [33]

Here, more so than anywhere else in the text, we readily observe the development of thought with respect to work in the Church's social doctrine. Earlier encyclicals viewed work as necessary, personal and to some extent social, but in *Laborem Exercens* work is understood in relation to an explicit theology of creation. Work, in its subjective meaning, is prior to and more fundamental than its objective content. It is Christ who explicitly reveals this to us, so much so that John Paul II can speak of the Gospel of Work.

> By broadening certain aspects that already belonged to the Old Testament, Christianity brought about a fundamental change of ideas in this field, taking the whole content of the Gospel message as its point of departure, especially the fact that the one who, while *being God,* became like us in all things devoted most of the years of His life on earth to *manual work* at the carpenter's bench. This circumstance constitutes in itself the most eloquent "Gospel of work," showing that the basis for determining *the value of human work is not primarily the kind of work being done but the fact that the one who is doing it is a person. The sources of the dignity of work are to be sought primarily in the subjective dimension, not in the objective one.*[34]

So while it cannot be denied, as we have seen, "that man is destined for work and called to it," nevertheless, "work is 'for man' and not man 'for.'"[35] The personalist and subjective dimensions of work lie at the heart of a proper theology of work. Thus, no matter what the circumstances of his work—whether man is the sole owner of an enterprise, the joint owner or one of the employees of a small or large corporation—man works *"for himself."*[36] That is, man works in order to build his humanity. While in paragraph nine the Holy Father refers to "the sometimes heavy toil" that accompanies work, nevertheless work is useful, something to enjoy and is worthy of man, since it helps man achieve his fulfillment. Work, is therefore, a basic good in itself.

> And yet, in spite of all this toil—perhaps, in a sense, because of it—work is a good thing for man. Even though it bears the mark of a *bonum arduum*, in the terminology of St. Thomas, this does not take away the fact that, as such, it is a good thing for man. It is not only good in the sense that it is useful or something

to enjoy; it is also good as being something worthy, that is to say, something that corresponds to man's dignity, that expresses this dignity and increases it. If one wishes to define more clearly the ethical meaning of work, it is this truth that one must particularly keep in mind. Work is a good thing for man—a good thing for his humanity—because through work man *not only transforms nature*, adapting it to his own needs, but he also *achieves fulfilment* as a human being and indeed, in a sense, becomes "more a human being."[37]

The teaching of *Laborem Exercens* is entirely consistent with, while at the same time expanding, the teaching of Vatican II.

Subjective Work: Philosophical Considerations

Finnis notes that much of *Laborem Exercens* can be understood as a commentary on Vatican II's analysis of human work. "But so, too," he adds, "is much of Karol Wojtyla's philosophical work on human personality and action."[38]

> The central chapter of his book *The Acting Person* begins with the assertion that "the performance of an action brings fulfillment" and with the comment:
>
> > All the essential problems considered in this study seem to be focused and condensed in the simple assertion of fulfillment in an action (*The Acting Person*, 149).[39]

For Wojtyla, a person is revealed and fulfilled in human action. The Second Vatican Council speaks of man going outside himself and beyond himself. This is referred to by Wojtyla as transcendence. In *The Acting Person*, Wojtyla introduces the term transcendence and notes that "etymologically 'transcendence' means to go over and beyond a threshold or a boundary (*trans-scendere*)."[40] For Wojtyla, there is both horizontal and vertical transcendence. Schmitz gives a more than adequate explanation of what is intended.

> Action, then, redounds upon the whole person, so that self-determination is also self-formation and self-development. Herein lies the reason why an action is not merely a quality or property of a person, and why it leaves the whole person either better or worse. Only in transcendence do we go beyond ourselves toward the promise of each one's unique humanity. Part of our fulfillment consists in a horizontal transcendence, that is, in our going out to things around us, in coming to know them, in interacting with them and being affected by them. But such horizontal transcendence is only a condition of our fulfillment: it is not its key.[41]

Horizontal transcendence is the self (the person) going out to meet and encounter objects. The person perceives and knows objects, intends and wills them.[42] But then the choice of object is not just the object itself, but simultaneously the self. This is vertical transcendence. The person, having chosen an object of choice, also chooses himself and through the action becomes more (or less as the case may be) of a person. Through choosing a certain action, a certain object, man chooses at one and the same time himself. Schmitz writes that horizontal transcendence, the choice of object where the person goes out to meet what is chosen, is the condition for self-fulfillment. Horizontal transcendence does not effect personal change, but is a necessary condition for it to take place. May we perhaps say that it is an avenue for self-fulfillment, for without it vertical transcendence would be impossible?

So there is an intimate bond between horizontal and vertical transcendence. Both are required if the person is to transcend self. But the key to self-fulfillment lies with vertical transcendence, the surrendering of the self that we presently are to the self that we might become. In this sense it is possible to say that choice is a symptom of freedom. We can choose because we are free.[43] Man can choose objects of choice, but at a deeper level he can choose the person he wills to become. He has the capacity for self-surrender.

> One's choice is not only transitive toward the chosen behavior and the further results and products of that behavior. It also is intransitive, an act by which, willy nilly, I who am choosing constitute myself as the person I will henceforth be, as the person I will remain unless and until I repent of that choice.[44]

Self-determination is intimately related to Wojtyla's vertical transcendence. In a sense, they are almost indistinguishable, although Wojtyla[45] and Finnis note that vertical transcendence "is the fruit of self-determination."[46] Might it not also be true that self-determination is the result of the person's capacity for vertical transcendence?

Applying this reasoning to work we can say this that when a person works, he is not just involved in a transitive activity, but is, at the same time, intimately involved in actualizing his human potential. Working away at the carpenter's bench, a workman is transforming a piece of wood into a table or chair, but he is also working away at himself. He is becoming more human, acquiring greater skill, expertise, experience and many moral virtues that are shaping him as much as he is shaping the wood. The object of his work, the work itself, redounds back on him, determining him to be a human person full of maturity, with a greater depth of virtue than he had before he began his work. He is actualizing his potential and fulfilling the task—the vocation—that God had assigned to him at the beginning of Creation and of his own personal existence.

Work thus takes its dignity, not from the type of work done, but from the fact that it is a person who is doing it—a person called beyond self to horizontal and vertical transcendence and thus to a new self. It is precisely in and through the experience of work that man is able to build his humanity, so to speak, and experience himself as a person. This does not imply that one cannot make objective or even qualitative distinctions between different types of work. The primacy of subjective work does not deny the importance of works of magnificence that are discovered, pursued and performed by entrepreneurs. It is these projects that enable men and women to be employed and thus enter into the objective and subjective meaning of work.

Subjective Work and the Entrepreneur

John Paul II, consistent with his thought in *Laborem Exercens*, teaches that the entrepreneur must discover and pursue with diligence the subjective dimension of his work. In an address to entrepreneurs in Buenos Aires in 1987, John Paul II spoke directly to the subjective dimension of entrepreneurial work. In a sense, he told the entrepreneurs that they should be entrepreneurs with themselves. He affirms the entrepreneurs in their work that is critical for the common good. Entrepreneurial work has an important objective character.

> [T]he degree of well-being that society enjoys today would have been impossible without the *dynamic figure of the entrepreneur*, whose function consists in organizing human labor and the means of production in order to produce goods and services. Without any doubt, your task is of the first order for society. That reality is based on your having received the "inheritance" of a twofold patrimony, that is, the natural resources of the country and the fruits of the work of those who have preceded you (See *Laborem Exercens*, 15).[47]

The gift granted by God and received by the entrepreneur calls forth responsibility. The work of the entrepreneur evokes the parable of the steward in the Gospel of Luke.[48] Entrepreneurs, accordingly, are asked to draw up an account of their stewardship. Their God-given gifts are meant for others. The pope then suggests an intimate connection between the objective and subjective meanings of work. By working for the common good, the entrepreneur facilitates the subjective meaning of work.

> [B]usiness is called *to fulfill*, under your influence, *a social function*, which is *profoundly* ethical: that of contributing to the perfection of man without discrimination, by creating conditions that will make it possible for work not only to develop the capacities of the person, but also at the same time to achieve an effective and reasonable production of goods and services, and will make the worker aware of working on something that is really his own.[49]

These goals of the common good and the perfection of man call forth the potential of the entrepreneur. The work of businessmen and women, therefore, is not unlike that of the shepherd.

> A business that respects these social goals evidently requires a model of a *deeply human* entrepreneur, who is aware of his duties, [is] honest, competent and imbued with a profound social sense that makes him capable of rejecting the inclination to selfishness, to prefer the wealth of love to the love of wealth. We can say by

way of analogy that there is a certain biblical similarity between the businessman and the Shepherd. It is an analogy.[50]

Thus in exercising his profession, in pursuing works of magnificence, the entrepreneur creates those conditions that make material prosperity a reality. In this the entrepreneur is akin to a shepherd. This not only facilitates opportunities for employment (and thus objective work), which is an absolutely essential aspect of solving problems related to the distribution of income and poverty, but at the same time, and in a sense of more importance, the entrepreneur provides people with the chance of fulfilling the subjective meaning of work. Without the creation of employment through works of magnificence, subjective work is not possible.

After these reflections, the pope speaks directly of the subjective nature of work as it applies to the entrepreneur. *The entrepreneur is called to be an entrepreneur with himself.* Then John Paul II speaks of the importance of working toward a more just and peaceful society.

> Beloved businessmen and women, we have already spoken about the highly complex and delicate environment in which you exercise your professional activity. Likewise, I also know the various kinds of difficulties that hinder your work, problems that are related to trade cycles, the sometimes difficult relations with your collaborators and workers, misunderstandings and accusations that sometimes make you their favourite target, economic concerns...
>
> I insist that I am aware of the existence of these problems, which are often objectively more serious. However, permit me to remind you that the great concern, *the great business affair that you must conduct in your life, is to conquer heaven, eternal life.* The Lord says to you: "What gain is it for a man to have won the whole world and to have lost or ruined his very self? (Lk. 9:25)... Never forget that the real dangers are the temptations that can lead your consciences and activity astray, namely, easy and immoral gains, waste, the temptation of power and pleasure, limitless ambitions, uncontrolled selfishness, dishonesty in business affairs and injustice towards your workers..."
>
> Businessmen and women who are by majority Christians, you should be the architects of a more just, peaceful and fraternal society. Be men and women of dynamic ideas, creative initiatives, generous sacrifices and a firm and sure hope.[51]

A Spirituality of Work

Section five of *Laborem Exercens* addresses *Elements for a Spirituality of Work.* John Paul's preceding analysis sets the tone. Work, considered in the light of creation, is a gift from God. Man, made in the image and likeness of God, is called to perfect the world and himself and in so doing "*shares by his work in the activity of the Creator.*"[52] But in light of the mystery of the Incarnation and Redemption, work now takes on an added meaning. Work is now a particular sharing in the activity of the Redeemer Jesus Christ. His death and Resurrection is a work of salvation and Christians share in this redeeming activity through their daily work. That work is not only creative, but also redemptive, is undoubtedly a strong theme in this part of the encyclical. But the Book of Genesis presents God's creative *activity* under the form of *work* and *rest*.

Redemptive Work

Christ was *"himself a man of work."*[53] John Paul II observes that the Gospel contains no special command to work. It is rather Christ's life—his example of work—that speaks to us eloquently.

> [H]e belongs to the "working world," he has appreciation and respect for human work. It can indeed be said that *He looks with love upon human work* and the different forms that it takes, seeing in each one of these forms a particular facet of man's likeness with God, the Creator and Father.[54]

Then after some further considerations he returns to the theme of toil annunciated by the Book of Genesis and experienced by each human person. The toil of man's work can be a sharing in Jesus Christ's supreme toil—his suffering and death on a cross.

> Sweat and toil, which work necessarily involves in the present condition of the human race, present the Christian and everyone who is called to follow Christ with the possibility of sharing lovingly in the work that Christ came to do. This work of salvation came about through suffering and death on a Cross. By enduring the toil of work in union with Christ crucified for us, man in a way collaborates with the Son of God for the redemption of humanity. He shows himself a true disciple of Christ by carrying the cross in his turn every day in the activity that he is called upon to perform.[55]

This gift of sharing in Christ's redemptive work is confirmed by the resurrection, enabling Christians to sense and feel the animating, purifying and strengthening action of the Spirit in their lives. So in and through their work, Christians have the possibility of dying with Jesus Christ in his death and rising with him in his Resurrection to a new life. Work becomes the privileged place of living out the reality of the sacrament of baptism. Work, because of the Paschal Mystery, receives a newness or freshness. Sweat and fatigue are never absent, but nevertheless, it is forged anew and becomes a new good.[56] Man, like Christ, is called to accept the redemptive nature of work. It too is a gift from the Father. So the original blessing and gift of work that accompanied the gift of man's creation is affirmed and renewed by Jesus Christ. It takes on the added dimension of the gift of redemption by means of Christ's life of work in Nazareth and his work on Calvary. The toil and fatigue of work is thus raised to the dignity of a new gift, a new good. The new good of work is now obedience to the Father's will and the redemption of men and women. By his work, man participates intimately and fully in the development of the Kingdom of God.

God's Activity: Work and Rest

John Paul II notes that while Christ gave no special command to work, he did speak "on one occasion a prohibition against too much anxiety about work and life."[57] Work is a good, but it serves a higher good—man. And man, as we have seen, is to be understood in light of the revealed Word of God. Here, then, in section five of the encyclical as with the previous analysis, it is the Book of Genesis that reveals the spiritual meaning of work.

Work is a participation in the work of God. But now this *actio* of God is defined in terms of work (*opus*) and rest (*requies*). It will be necessary, therefore, to examine the spiritual meaning of work in light of God's *opus* and *requies*. It is true that the encyclical does occasionally use *opus* to denote man's work. But for the most part it uses *labor* when referring to man's work. Here in paragraph twenty-six, the emphasis, however, is on *opus* and it is directly related to God's *opus*. Work is not so much *labor*, as it is *opus*—a work of art.

> The word of God's revelation is profoundly marked by the fundamental truth that *man*, created in the image of God, *shares by his work in the activity of the Creator* and that, within the limits of his own human capabilities, man in a sense continues to develop that activity, and perfects it as he advances further and further in the discovery of the resources and values contained in the whole of creation. We find this truth at the very beginning of Sacred Scripture, in the book of Genesis, where the creation activity itself is presented in the form of "work" done by God during "six days," "resting" on the seventh day.[58]

God's activity is *opus*. His creation is an *opus*—a work of art. The created world is the fruit of the Creator's inner freedom and it is in that sense entirely unnecessary. God's work is effortless and is entirely the overflow of his eternal love and freedom. There is no compulsion or toil. It is *opus*—free and magnificent. Man, created in the image of God, is called to participate in this *opus*. Man is called to see and live, albeit with difficulty because of Original Sin, that his work is not only necessary, but also free. After the example of the Creator, man's work is an act of inner freedom, and not just obligation and necessity. Hence, John Paul says that the Book of Genesis shows itself to be *"the first 'gospel of work.'"*[59] In this regard, *Laborem Exercens* makes four critical points.[60]

First, God's creative and free activity—God's *opus*—is presented by the sacred text under the form of *working* and *resting*. God continues to work and rest in the world. Second, man is called to imitate God in his working and resting, in his *opus*. But man discovers and experiences that his work is also *labor*. Nevertheless, man is still called to imitate the *opus* of God. Third, it is imperative that man rest every "seventh day." This allows man to move beyond work as *labor* to work as *opus*. It allows man, in other words, to become more and more, and thus fulfill the will of God. It is the will of God that man rest in God. Fourth, the sabbath not only permits man to rest and gain a proper perspective about his work, it is also a foretaste of the eternal sabbath. Therefore, the sabbath is God's instrument allowing man to discover, experience and understand the meaning of human freedom.

Seen from the perspective of the eternal rest that God prepares for his elect, human work receives its proper value—good. It is subservient to the human person. For it is the human person that God desires, not so much his work. It is precisely the rhythm of the "seventh day" that allows man not only to receive a foretaste of the final rest in heaven, but it also enables him to order his work toward its true spiritual meaning. Observing the Sabbath is an aid to man, helping him see that his work is not simply an external activity, but one in which, through freedom, he attains the will of God. Can it not be said that the Sabbath is that interior space allowing man to discern the true meaning of work in its objective and subjective value? The Sabbath rest is that "space" in which the work (*labor*) having been completed now receives its full value. *Labor*, through rest, becomes *opus*. Man participates, through rest, in God's free work—in God's freedom. Lack of observance of the sabbath, therefore, will have grave repercussions for man's freedom and activity. In fact, the sacred text itself speaks of God finishing his work of creation *by resting on the Sabbath*. Work and rest form an organic unity of action for God and it is God's intention that man respects and pursues this organic connection.

> And on the seventh day God finished his work which he had done, and he rested on the seventh day from all his work which he had done. So God blessed the seventh day and hallowed it, because on it God rested from all his work which he had done in creation.[61]

God's creative activity—his *opus*—is presented as taking place within six days of work and one day of rest. The *Creatoris opus* is not finished until the Creator takes his rest. In resting, God *contemplates* his work and *finishes* it. God rests, contemplates his work and sees that it is good—indeed very good—and thereby finishes his *opus*.[62] And man, made in the image of God, is called to observe the Sabbath for that very reason. Without the Sabbath rest, man cannot bring to fulfillment the task of perfection that God has called him to. Without the rest of the seventh day, man is unable to contemplate his work and finish it. He is unable to imitate God in his free creative work.

Conclusion

Understood in light of the mysteries of creation and redemption, work itself is a mystery. The Book of Ecclesiastes tells us so. Work is gift, mystery and toil.

I have seen the business that God has given to the sons of men to be busy with. He has made everything beautiful in its time; also he has put eternity into man's mind, yet so that he cannot find out what God has done from the beginning to the end. I know that there is nothing better for them than to be happy and enjoy themselves as long as they live; also that it is God's gift to man that every one should eat and drink and take pleasure in all his toil.[63]

Through the revealed word of God, man knows that his work is a share in God's work of creation and redemption. Man can see and discern through the gift of faith and human reason that he is to be about God's business. But precisely because work is about God's business, it is a mystery that man will never exhaust. God's work is *opus* and man is called to participate in it. Man, therefore, in his work, is prolonging and perfecting the *opus* of his Father and Creator. It is an *opus* that is both creative and salvific—a point further underlined in John Paul II's second and third social encyclicals.

Notes

1. *Quadragesimo Anno*, 61.
2. *Laborem Exercens*, 3.
3. *Laborem Exercens*, Introductory paragraph.
4. *Laborem Exercens*, 2.
5. Ibid., Introductory paragraph.
6. Ibid.
7. Ibid.
8. John Finnis, "The Fundamental Themes of John Paul II's *Laborem Exercens*," in William E. May and Kenneth D. Whitehead, eds., *The Battle for the Catholic Mind: Catholic Faith and Catholic Intellect in the Work of the Fellowship of Catholic Scholars 1978-95* (South Bend, IN: St. Augustine's Press, 2001), 222.
9. Ibid. Emphasis added.
10. *Laborem Exercens*, Introductory Paragraph.
11. Ibid., 4.
12. Ibid., 4.
13. See Gen. 1:27.
14. *Laborem Exercens*, 4.
15. CCC 2427.
16. *Laborem Exercens*, 12. Emphasis added.
17. Finnis, "The Fundamental Themes" in *Battle for the Catholic Mind*, 222.
18. Ibid.
19. *Laborem Exercens*, 4. Emphasis added.
20. Schindler, *Heart of the World*, 117–18.
21. *Laborem Exercens*, 12, 15. Emphasis added.
22. Ibid., 12.
23. Ibid.

24. Ibid. The English uses *intellect*, while the Latin uses *ingenium*. The Latin gives rise to an appreciation of the work of the entrepreneur—if not explicitly, then most definitely implicitly. The English translation here is unfortunate.

25. Ibid.

26. Ibid., 13.

27. Ibid.

28. Ibid.,15.

29. *Laborem Exercens*, 13. (The scripture reference is to John 4:38.)

30. *Laborem Exercens*, Introductory paragraph.

31. *Laborem Exercens*, Introductory paragraph.

32. *Laborem Exercens*, 6. Emphasis added.

33. Ibid., 6. Emphasis added.

34. *Laborem Exercens*, 6. Emphasis added.

35. Ibid.

36. Ibid., 15. Emphasis added.

37. Ibid., 9.

38. Finnis, "Fundamental Themes" in *Battle for the Catholic Mind*, 224.

39. Ibid.

40. Karol Wojtyla, *The Acting Person*, trans. Andrzej Potocki, ed. Anna-Teresa Tymieniecka, vol. 10, *Analecta Husserliana: The Yearbook of Phenomenological Research* (Boston: D. Reidel Publishing Company, 1979), 119.

41. Kenneth L. Schmitz, *At the Center of the Human Drama: The Philosophical Anthropology of Karol Wojtyla/Pope John Paul II* (Washington, DC: The Catholic University of American Press, 1993), 86.

42. See Finnis, "The Fundamental Themes" in *Battle for the Catholic Mind*, 224. "Horizontal transcendence, then, is the fact that we can get outside ourselves by perceiving and knowing objects, and by intending and willing objects (including events and states of affairs) outside, beyond ourselves."

43. I owe these thoughts and their phrasing to Fr. Francis Martin, revealed in personal conversation.

44. Finnis, "The Fundamental Themes" in *Battle for the Catholic Mind*, 225.

45. See Wojtyla, *The Acting Person*, 119.

46. Finnis, "The Fundamental Themes" in *Battle for the Catholic Mind,* 224.

47. John Paul II, "An Economic and Ethical Challenge That Must Be Faced By Overcoming Egoism," *L'Osservatore Romano: English Weekly Edition*, May 18, 1987, 12–13, 12.

48. Ibid.

49. Ibid., 13.

50. Ibid.

51. Ibid.

52. *Laborem Exercens*, 25.

53. Ibid., 26.

54. Ibid.

55. Ibid., 27.

56. Ibid., 27.

57. Ibid., 26.

58. Ibid., 25. Clearly the English text does not distinguish between the Latin words *actio* and *opus*, but simply lumps them together under the phrase "God's creative activity." It is a significant omission.

59. Ibid.

60. Ibid.

61. Gen. 2:2–3.

62. This line of thought I owe to Fr. Francis Martin revealed in class discussion and in personal conversation.

63. Eccl. 3:10–13.

7

From Work to Entrepreneurship:
The Revolution of *Centesimus Annus*

Centesimus Annus is not addressed to those who are fond of abstract diatribes on what the best socio-economic system may be, but to "this man," to "each man," who toils daily to seek solutions to his needs and others' needs.

—Marco Martini[1]

With the collapse of Communism, the question for many Catholics was: Is the remaining system—capitalism—the answer to the social question? Or might there be a third way? To the first question John Paul II gives a qualified yes. John Paul II affirms not capitalism, but a "business economy," "market economy" or simply "free economy."[2] To the latter question the answer is a resounding no. The Church does not suggest a third way between communism and capitalism. This is clearly beyond her competence. The Church restricts herself to enunciating principles, especially those pertaining to the truth about the human person. Specific solutions to the social question are the domain of the laity.

While *Centesimus Annus* has to be read in light of *Rerum Novarum*, the encyclical engages the issues of the day and underlines two great themes of John Paul's pontificate—the importance of culture and the centrality of man in sections five and six. In this chapter we focus on *Centesimus Annus'* attention to the virtues of the entrepreneur. We then ask whether *Centesimus Annus* represents a novel approach to the social question, especially with respect to entrepreneurial work and the free-market economy. This is followed by a discussion of *Centesimus Annus'* view of the difference between a free market economy or business economy as opposed to a capitalist society, as well as John Paul's call for a society of *free work, enterprise and participation*. The final section examines the call for a business firm to be a *communion of persons*.

Entrepreneurship and Property

First, consistent with *Laborem Exercens*, John Paul II locates entrepreneurial work within the creative act of God. Entrepreneurial work, and all work, obtains its original meaning from creation. Second, the pope continues to reflect on the relational dimension of work and suggests that this dimension is becoming clearer in the modern age. Finally, the Holy Father takes stock of the fact that in the modern world it is work, and not so much land, that is becoming the decisive factor in an economy. These three points allow him to develop the social teaching with respect to the entrepreneur.

John Paul II repeats and affirms Church's insistence upon the right to private property, but affirms previous papal teaching that it is not an absolute right. The pope then re-reads this teaching in light of creation. He then re-reads the relationship between land and work and then introduces the new form of ownership: "*the possession of know-how, technology and skill.*"[3]

John Paul II asks his readers to consider what has taken place in the relationship between land and work in the past one hundred years? To be sure, at the time of *Rerum Novarum*, work was beginning to dislodge land as the prime factor of wealth. But now with the benefit of hindsight and the experience of continued changes in the workplace, we can clearly acknowledge the shift. "At one time *the natural fruitfulness of the earth* appeared to be, and was in fact, the primary factor of wealth, while work was, as it were, the help and support for this fruitfulness." But now, in the twentieth and twenty-first centuries, the scales are tilting more and more in favor of work. "In our time, *the role of human work* is becoming increasingly important as the productive factor both of nonmaterial and of material wealth."[4]

This change in the relationship between work and the natural fruitfulness of the land yields this important insight.

> In our time, in particular, there exists another form of ownership which is becoming no less important than land: *the possession of know-how, technology and skill*. The wealth of the industrialized nations is based much more on this kind of ownership than on natural resources.[5]

With work becoming increasingly decisive in the production of wealth, land is accompanied by knowledge as something to be desired and possessed. As a resource, it enters the market. There is thus a price for it and it too, like land, will be determined by demand and supply. Knowledge is truly a new form of possession.

The Entrepreneur in *Centesimus Annus*

It is knowledge—alertness to information—that is essential for the entrepreneur. Thus the changes in work, particularly the new form of possession, lead John Paul to identify and appreciate all of the key elements of the definition of entrepreneurial work that has been developed in Chapter 1. In the following citation, John Paul mentions all the key elements of that definition:

> Mention has just been made of the fact that *people work with each other*, sharing in a "community of work" which embraces ever widening circles. A person who produces something other than for his own use generally does so in order that others may use it after they have paid a just price, mutually agreed upon through free bargaining. It is precisely the ability to foresee both the needs of others and the combinations of productive factors most adapted to satisfying those needs that constitutes another important source of wealth in modern society. Besides, many goods cannot be adequately produced through the work of an isolated individual; they require the cooperation of many people in working towards a common goal. Organizing such a productive effort, planning its duration in time, making sure that it corresponds in a positive way to the demands which it must satisfy, and taking the necessary risks-all this too is a source of wealth [*fons divitiis fecundus*] in today's society. In this way, the role of disciplined and creative human work and, as an essential part of that work, initiative and entrepreneurial ability becomes increasingly evident and decisive [*Ita evidentiores et usque praestantiores fiunt rationes laboris humani ordinate et efficientis et, sicut est huius laboris pars praecipua, facultatis consilia capiendi et opera conducendi*].[6]

Thus entrepreneurial work is a source of wealth in today's society (*fons divitiis fecundus*). It is, in fact, increasingly evident and decisive or excellent (*evidentiores et usque praestantiores*). The Latin text does not explicitly mention entrepreneurial ability. Rather, it speaks of *facultatis consilia capiendi*. Perhaps the official English version could have used *inceptum* or *conatus* or may have even referred back to the spirit of enterprise (*spiritui innovationis*) as used in *Gaudium et Spes*, 64. Nevertheless, these last few lines of the citation from paragraph thirty-two make it clear that we are dealing with entrepreneurial work. A better translation would be the following:

> Thus the efficient and orderly method of human work is made evident and excellent. A particular part (aspect) of this work is the *seizing* (or grasping) of the *faculty* (capacity) for counsel (or judgment or *invention*) and the *bringing together* of this work.[7]

The text, therefore, is clearly an affirmation of entrepreneurial work. The work described in the above passage is one of uniting productive factors and people together, taking precautions because of the duration of the project, taking care to make sure that it responds to the necessities which it ought to satisfy and the taking up of the dangers which are required of such a project.

Consistent with *Laborem Exercens*, John Paul II sees the work of the entrepreneur as being truly an *opus: sociale opus*.[8] Clearly, entrepreneurial work is *labor*. It is fraught with dangers and risks, requires long hours and perseverance. Like all work it, too, is toilsome. But at the same time entrepreneurial work is a work of magnificence, as St. Thomas reminds us. The entrepreneur participates in this work in an intimate way, since he is the source and origin of such a work. He is an intimate participant, not spectator, of a *sociale opus*—a work that shares in the *opus Creatoris*. For John Paul, the work of the entrepreneur is decisive and evident. It plays a key role in man's participation in God's work—in God's *opus*. Just as God's work is a work of freedom, so too is that of the entrepreneur. His is a work of discovery, alertness and risk taking. In this light, it is not so much a responsive (and thereby necessary) work, as it is one of initiative, ingenuity and energy.

But it is the relational dimension of entrepreneurial work that appears foremost in the pope's mind. Entrepreneurs work with others, foreseeing the needs of others and satisfying these needs through the engagement of the factors of production. Thus John Paul II is entirely consistent with his teaching found in *Laborem Exercens*. The principal characteristic of work is thereby confirmed by the experience of entrepreneurs and the experience of modern developments in work.

Centesimus Annus also highlights the relational dimension of entrepreneurial work. Work gains its fundamental meaning from the other, for like man himself, work is ordered to the other. The repetition of *other* is a distinctive mark of the text.

> Moreover, it is becoming clearer how a person's work is naturally interrelated with the work of others. More than ever, work is *work with others* and *work for others*: it is a matter of doing something for someone else. Work becomes ever more fruitful and productive to the extent that people become more knowledgeable of the productive potentialities of the earth and more profoundly cognizant of the needs of those for whom their work is done.[9]

Thus while John Paul appreciates many of the elements that characterize the entrepreneur's work, it is the orientation to the *other*—to the *needs of others*—that also captures his attention. Entrepreneurial work has a power to unite people; it has an ability to foresee the needs of others, to combine the energy of materials and labor to achieve an outcome that will satisfy these needs. Entrepreneurial work is able to take an isolated individual and situate him in a community with other men and women and thus become involved in a *sociale opus*. This, for John Paul II, appears to be a fundamental characteristic of entrepreneurial work.

Paragraph thirty-two then proceeds to make an extraordinary claim. *Entrepreneurial work affirms a truth about the human person*. The process of entrepreneurial work actually sheds light on the nature of human persons created in the image and likeness of God!

> This process, *which throws practical light on a truth about the person which Christianity has constantly affirmed*, should be viewed carefully and favorably.

Indeed, besides the earth, man's principal resource is *man himself.* His intelligence enables him to discover the earth's productive potential and the many different ways in which human needs can be satisfied. It is his disciplined work *in close collaboration with others* that makes possible the creation of ever more extensive working communities which can be relied upon to transform man's natural and human environments. Important *virtues* are involved in this process, such as diligence, industriousness, prudence in undertaking reasonable risks, reliability and fidelity in interpersonal relationships, as well as courage in carrying out decisions which are difficult and painful but necessary, both for the overall working of a business and in meeting possible setbacks.[10]

Entrepreneurial work, in fact, confirms the teaching of the Church: at the center of the social question is *man himself*—a personal and social being. Entrepreneurial work is thus a kind of light—a practical light—that enables modern man to perceive the truth that it is man, not capital or land, that is the crucial element in the economic and financial sphere.

Thus using his intelligence and free will man is able to subdue the earth. At the same time he is able to develop and deepen the social sense of work. He can use his intellectual and moral qualities for man himself and for others. He is able to mold human activity according to his personal and social nature. Here again the Latin text does give a slightly different sense than the English. In some ways, it gives a more intimate sense of work. Work is where one develops and sustains interpersonal relationships. It speaks of tempered work and not disciplined work (a significant difference in meaning). This tempered work acts and unites, in cooperation with others, in bringing about communities of work that are constituted by great and worthy trust in changing man's natural and human environment.

It appears, therefore, that for John Paul II, there are three fundamental reasons as to why entrepreneurial work is important. First, it is based on a correct anthropology. Because the human person possesses freedom and intelligence, the State must play a subsidiary role in economic and financial development. Socialism is to be rejected because it represents not only an *overplay of the State*, but an *underplay of the person.*

Second, the work of the entrepreneur demonstrates a profoundly relational dimension. It sheds light on the fundamental characteristic of human work—its ability to unite people and establish communion among them. Finally, John Paul II sees the entrepreneur as intimately involved in a great *sociale opus*. Entrepreneurial work, with its sense of initiative, alertness and discovery, shares intimately in, prolongs and perfects God's *opus*—his creative work. Because it involves risks, diligence, industriousness, difficult and painful decisions, and hence toil, the entrepreneur participates in the redemptive work of Jesus Christ. Entrepreneurial work participates, perfects and prolongs the creative and redemptive work of God himself.

Centesimus Annus: Nova et Vetera?

These then are the major elements of the encyclical as they relate to the entrepreneur. But how does this relate to what John Paul's call for a society of *free work, enterprise, and participation.* Can it be said that *Centesimus Annus* represents a radical shift in Catholic social teaching with respect to private initiative (as some commentators have claimed)? Or can it be viewed as consistent with past teaching on private initiative, while at the same time developing this teaching? The latter appears to be the case, in as much as critical elements of *Centesimus Annus* draw upon *Rerum Novarum*'s emphasis on private property, *Quadragesimo Anno*'s affirmation of private initiative, and Pius XII's praise and encouragement of business and entrepreneurial activity.

But we also need to consider a brief passage in the second of John Paul's social encyclicals *Sollicitudo Rei Socialis.*[11] In the midst of deepening the meaning of human development, John Paul wrote this about the crucial role played by private initiative, both for the good of the human person and the common good.

> It should be noted that in today's world, among other rights, *the right of economic initiative* is often suppressed. Yet it is a right which is important not only for the individual but also for the common good. Experience shows us that the denial of this right, or its limitation in the name of an alleged "equality" of everyone in society, diminishes, or in practice absolutely destroys the spirit of initiative, that is to say the *creative subjectivity of the citizen.* As a consequence, there arises, not so much a true equality as a "leveling down." In the place of creative initiative there appears passivity, dependence and submission to the bureaucratic apparatus which, as the only "ordering" and "decision-making" body—if not also the "owner"—of the entire totality of goods and the means of production, puts everyone in a position of almost absolute dependence, which is similar to the traditional dependence of the worker-proletarian in capitalism. This provokes a sense of frustration or desperation and predisposes people to opt out of national life, impelling many to emigrate and also favoring a form of "psychological" emigration.[12]

The passage is in some ways more evocative than *Centesimus Annus* in its confirmation of the spirit of initiative and the negative results that ensue when it is ignored. The term "psychological emigration" is thought-provoking, to say the least.

Some commentators argue that *Centesimus Annus* represented an almost complete shift in the Church's understanding of capitalism, private initiative, and free markets. Jeffrey Tucker argues:

> Surely, the distinctive mark of the encyclical—*especially in light of previous social encyclicals*—is its highly sympathetic explication of the workings of the market economy, as many commentators have already pointed out.[13]

Michael Novak also maintains that John Paul II significantly departed from previous social encyclicals.

All in all, *Centesimus Annus* breaks truly new ground. Not only does it make "creative subjectivity" the central focus of its logic and the key to its understanding of humane capitalism, it deploys its own creative spirit in practically every section.[14]

But creative subjectivity is not its focus. The human person, created in and through Christ, is the central focus. John Paul II makes this clear, as we have seen, by devoting the final section of the encyclical to man (*Man is the Way of the Church*). It is man—the full truth of man—that is essential to John Paul. Man is assuredly creative. He is free. But, as noted in Chapters 4 and 5, this freedom is received and therefore is to be exercised according to the original ordering that God intends. God intends man to be a providential being. Man is called upon to use his freedom to subdue the world and, in light of the subjective meaning of work, he is called upon to subdue himself. Freedom is ordered to the truth of man. And, as John Paul II reminds us in *Centesimus Annus*, one cannot forget the truth of man's frailty. Man lives within the perspective not only of creation (and therefore freedom), but also of Original Sin and his own personal sin. Because of this, there can exist no utopian economic or financial system. All carry within them the seeds of disharmony and fragility.

Therefore, it seems more correct to say that *Centesimus Annus* is the extension and development of previous Catholic social teaching, rather than an encyclical that breaks new ground or somehow represents an earthquake in the Church's social doctrine. John Paul II writes within the perspective of *Rerum Novarum*, *Quadragesimo Anno*, and the social teaching of Pius XII. He also writes within the perspective of his own theological and social teaching. From this latter perspective it is quite clear that what John Paul II brings to his social thought is a clearer and loftier vision of man, but at the same time a more realistic view of the human person. Anthropology is his contribution. John Paul II approves of a free economy because he acknowledges, with profound insight, that man is free. But he in no way accedes to a merely libertarian view of man. The State, intermediary bodies, and therefore culture, have their roles to play. Their roles, however, are not the replacement or usurping of individual freedom. Rather, they exist to promote the common good, part of which must be the protection of those less fortunate—those unable to defend themselves against a freedom not orientated to the truth of man.

Nonetheless, as Novak notes, there is something is fresh and exciting about the encyclical. This undoubtedly pertains not only to its treatment of the entrepreneur. John Paul II brings to light the relational dimension of the entrepreneur in a way that no other pope before him has done. The work of the entrepreneur is fundamentally oriented to the other (as we have noted). The entrepreneur is able to foresee the needs of others and work with others to satisfy the needs of the other. This is what truly fascinates John Paul II. His contribution in this area is unique and definitely new.

A "Business," "Market," or "Free Economy": Not Capitalism

Having considered the entrepreneur, his work and the virtues that are required of such a work, John Paul now moves on to make some subtle distinctions. He is not praising "capitalism"—a word he clearly dislikes—but rather a business, market or free economy. He sees many virtues in the "modern *business economy*" and the functioning of "*the free market*."[15]

> The modern *business economy* has positive aspects. Its basis is human free-dom exercised in the economic field, just as it is exercised in many other fields. Economic activity is indeed but one sector in a great variety of human activities, and like every other sector, it includes the right to freedom, as well as the duty of making responsible use of freedom. But it is important to note that there are specific differences between the trends of modern society and those of the past, even the recent past. Whereas at one time the decisive factor of production was *the land*, and later capital—understood as a total complex of the instruments of production—today the decisive factor is increasingly *man himself*, that is, his knowledge, especially his scientific knowledge, his capacity for interrelated and compact organization, as well as his ability to perceive the needs of others and to satisfy them.[16]

So the business or free economy is not the result of chance. Rather, it is the result of intelligent human beings exercising their right to freedom in the economic sphere. William McGurn writes of the temptation to regard the market system as a random and disorderly process. The temptation should be rejected. The market and business economy is not a matter of chance, but is the direct result of human ingenuity and freedom.

> For example, the millions of small, individual actions that occur every hour in a place like Hong Kong, might seem random and disorderly to the casual observer. Yet it is not a matter of chance that in Hong Kong there is food on the shelves, abundant water (though the territory has no water supply of its own), and no short-age of commodities (despite an absence of natural resources). In her history of the territory, British author Jan Morris put it this way: "In a small Chinese shop on Cheung Chau [island] I once bought myself a packet of candies made in Athens, and even as I opened it I marveled at the chain of logistics that had brought it from the shadow of the Acropolis to be chewed by me on the corner of Tung Wan Road. While not the outcome of any specific human plan, the obvious ease with which capitalism literally delivers the goods demonstrates that a capitalist system is not the chaotic process it appears to be at first glance.[17]

This social dimension of the market is brought out well by Rocco Buttiglione.

> The market is not a natural state of affairs; it is a social institution. As such, it must be created and it must be defended; it may be enlarged and may be restricted. In order to enter into the market, to be able to sell and to buy in the market place,

there are many necessary assumptions. Some of these assumptions are of a legal and objective nature. For example, we need laws defending the freedom of individuals and their property, and we need a law of contracts. It is impossible to buy and sell if somebody can take forcefully what he wants. We need efficient communications and transportation systems, in order to take our commodities to market. We need information concerning the kinds of commodities in demand; we need educational and technical skills in order to produce them. Those who will take the responsibility of production need a minimum of capital to allow them the chance to expose their good ideas to an intelligent and active banker who can provide them with needed capital.[18]

For the creation and establishment of the free market there must be protection, through the legislative and judicial system, of the right to private property. *Rerum Novarum* made this abundantly clear. But then, as Buttiglione remarks, the free market is not a law unto itself—it is an institution that must be created and defended. It may, if necessary, be enlarged or restricted. The free market, established and maintained for the common good, must itself operate under the umbrella of the common good. Private action may need to be restricted when the common good requires it—when legitimate human needs are not satisfied by the market.

Freedom and Truth: Fallen Man

Two issues arise here. There is first the doctrine of original (and personal) sin. On the one hand human freedom leads to creativity in the marketplace. This clearly benefits the common good. Yet, as experience and history shows, the human heart wounded by sin can also turn against the good of others. McGurn underlines this curious paradox.

Capitalism curiously nurtures within its success vices that, left unchecked by other institutions such as church and family, carry the seeds of the system's destruction. The ironies are almost diabolical. It is in capitalist lands that the family appears most threatened—not by poverty, but by riches. This, in turn, threatens to undermine the very virtues by which wealth is acquired.[19]

The free-market system promises a level of material wellbeing. It promises success and often fulfills this promise. It does not, however, promise human virtue. Freedom may lead to vice and often does. This is the risk of freedom. Other institutions, therefore, will be required to check its behavior to "weed out" the seeds of destruction. But these, too, will prove to be fruitless if they are not based on a correct anthropology.[20] The free market, as Buttiglione notes, presupposes the free man.[21] But freedom presupposes truth—the truth of the human person. John Paul II restates this themes in *Centesimus Annus.*

A person who is concerned solely or primarily with possessing and enjoying, who is no longer able to control his instincts and passions, or to subordinate them by obedience to the truth, cannot be free: *obedience to the truth* about God and man is the first condition of freedom, making it possible for a person to order his needs and desires and to choose the means of satisfying them according to a correct scale of values, so that ownership of things may become an occasion of personal growth.[22]

When human action is not guided by the truth about man, it will require the State to act in such a way that the basic rights and needs of its citizens are satisfied. The right to life, the right to education, to housing, to food, and to health are essential for human existence. The State should intervene when these rights are threatened and intermediary bodies have an even more important role to play in helping form a culture based on a correct anthropology. Only in this way will justice be implemented and the wound of Original Sin healed.

The Jurisdiction of the Free Market

The second issue relates to the limits of the market economy. The free market has its field of action, its area of jurisdiction and its field of expertise. John Paul II is insistent on this. "It would appear that, on the level of individual nations and of international relations," writes the Holy Father, "*the free market* is the most efficient instrument for utilizing resources and effectively responding to needs."[23] But the market, like all human realities, has its own shortcomings and frailties. John Paul II sees two problems here. One is essentially related to the nature of the market itself. The other has more to do with the conditions that would render the market fruitful. He treats the latter first.

It would be futile to institute a market economy where the necessary conditions for its functioning do not exist. Thus, for instance, it would be highly unwise for a country to institute a market economy where there did not exist the right or protection of private property.[24] The prior task of property rights and their protection awaits that kind of society. The pope mentions the difficulties of a lack of access to basic knowledge. This clearly hinders people from participating in the business economy. Likewise, communication and transportation systems must be in place for the free market to function adequately.

The second limitation concerns the nature of goods that are to be traded in a market. Can everything be subject to the rules of free competition? Or are there human needs that cannot be valued—that do not admit a market price? Or even if they do admit a market price, should this be the price charged to the consumer? This is a very difficult and delicate issue, touching as it does, upon the relationship between the State, intermediary bodies and the free market and the legitimate jurisdiction of the parties concerned. The free market "is the most efficient instrument for utilizing resources and effectively responding to needs,"[25] but there would appear to be many exceptions in the mind of the Pontiff.

But this is true only for those needs which are "solvent," insofar as they are endowed with purchasing power, and for those resources which are "marketable" insofar as they are capable of obtaining a satisfactory price. But there are many human needs which find no place on the market. It is a strict duty of justice and truth not to allow fundamental human needs to remain unsatisfied, and not to allow those burdened by such needs to perish. It is also necessary to help these needy people to acquire expertise, to enter the circle of exchange, and to develop their skills in order to make the best use of their capacities and resources. Even prior to the logic of a fair exchange of goods and the forms of justice appropriate to it, there exists something which is due to man because he is man, by reason of his lofty dignity.[26]

The issue is complex. John Paul II is not specific as to which basic needs find no place in the market. Food, for instance, which is clearly a basic human need, is for the most part left to market conditions.

A Society of Free Work, of Enterprise, and of Participation

In light of these considerations, John Paul II proposes a *societas liberi operis, conductionis et participationis.*[27] As regards developing a society of free work, little is said here, except for the need to reduce barriers and monopolies, and so it seems safe to assume that all the aspects of work that appear in *Laborem Exercens* apply here. There is clearly a need for intermediary bodies—the family, churches, social institutions of goodwill, etc.—to educate people concerning the nature of work, not only as necessary, but as a free cooperation in the *opus* of God.

Significantrly, the Latin text uses *conductionis* (bringing together, uniting or hiring)[28] and not *spiritus innovationis* (enterprise).[29] The difference in meaning is significant. No doubt *conductionis* does not exclude *enterprise* in its work of bringing together, but the reverse is probably not admissible. An individual can be enterprising without others. Once again, John Paul appears to be emphasizing the relational dimension of entrepreneurial work, without thereby discounting the other elements of such work. It might be more appropriate, therefore, to speak of John Paul II's call for a *society of free work* (*opus*), unity *and participation.*[30]

Such an interpretation seems warranted. In the five paragraphs that follow the call for a *societas liberi operis, conductionis et participationis*, the pope directly addresses modern problems of disintegration. *Centesimus Annus* addresses "the phenomenon of consumerism,"[31] "the ecological question"[32] (brought about by false aesthetic attitudes that are not born of wonder),[33] and problems related to marriage and family (and the sanctity of life).[34] Hence, the call is for a society that "unifies" or "brings together." The English text's use of the word "enterprise" (instead of the suggested word "unity") inadvertently directs the reader's attention away from the problems of disintegration and the subsequent need to pursue a society of unity (*conductionis*).

The Meaning of Participation in Wojtyla's Writings

Centesimus Annus' call for a society of *participation* is dealt with in the later part of section four of *Centesimus Annus*. It is introduced via the concept of alienation—the reverse, so to speak, of participation. Marxists objected to the experience of alienation in capitalist societies. But the Marxist objection to capitalism, says John Paul II, was "based on a mistaken and inadequate idea of alienation"—a "materialistic foundation" paying regard only to the "sphere of relationships of production and ownership."[35] The experience of socialist countries confirmed this inadequate analysis.

But the Marxist analysis, even if wrongly grounded, is correct in its claim that man experiences alienation in Western modernity. According to the pope, it occurs through "consumerism, when people are ensnared in a web of false and superficial gratifications rather than being helped to experience their personhood in an authentic and concrete way."[36] For Wojtyla this experience of personhood—of self—is intimately related to self-determination. John Paul II continues noting that not only does consumerism contribute to alienation, but so too does a workplace in which each person "is considered only a means and not an end."[37] Paragraph forty-one of the encyclical reminds us, once again, of the principal characteristic of work. It is, as we have seen, John Paul's striking and repetitive use of the word "other" (*alius*) that alerts us to this characteristic and reinforces it in *Centesimus Annus*. All work is done with and for others. Thus self-determination, achieved in and through horizontal and vertical transcendence, cannot be an isolated act of the individual. Rather, as Wojtyla wrote in *The Acting Person*, self-determination is achieved by action with and for others.

> The progress toward vertical transcendence is not a solitary journey, however. For actions that transform a person are for the most part taken together with others. And so, in the final chapter, the author takes up the topic of interpersonal relations and of participation in community with others for the benefit of the whole.[38]

Wojtyla devotes Chapter 7 in *The Acting Person* to participation. It has a precise meaning that he himself develops and summarizes in other places.[39] Buttiglione notes that along with transcendence and integration, participation is "one of the fundamental characteristics of the acting person."[40] Buttiglione observes, therefore, that participation is not accidental to the philosophical method of Wojtyla. Rather, it is essential to man's fulfillment realized through freedom.

> Without it, man would not be able to act in relation with other men, and therefore, this relation would be for him nothing but a conditioning, instead of being an occasion for the realization of his freedom... Participation is therefore the condition through which man can remain free and at the same time experience himself as such in relationship with other men and in social life. Participation allows him to avoid either treating the other as an object, or being treated in that way by him, when they are doing something together.[41]

Participation is therefore integral to the affirmation of the human person through experience—through action. Through participation, persons are affirmed in their subjectivity and they are not looked upon, or treated as objects. Likewise, the person himself, through participation, treats the other as person, and not as object. When man is not treated as a personal subject, he then experiences alienation.

Crossing the Threshold of Love, Mary Shivanandan comments that Wojtyla's thought on "[b]oth participation and alienation are linked to man's personal subjectivity. Man is alienated when, without ceasing to be a member of the human species, *he is not considered a personal subject*."[42] In this sense, it is possible to say that, participation (unlike transcendence) has a normative value. Through participation, man acts with others and this provides him with the possibility of realizing his freedom. But if this action with others is not for others but is against others or against oneself—i.e., the person is treated as an object and not as a subject—alienation will ensue. Participation is lost.

Wojtyla himself gives a clear and succinct statement of what he intends by participation.

> This notion of participation does not have much in common with the Platonic or Scholastic notion. It serves, instead, to specify and express what it is that safeguards us as persons along with the personalistic nature and value of our activity as we exist and act together with others in different systems of social life. That is precisely what I meant by participation in *Osoba i czyn*, namely, the ability to exist and act together with others in such a way that in this existing and acting we remain ourselves and actualize ourselves, which means our own *I*'s.[43]

The connection with self-determination and transcendence is clear. Man being a person experiences himself precisely as an *I* in and through action that redounds on the self. He becomes conscious, not only of his own efficacy. Man is, to be sure, the efficient cause of his own actions. But human activity is not limited to a reaching out to and interaction with objects outside of man—horizontal transcendence. In addition, in his free decisions, man reaches out *to choose himself.* In choosing an object of choice, man simultaneously chooses himself. By means of vertical transcendence, man goes out of himself to values that transcend him, only *to return to himself with a new self.* Action has a redounding nature.

This is the first sense of action having a personalistic value which should not be confused with the ethical value of action.[44] Prior to any reaching out to an object of ethical value, man is engaged in actions that are personal. Wojtyla's point in introducing the concept of participation is to fulfill the personalistic structure or value of action. When man acts, he acts with other persons. He lives in a community of persons. He does not live in a vacuum. The experience then of self-determination leads man to an awareness, through consciousness, of self-governance and self-possession, but this process takes place in union with other men and women and rarely, if ever, in isolation from others. Man thus experiences himself not only via transcendence, but also via participation. The personalistic value of action, then, requires not only that an action be done by a person, but with other persons. Because man is a social being, he encounters in his choices other men and women. *His experience of himself is simultaneously an experience of others.* Both transcendence and participation affirm his experience of self.

Clearly Wojtyla believes that all personal action has this participatory personal value. The human person is called to recognize it, to embrace and so fulfill the ultimate meaning of the personalistic value of action. To repeat: The personalistic value of an action gains its meaning from the fact that the action is done by a person (transcendence) with other persons (participation). So man's experience of himself is achieved by action that is transcendental and participatory. Man's experience of himself is always in some measure or degree related to the experience he has of working with and for others. He experiences the self—the *I*—not as an individualistic self-realization, but rather in a wholesome encounter with other men and women.

But a correct understanding of participation is not complete unless the person recognizes the *I* of the other. Man must recognize the other as his neighbor. It is here that reason and revelation meet. If Wojtyla's insights about the importance of participation have a certain novelty about them, then this latter point is just as compelling. Participation requires not just a recognition that in acting with others I experience myself as a person. Participation is not just about the self. No, participation is simultaneously about the recognition of the other precisely as an *I*.[45]

Wojtyla thus suggests that in order for participation to be fully actualized, I must become aware of and experience the other person in a way that is analogous to my own experience of self and fully accept the other as another *I* like myself. Is this another way of saying that just as I experience my own dignity in and through action, so too I can now recognize the dignity of the other? Certainly "I cannot experience another as I experience myself, because my own *I* as such is nontransferable."[46] But, nevertheless, I come to understand the other as *I* by means of my own experience of myself as *I*. In this sense, then, we can say that it is analogous.

Transcendence, Participation, and the Entrepreneur

Our brief discussion on Wojtyla's notion of participation is important for a correct understanding of the meaning of work, particularly entrepreneurial work. In working with others and for others, the entrepreneur has the opportunity to experience himself and his neighbor. Through participation and gift of himself (transcendence) he is able to establish communion with his fellow man — a vision that emerges in *Centesimus Annus'* discussion of alienation makes this clear.

> The concept of alienation needs to be led back to the Christian vision of reality, by recognizing in alienation a reversal of means and ends. When man does not recognize in himself and in others the value and grandeur of the human person, he effectively deprives himself of the possibility of benefiting from his humanity and of entering into that relationship of solidarity and communion with others

for which God created him. Indeed, it is through the free gift of self that one truly finds oneself. This gift is made possible by the human person's essential "capacity for transcendence." Man cannot give himself to a purely human plan for reality, to an abstract ideal or to a false utopia. As a person, he can give himself to another person or to other persons, and ultimately to God, who is the author of our being and who alone can fully accept our gift. Man is alienated if he refuses to transcend himself and to live the experience of self-giving and of the formation of an authentic human community oriented toward his final destiny, which is God. A society is alienated if its forms of social organization, production and consumption make it more difficult to offer this gift of self and to establish this solidarity between people.[47]

As can be seen, John Paul II applies these important philosophical and theological principles to the social sphere. The implications for entrepreneurs are clear: in their work, they must structure their business and its activities in such a way that people are able to respond to the call of God to transcend themselves, participate with others in their work environment and thus establish communion. The call is lofty and the responsibility demanding. John Paul II in no way waters down the call to sanctity. More importantly, he makes it attractive by appealing to concepts that are not foreign or extraneous to the entrepreneur. The entrepreneur needs to work with others. It is from this experience of entrepreneurs themselves—from this truth that their activity is profoundly relational—that John Paul's call and challenge surely resonates with the entrepreneur. The call comes from deep within the entrepreneur himself, affirms his humanity and activity, and elicits a process of conversion away from sin to newness of life.

The Business as a "Community of Persons"

Centesimus Annus, therefore, provides an affirmation of the entrepreneur and his activities and at the same time a clear vision of how this activity is to be conducted in light of the Gospel and some key philosophical concepts. Along with John Paul's call for a society of *free work, unity and of participation*, he teaches that "the purpose of a business firm is not simply to make a profit [*iustas quaestus*], but is to be found in its very existence as a *community of persons* [*hominum communitas*]."[48]

A business firm is clearly concerned with carrying out a specific task and service to community. This is its primary task. Business firms are "in various ways endeavoring to satisfy their basic needs, and who form a particular group at the service of the whole of society."[49] Hence, this firm cannot function without profit. It is needed for future activities and is a sign that the business is functioning well.[50] But this is not the only factor that must be considered.

It is possible for the financial accounts to be in order, and yet for the people—who make up the firm's most valuable asset—to be humiliated and their dignity offended. Besides being morally inadmissible, this will eventually have negative repercussions on the firm's economic efficiency.[51]

The principal task of a business firm—proceeding from the *transcendence of the human person* and his call to *participation*—is to form a communion of persons. This is not, as we have seen, a vague or general concept. Rather, this communion will flow from the formation of *I-other* relationships deepening, wherever possible and appropriate, into *I-thou* relationships. Only when these are formed in the workplace will there be communion. This is clearly a magnificent and sublime challenge to all in the business world.

Conclusion

Centesimus Annus' teaching on entrepreneurship is clearly within the tradition of the social teaching of the Catholic Church. His defense of the right to private property and private action is clearly consistent with that of his predecessors. But he brings to the social doctrine his fascination for man. Man is the reason. He is free and he must be guided by the truth about himself. John Paul's call for a society of free work, unity and participation is clearly a development in social thought. Likewise, his insistence on a business firm being a communion of persons is novel. It is based, to be sure, on the call to communion found in *Gaudium et Spes*, but it now has a particular application in the financial and economic sphere. His contribution is via transcendence and participation and these philosophical concepts are extremely important to a correct understanding of man and his activity.

Finally, Pope John Paul II affirms and magnifies the esteem with which the Church holds private initiative and entrepreneurial work, underlining its communal dimension. In *Laborem Exercens*, he highlights the communal dimension of work as being the essential characteristic of work. The fundamental characteristic of work is its ability to unite people. It is the other that seems to echo throughout the passages that deal with the entrepreneur. The entrepreneur's work is characterized by work with others. He is called to work for others. The personalistic value of action, first derived from transcendence, is then fulfilled by the introduction of participation. It receives normative value. The entrepreneur, like all men, is called to recognize the dignity of the human person. Expressed negatively, man should never use another human person as if he were an object. He must work for others. The personalistic value of action is the source not only of allowing man freedom in the work environment, but also of the personalistic norm, informed by participation, becomes a source of continual conversion, urging the entrepreneur to treat the other as an I.

Notes

1. Marco Martini, "Gospel is Basis for Action," *L'Osservatore Romano: English Weekly Edition*, 22 July 1991, 9–10, 9.

2. Ibid., 42.

3. *Centesimus Annus*, 32.

4. Ibid., 31.

5. Ibid., 32.

6. *Centesimus Annus*, 32.

7. Author's translation.

8. The English text, unfortunately, does not alert the reader to the meaning contained in the Latin text. It speaks rather of a "community of work."

9. *Centesimus Annus*, 31. Emphasis added.

10. Ibid., 32. Emphasis added.

11. John Paul II. Encyclical Letter *Sollicitudo Rei Socialis* in: Miller, *The Encyclicals*, 379–420. The Latin text is from AAS 80 (1988), 511–86.

12. *Sollicitudo Rei Socialis*, 15.

13. Jeffrey A. Tucker, "Papal Economics 101: The Catholic Ethic and the Spirit of Capitalism," *Crisis* 9, no. 7 (1991), 16–21, 16. Emphasis added.

14. Michael Novak, "Magnificentesimus," *Crisis* 9, no. 7 (1991), 2–3.

15. *Centesimus Annus*, 32, 34.

16. Ibid., 32.

17. Ibid., 195.

18. Rocco Buttiglione, "Behind Centesimus Annus," *Crisis* 9, no. 7 (1991): 8–9.

19. McGurn, *The Turn Towards Enterprise*, 203.

20. Schall quotes Solzhenitsyn, who notes the practical consequences of divorcing freedom from truth. Schall remarks that a response to the Marxist system "would have to be primarily effected through a spiritual understanding of man's nature and being, through a 'turning' in the heart of each person." Thus, gaining freedom is not enough. Rather, freedom must be firmly rooted in the truth of the human person, otherwise shallow and superficial personalities ensue. What is at stake is the need for a correct anthropology. Schall then cites Solzhenitsyn: "A fact which cannot be disputed is the weakening of the human personality in the West while in the East it has become firmer and stronger. Six decades for our people and three decades for the people of Eastern Europe; during that time we have been through a spiritual training far in advance of Western experience. The complex and deadly crush of life has produced stronger, deeper, and more interesting personalities than those generated by standardized Western wellbeing." (James V. Schall S.J., "The Teaching of Centesimus Annus," *Gregorianum* 74, no. 1 (1993): 17–43, 21–22.)

21. Buttiglione, *Behind Centesimus Annus*, 9.

22. *Centesimus Annus*, 41.

23. Ibid., 34.

24. See Hernando De Soto, *The Mystery of Capital: Why Capitalism Triumphs in the West and Fails Everywhere Else* (New York: Basic Books, 2000), 6–7. Soto argues strongly that property rights are a necessary condition for private initiative and action. John Paul does not mention this crucial fact, but given the preceding analysis he surely hints at it.

25. *Centesimus Annus*, 34.

26. Ibid.

27. Ibid.

28. See *Dictionary of Ecclesiastical Latin* s.v. *conductionis*.

29. The phrase *spiritui innovationis* was used in *Gaudium et Spes*, 64. It has not been used by Pope John Paul II in *Centesimus Annus*. He has preferred other phrases, as we have seen.

30. This is my suggested translation.

31. *Centesimus Annus*, 36.

32. Ibid., 37.

33. Ibid.

34. Ibid., 39.

35. Ibid., 41.

36. Ibid.

37. Ibid.

38. Schmitz, *At the Center of the Human Drama*, 86.

39. See Wojtyla, "Participation or Alienation?" in *Person and Community*, 197–207.

40. Rocco Buttiglione, *Karol Wojtyla: The Thought of the Man Who Became Pope John Paul II*, trans. Paolo Guietti and Francesca Murphy (Grand Rapids, MI: William B. Eerdmans Publishing Company, 1997), 169.

41. Ibid., 169.

42. Mary Shivanandan, *Crossing the Threshold of Love: A New Vision of Marriage in the Light of John Paul II's Anthropology* (Washington, DC: The Catholic University of America Press, 1999) xviii. Emphasis added.

43. Wojtyla, "Participation or Alienation?" in *The Acting Person,* 200.

44. See Wojtyla, *The Acting Person*, 264.

45. Wojtyla, "Participation or Alienation?" in *The Acting Person,* 202.

46. Ibid.

47. *Centesimus Annus*, 41.

48. Ibid., 35.

49. Ibid.

50. Ibid.

51. Ibid.

FURTHER READING

Introduction

For a summary of the pre-Leonine period not covered in this book I refer the reader to:

Schuck, Michael J. *That They Be One: The Social Teaching of the Papal Encyclicals 1740-1989*. Washington, DC: Georgetown University Press, 1991, 1–43.

The two economic issues dealt with in this period are immoral business practices and theft.

For a more systematic treatment of the issue of development of social doctrine see:

Gregg, Samuel. *Challenging the Modern World: Karol Wojtyla/John Paul II and the Development of Catholic Social Teaching*. Lanham: Lexington Books, 1999, 14–16.

One might also consult the brief, but very helpful explanation by the following:

Martin, Francis. *The Feminist Question: Feminist Theology in the Light of Christian Tradition*. Grand Rapids, MI: William B. Eerdmans Publishing Company, 1994, xii.

Chapter One

For a more in-depth treatment of a "theology of work" one may consult:

Chenu, M. D. *The Theology of Work*. Translated by Lilian Soiron. Chicago: Henry Regnery Co., 1966.

Goosen, Gideon. *The Theology of Work*. Edited by Edward Yarnold, vol. 22. *Theology Today*. Hales Corners: Cergy Book Service, 1974.

Kaiser, Edwin G. *Theology of Work*. Westminister: The Newman Press, 1966.

Kuic, Vukan (Editor). *Work, Society and Culture*. New York: Fordham University Press, 1986.

Schoonenberg, Peter. *God's World In The Making*, vol. 2. *Duquesne Studies Theological Series*. Pittsburgh: Duquesne University Press, 1964.

For writings that are theological but more practical, one may find helpful the following:

Escrivá, Josemaría. *Friends of God*. Princeton: Scepter, 1989.
Wyszynski, Stefan. *All You Who Labor*. Translated by J. Ardle McArdle. Manchester: Sophia Institute Press, 1995. (Wyszynski's work is excellent. It treats twenty-two topics related to work and one's spiritual life.)

For a study of the teachings of Escrivá one may consult:

Belda, M. et al., eds. *Holiness and the World: Studies in the Teachings of Blessed Josemaría Escrivá*. Princeton: Scepter Publishers, 1997.

For a more recent and comprehensive study of corporate finance see:

Brealey, Richard A., Stewart C. Myers, and Alan J. Marcus. *Fundamentals of Corporate Finance*, 2d ed. Boston: Irwin/McGraw-Hill, 1999.

A very useful summary of the way the entrepreneur has been considered during the last two hundred years of economic thought is provided by Kirzner in his 1985 work:

Kirzner, Israel M. *Discovery and the Capitalist Process*. Chicago: The University of Chicago Press, 1985, 1–2.

For a comprehensive study of risk and return see:

Brealey, Richard A., Steward C. Myers, and Alan J. Marcus. *Fundamentals of Corporate Finance*, 2d ed. Boston: Irwin/McGraw-Hill, 1999. Chapters 8, 9, and 10 deal with this issue.

Chapter Two

For a good overview of the social teaching of the Fathers of the Church, apart from the entrepreneurial aspect dealt with in this work see:

Charles, Rodger, S.J. *Christian Social Witness and Teaching: The Catholic Tradition from Genesis to Centesimus Annus*, vol. 1. Trowbridge: Cromwell Press, 1998, 74–98.
Phan, Peter C. *Social Thought*. Edited by Thomas Halton, 22 vols., vol. 20. *Message of the Fathers of the Church*. Wilmington: Michael Glazier, Inc., 1984.

For an overview and discussion of the economic situation of the Middle Ages see:

Charles, Rodger, S.J. *Christian Social Witness and Teaching: The Catholic Tradition from Genesis to Centesimus Annus*, vol. 1. Trowbridge: Cromwell Press, 1998, 101–239.

On usury one could consult the third chapter of Flynn's work where he deals with the question of commerce in the following:

Flynn, Frederick E. "Wealth and Money in the Economic Philosophy of St. Thomas," Doctoral Dissertation, Notre Dame, 1942, 39–55.

For a good discussion of a just price see:

Charles, Rodger, S.J. *Christian Social Witness and Teaching: The Catholic Tradition from Genesis to Centesimus Annus*, vol. 1. Trowbridge Press, 1998, 198–99.

Chapter Three

On the relationship between private property and wealth see:

De Soto, Hernando. *The Mystery of Capital: Why Capitalism Triumphs in the West and Fails Everywhere Else*. New York: Basic Books, 2000.

For a discussion of the social teaching of Pius X and a summary of that teaching one may consult:

Charles, Rodger, S.J. *Christian Social Witness and Teaching: The Catholic Tradition from Genesis to Centesimus Annus*, vol. 2. Trowbridge: Cromwell Press, 1998, 34–41. Likewise the same reference is excellent for Benedict XV, 44–51.

For a treatment of solidarity in the thought of John Paul II see:

Doran, Kevin P. *Solidarity: A Synthesis of Personalism and Communalism in the Thought of Karol Wojtyla/Pope John Paul II*. New York: Peter Lang, 1996.

This is a splendid study on this topic. See especially Chapter 3 on the concept in the social teaching of the Catholic Church, 1891–1978. Also, Chapters 4 and 5 deal with John Paul's treatment of the subject both before and during his pontificate.

Chapter Five

To locate John Paul II's social teaching within the broader context of his theological and moral teachings one might consult:

Beigel, Gerard. *Faith and Social Justice in the Teaching of Pope John Paul II*. New York: Peter Lang, 1997.

Doran, Kevin P. *Solidarity: A Synthesis of Personalism and Communalism in the Thought of Karol Wojtyla/Pope John Paul II*. New York: Peter Lang, 1996.

Both these works are excellent and bring together the philosophical and theological teaching of John Paul II and its application in his social encyclicals.

With respect to philosophical works of Karol Wojtyla one may consult the works of Beigel and Doran cited above as well as the following ones:

Schmitz, Kenneth L. *At the Center of the Human Drama: The Philosophical Anthropology of Karol Wojtyla/Pope John Paul II*. Washington, DC: The Catholic University of America Press, 1993.

Buttiglione, Rocco. *Karol Wojtyla: The Thought of the Man Who Became Pope John Paul II*. Translated by Paolo Guietti Francesca Murphy. Grand Rapids, MI: William B. Eerdmans Publishing Company, 1997.

Kupczak, Jaroslaw. *Destined for Liberty: The Human Person in the Philosophy of Karol Wojtyla/John Paul II*. Washington, DC: The Catholic University of America Press, 2000.

Shivanandan, Mary. *Crossing the Threshold of Love: A New Vision of Marriage in the Light of John Paul II's Anthropology*. Washington, DC: The Catholic University of America Press, 1999.

For the relationship between *Gaudium et Spes* and *Veritatis Splendor* see:

Welch, Lawrence J. "Gaudium et spes, the Divine Image, and the Synthesis of Veritatis splendor." *Communio* 24, no. Winter (1997): 794–814.

Chapter Six

For further reactions to *Centesimus Annus* see:

Phan, John-Peter, ed. *Centesimus Annus: Assessment and Perspectives for the Future of Catholic Social Doctrine*. Citta Del Vaticano: Libreria Editrice Vaticana, 1998.

INDEX

ABOUT THE AUTHOR

FR. ANTHONY G. PERCY is a diocesan priest of the Archdiocese of Canberra-Goulburn, Australia. His undergraduate studies were in commerce and finance at the University of New South Wales. He received his doctorate in sacred theology from the John Paul II Institute for Studies on Marriage and the Family, at the Catholic University of America, Washington, D.C., in 2003. He is also the author of *Theology of the Body Made Simple* (2006). Since 2009, he has been Rector of the Good Shepherd Seminary in Sydney, Australia.

Breinigsville, PA USA
20 July 2010
242080BV00001BA/1/P

9 780739 125144

3 4711 00209 2957